EARTHLY THINGS

Also by Olov Hartman
Holy Masquerade (tr. Karl A. Olsson)

EARTHLY THINGS

Essays by
OLOV HARTMAN

Translated, with an Introduction, by
ERIC J. SHARPE

WILLIAM B. EERDMANS PUBLISHING COMPANY
GRAND RAPIDS, MICHIGAN

Essays 4, 5, and 14 are taken from *Medmänskligt*, published by Rabén and Sjögren, Stockholm, in 1952.
Essays 2, 15, 16, 17, and 20 are taken from *Jordiska Ting*, published by Rabén and Sjögren, Stockholm, in 1956.
Essays 1, 3, 18, and 19 are taken from *Stället om törnbusken*, published by Rabén and Sjögren, Stockholm, in 1961.
Essays 6, 9, 10, and 11 are taken from *Ett fritt evangelium*, published by Svenska Kyrkans Diakonistyrelses Bokförlag, Stockholm, in 1963.
Essays 7, 8, 12, and 13 have not previously appeared in book form; they were originally published in *Svenska Dagbladet, Vår Kyrka, Livets ord,* and *Vår Lösen* respectively.
"The Christian Faith" was first published in *Västerås stiftsbok* for 1964, and has since appeared in *Vad är det?*, published by Rabén and Sjögren, Stockholm, in 1965.
Biblical quotations are from the Revised Standard Version of the Bible.

CONTENTS

Introduction

Some thirty miles north of Stockholm, on the shore of Lake Mälar, lies one of Sweden's smallest cities, Sigtuna. Once the capital of the kingdom of Svea, with a history going back to the Viking period and beyond, the Sigtuna of today, despite (or perhaps because of) its size and idyllic character, is one of Sweden's leading intellectual centers. Its educational establishments include two of the country's most famous boarding schools, while for fifty years now the life of the city has been closely bound up with the life and activities of the Church of Sweden's Sigtuna Foundation (*Sigtunastiftelsen*), of which Olov Hartman has been director since 1948.

Opened in 1917 on the initiative of Manfred Björkqvist, Einar Billing, Nathan Söderblom, J. A. Eklund, and others as a forum for what was then the new dialogue between the Church and the social, political, and cultural activities of a rapidly developing country, the Sigtuna Foundation has held to the intentions of its founders without ever becoming an anachronism. What its existence has meant to the life of the Church in Sweden it is still too early to calculate, but it is certain that to Swedish churchmen "Sigtuna" is more than a mere place name. It stands, rather, for an attitude and a mode of thought—expectant, open, and courteous towards the secular world, and yet uncompromising (whatever its opponents may say or think) in its Evangelical centrality. Besides conference and guest rooms, the Sigtuna Foundation has a chapel; and it is no accident that the chapel bears the name of the first and greatest of Swedish reformers, Olaus Petri (1493-1552).

For twenty years now, Olov Hartman's work has been inseparable from the work of the Sigtuna Foundation. Most of its conferences, on all manner of subjects connected with the dialogue between the church and the world, he contrives to address at least once, and most of the essays contained in this book were first delivered as conference lectures. This constant demand on his time and energies is one of the reasons why he has never written any of the heavyweight, "definitive" works that some people feel he ought to write. His most sustained writing is to be found in his novels and his church dramas; his theological, pastoral, and cultural writing, on the other hand, has almost all appeared in concentrated essay form. But there is a deeper reason why Hartman has never written anything approximating to a "systematic theology": he simply does not believe in it. More and more he has come to believe that the worst thing that can happen to a theologian is to be fettered by a system of his own (or someone else's) making. Theology, he believes, is a kaleidoscopic vision of reality, constantly changing and shifting around the fixed point of the revelation of God in Christ Jesus; to write theology is to rise repeatedly to the specific challenge of the gospel, not to formulate once and for all an ideal and therefore unreal solution to artificial problems. He cites with approval the example of the "grand old man" of Swedish theology, Gustaf Aulén, whose systematic theology, *The Faith of the Christian Church*, recently appeared in its sixth revised edition. It is not surprising, then, that he refuses to consider himself as the leader of a "school." True, his influence is widespread, and growing, but the mere suggestion on someone's part that he reckons himself a Hartman disciple is more likely to provoke his anger than his gratitude. Idolatry, however it may be disguised, he treats after the manner of an Old Testament prophet.

Similarly, Hartman makes no claim to belong to a school or a party. Influences there have been; but they have been temporary, *ad hoc*, stages to be passed. Only in Augustine and Luther does he recognize permanent forces at work on his own mind. He speaks of his intellectual and spiritual development as a process of rediscovery—rediscovery of Evangelical insights first encountered, though not then fully understood, under the banner of the Salvation Army.

The Salvation Army was Olov Hartman's first spiritual home, and he acknowledges a threefold debt to the company of "Blood and Fire." First, in respect of its central Evangelical doctrine of individual repentance and forgiveness, the "penitent form," to which the sinner may come in order to receive the assurance of the forgiving grace of God, has always been a tangible reality in Hartman's thought, even when transmuted into an altar. His deep love and knowledge of the Holy Scrip-

tures—Old and New Testaments alike—is a further closely
related inheritance, which his thirty-five years as a Lutheran
minister have only served to strengthen and deepen. The central message of Scripture is the message of the infinitely costly,
seeking and forgiving love of God, demonstrated once and for
all in the passion and death of Jesus Christ, and this, too, is
the heart of Hartman's theology. But the Army went a step
further. From Methodism came its doctrine of holiness (or
sanctification, Christian perfection, perfect love), which it set
forth as the only goal of the Christian life on earth. But what
did it mean to be "holy," in practical terms? Were some Christians holy and others not? Where did the line go?

When Olov Hartman was five years old (he was born in
1906), his father gave up a successful business to become a
cadet in the Salvation Army. This was an absolutely unheard-of
step to take in the early years of the century, when the boundary between what was permitted to respectable people and
what was not was very sharply drawn. Among the stories told
of his father was the occasion when, as a cadet, he had been
ordered to take a handcart and move some boxes; on the way
he met some of his former errand-boys. Imagine: the boss in
uniform, pushing a handcart through the streets! Middle-class
convention could not have been more thoroughly flouted, nor
at greater social cost. But there was another occasion, which
left still deeper traces on his son:

> I said [writes Hartman] that my father defied middle-class
> convention, and did it in the name of Christ. But there was
> the matter of Salvationist convention, too. My father's holiness
> sermons took little account of it. In the Salvation Army, the
> pursuit of the devil was not given up so easily. These sermons
> contained a demand for wholeness that was capable of burn-
> ing through every armor and every uniform. . . . Once, to my
> horror, my father turned over the meeting to someone else,
> and went to the penitent form, to kneel among the sinners.
> This was, to say the least, not customary in the Army. His own
> words had convicted him. What did it matter whether it was
> customary or reasonable?

In time, the lesson came home: that in the face of the holy
love of God, all are equally sinners, equally in need of redemp-

tion; if there is sanctification, it is to be found in continual
forgiveness, not in some static "second blessing." This was the
teaching that Hartman found in Augustine and Luther. Even
in his first (temporary) encounter with theological liberalism,
he found that when all else seemed to have been shaken, the
parable of the Prodigal Son was left. After his ordination in
1932, this was what he found in the Eucharist—the forgiving
grace of God. And it is this conviction that still shapes his
thought: his novels, his short stories, his church dramas, his
sermons, and (in the present case) his essays all circle around
the problem of human guilt—hidden, suppressed, and distorted
much of the time, but ever and again revealed and obliterated
in the clear light of the gospel.

The Salvation Army, secondly, gave Hartman a vision of
the gospel in action: a gospel in uniform, worn proudly for
the world to see, a gospel on the march, with bands playing,
drums beating, and flags flying, an unconventional gospel.
Closely connected with this is his sense of the dramatic, crys-
tallized in his conviction that "in the beginning was the drama,"
that the Christian revelation was dramatic before it was
verbal, and that what takes place day by day and week by
week at the altar is a re-presentation of the original drama
played out—in face of the whole world—in the night in which
the Lord was betrayed. The church has an errand to the world,
and woe betide the church if the errand should be forgotten
or ignored. It is incumbent on the church to clothe her message
in symbols—verbal, plastic, oral—for, after all, this was the way
chosen by her Lord. The Word and the sacraments, even
more than the uniforms and the bass drums, are symbolic
actions, carried out in the presence of the world, that the world
might be saved; but beyond all the symbols is the drama, the
action, the event—and this is what the church is commissioned
to proclaim, whatever may be its reception. The officers and
soldiers of the Army were brought up to believe that the light
of the world was foreordained to shine in the midst of a great
darkness: that the marching company was passing through
enemy-occupied territory. Persecution, scorn, hatred, amuse-
ment—these were the signs of faithful service. Hartman still
stresses that he is unable to understand the sense of superiority
that characterizes so much organized Christianity today, not

least in the Church of Sweden. The gospel, he argues, has never been "popular," and can never achieve what we understand by popularity without distortion. It must be made, not acceptable, but inescapable.

The third aspect of Hartman's Army inheritance has to do with the social dimension of the gospel. In his first novel, published in 1948, the year he came to Sigtuna, he described an encounter between an undergraduate brought up in the Swedish Free Church tradition (in some ways a reflection of the author himself) and a working-class girl, the daughter of a socialist of the old school. The barrier between them was partly a matter of class, but mostly a matter of ideology. To be a socialist in the early part of the century was often tantamount, in the eyes of the Swedish Church, to blasphemy and ungodliness. The problems of the working classes as a whole were dismissed or ignored, while the Church tended to identify itself (unconsciously, perhaps, but no less effectively) with the upper classes, the "establishment." That the Salvation Army refused to accept this identification, and took up the cause of the outcast, was just one more cause of friction. What is significant in this connection is that Hartman's undergraduate was prepared, however unwillingly, to learn from the young socialist something about the importance of people. Hartman recalls that it was not until he came to the Sigtuna Foundation that he came to recognize the political and social consequences of what the Army had been doing on the individual level for so many years. Once more it was a matter of rediscovery, but rediscovery in a deeper context, as he learned to place the social reality of the world in the context of the sacrament of the altar. An important word in Hartman's theological vocabulary is the New Testament term *diakonia*, "service": not service as a bait to catch the ungodly, or as sugar on the pill of the gospel, but as a necessary consequence of the work of Christ, who came not to be served but to serve. *Diakonia* is an aspect of the total life of the church in the world, and can be practiced in many ways: so, for example, there is a *diakonia* of culture and a *diakonia* of society over and above the traditional individual *diakonia* carried on by the Salvation Army and similar bodies. In every case, however, the impulse to serve comes from Christ himself, living and active in Word and sacraments.

It will be clear from what I have said so far that the Salvation Army provided Hartman with a point of departure; but he matured in a far different milieu, that of the Lutheran Church of Sweden. His break with the Salvation Army came in 1925. In 1928, after two and a half years of study at Fjellstedtska School in Uppsala, he entered the University of Uppsala as a theological student, and was ordained four years later in 1932. From 1932 to 1948 he served as a parish minister, mainly in the south of Sweden, where he came into contact with that type of strict Lutheran orthodoxy, and its pietist derivative, connected with the names of Henric Schartau and Peter Lorenz Sellergren, and learned to set high value on the classical doctrine of justification by faith. He encountered the "high church" movement (transplanted from England, though doctrinally Lutheran) with recognition, since the Eucharist had already begun to speak to him directly on its own terms of the drama of God's grace. He also encountered in these years the work of the Lundensian theologians, especially Nygren (in whom he recognized a kindred spirit) and Wingren (with whom he argued incessantly), deriving important impulses from both. The nineteenth-century Danish poet, theologian and educator N. F. S. Grundtvig was another new acquaintance, and his influence on Hartman was considerable. Hartman has always considered Grundtvig's work on the frontiers of Christianity and culture to be of the utmost significance.

However, the question of Christianity and culture was not without its problems for a man of Hartman's background. The Swedish Free Churches (and this of course includes the Salvation Army) have traditionally been rather suspicious of most of the creative arts. The "spirituality" of the pietist movement as a whole, and its descendants, left little or no room for novels, poetry, drama, and the plastic arts, except insofar as they could be adjusted to the demands of "edification"—the results, in these cases, being as a rule anything but encouraging. In 1945, Hartman submitted a nativity play to the Swedish radio; rather to his surprise, it was accepted for performance. But could one and the same man be a Christian and an author? Hartman discovered that he could—because he was. In his own words, the lid was off the volcano. The urge to write mastered him.

The following years saw the production of a stream of novels, short stories, essays, and church dramas, a record of almost incredible diversity. Two things have, however, been said about his production: first, that it is all Christian proclamation; and secondly, that it is all dramatic. This is a very fair judgment. Hartman has never written anything on the principle of "art for art's sake." He is always concerned to confront his readers with aspects of the ultimate human conflict: the distress of man with no refuge but himself, the judgment and salvation of man before God. And as I have said, for Hartman, the gospel *is* drama.

Although this is not the place to attempt a close analysis of Hartman's writing as a whole, some observations may be made. To date, he has written five novels: *Död med förhinder* (1948), *Helig maskerad* (1949), *Människor i rött* (1950), *Innanför* (1958) and *Brusande våg* (1959), only the second and the fourth of which have so far been translated into English.[1] These novels, like his short stories, are often hard on the reader: the purely aesthetic and the calm weather of untroubled faith are conspicuous by their absence, nor is there the slightest trace of sentimentality in them. As a novelist, he has more in common with Hemingway, Faulkner, and (especially) Graham Greene than with the hack writers of "Christian novels" (a term Hartman abhors). He is realistic—often brutally so. Concerned as he is to unmask false motives, hypocrisy, and humbug, he is capable of producing terrifying indictments of much that passes for religion. What Christian minister, for instance, can read *Holy Masquerade* without a shudder? But behind and beyond the revelation of human weakness there is always the gospel of unconditional mercy and forgiveness for the lonely and lost. The shabby little caretaker in his Salvation Army novel *Människor i rött*, tormented with guilt over his snuff-taking, finds the same mercy as Jenny Forsman, "the Knife," the officer who knows all about the Law and so little about the gospel. For the message is unconditional: mercy and forgiveness for man *as he is*—not as the church (or the Army) would make him. Mercy and forgiveness spring from one

[1] *Holy Masquerade*, tr. by Karl A. Olsson (Grand Rapids: Eerdmans, 1963); *The Sudden Sun*, tr. by Elsa Kruuse (Philadelphia: Fortress, 1964).

root, and from one root only—the drama played out in the
night in which the Lord was betrayed. Of conventional "happy
endings" there is, however, little or no trace in Hartman's
novels, even when it would have been so easy to have manipulated the material in a slightly different way. The minister's
wife in *Holy Masquerade*, who rescues the statue of the
Madonna and Child from the burning church, is taken to a
mental hospital. The Rural Dean in *Död med förhinder* dies
with his breviary in his hands, but its cover is stained with his
saliva, and the first thing his son has to do, before closing the
old man's eyes, is to brush off an inquisitive fly. Neither is quite
the idyll it might have been. This concern with realism is, no
doubt, partly due to the cultural climate of the 1940s and
1950s in Sweden, when the novels were being written, but is
also an expression of Hartman's theological concern for man
as he really is. I shall return to this subject in a moment.

Four of Hartman's church dramas have been published in
English: *Prophet and Carpenter*, *The Fiery Furnace*, *The
Crown of Life* and *Mary's Quest*. Neither their form nor their
content is a subject that can be discussed here, though I may
perhaps be forgiven for quoting what I have written elsewhere:

> Like the liturgical movement as a whole, it [the liturgical
> drama movement] is based on Eucharist and prayer; and it is
> typically Swedish in that it expresses itself in terms of the
> Evangelical Lutheran doctrine of the Word of God. Liturgical
> drama belongs to the Church. Separate it from the Church
> and you deprive it of its *raison d'être:* a liturgical drama per-
> formed outside the church building, deprived of its essential
> connection with the altar, becomes a contradiction in terms.
> . . . The liturgical drama as developed in Sweden presupposes
> the altar and the Eucharist; its time-scheme is that of the
> night in which the Lord was betrayed; and its terms of refer-
> ence are those of the living, worshipping and praying Church.
> As a modern art form, Swedish liturgical drama is *sui generis*.
> Though it has drawn on the Medieval drama, it cannot be
> equated with either the mystery plays or the miracle plays.
> . . . It has however this much in common with Medieval
> liturgical drama, that it is sacramental and secular in its prin-
> ciples. Sacramental because it is focussed on the drama of the

altar; secular because it is passionately concerned with men
and women as they are in God's world.[2]

These words were written with Hartman's massive dramas in
mind. Whatever the impression given by these dramas, one can
scarcely avoid feeling that one is here dealing with a creative
talent of the first order, who knows man and the church, but
who refuses to play off the one against the other. His respect
for human—and divine—reality is too great for that.

The reader who approaches Hartman for the first time, particularly through the medium of his essays, can hardly fail to
be struck by the fact that, while his theology is so firmly Evangelical in character, he demonstrates time and time again a
close acquaintance with and positive appreciation of the work
of the modern schools of depth-psychology. The combination
is an unusual one, and has rendered him suspect in the eyes
of many an old-fashioned orthodox Evangelical in Sweden.
But there is no question of the order of Hartman's priorities.
In his younger days, he was himself suspicious of the psychologists, and it was only as he gained a closer acquaintance with
their writings and practical methods that he recognized the
Evangelical relevance of what they were doing. Evangelical,
that is, by the standards of Paul, Augustine, and Luther, not
by the standards of post-Reformation scholasticism. The question is whether man is a completely rational being, guided and
directed in all things by a conscious will that is always perfectly under control—the primary assumption of all scholasticism, whether Catholic or Protestant—or whether there are in
the human makeup layers of subconscious resistance to the
gospel that can never be reached by the conventional methods
of preaching and teaching. It is Hartman's conviction that the
guilt with which the gospel alone can deal, is very often subconscious, and must be brought to the surface before it can be
cured. Hence Hartman can hail depth-psychology as a powerful ally, not to be treated with uncritical reverence as a pana-
cea for all the ills of this world (for its limitations must be

[2] Eric J. Sharpe, "Liturgical Drama in Sweden," in *Visible Proclamation: The Church and Drama* (Geneva: WCC Youth Department, 1963),
pp. 23f. See also my introduction to *Mary's Quest* (London: Faith Press,
1963).

clearly recognized), but to be used to reach down into the depths of the human subconscious, where guilt dwells. Psychotherapy can reveal, but it cannot cure. It can show that there is something in man that calls for forgiveness, but it cannot forgive. Hartman is profoundly concerned as a minister of the gospel with the neurotic aspects of modern civilization (see especially the essays in Part II of this book), but he is uncompromising in his insistence that healing is to be found only in the gospel. It is in this connection that he stresses the value of oral confession and the role of the minister as a mediator of absolution: in confession the individual can be confronted with his own self on all its levels, while in absolution (repeated as often as may be necessary) he can be assured of the unconditional love of God. In this, as in much else, he is genuinely a follower of Luther.

Hartman's interest in depth-psychology is motivated ultimately by his desire to see man as he really is. The same might perhaps be said of his concern with the relationship between the Christian gospel and what, for want of a better word, we call "secular" culture. The various expressions of this culture —the novel, drama, poetry, music, the mass media—must, he maintains, have a Christian dimension as long as they claim to reflect human experience in this world. If the heart of the gospel has to do with man's sin, guilt, and forgiveness (and this is the stance of faith on which his work rests), then there is an area of contact between Christian reality and the universal experience of mankind, as reflected in all human attempts at self-expression and communication. At the same time Hartman is profoundly suspicious of any kind of "Christian" culture that would attempt to reduce culture to the level of conventional piety, of whatever ecclesiastical color. Christian culture, for Hartman, is culture that is prepared to relate itself to the revelation of God in Christ, mediated to man through Word and sacraments; but this is not to say either that everything that claims the name of Christian has knowledge of this relationship, or that those who consciously reject the claims of the gospel are beyond the reach of Christ. Conventional, secure, systematized religion he knows to be a highly effective barrier against the gospel; and it is the gospel of the unconventional Christ—the Messiah who was the friend of tax-collectors and sinners, who prompted his father to push a barrow through the streets before the eyes of his former errand-boys—that must judge in order to save. As with psychoanalysis, the arts are to be taken for what they are, and not for what they are not: as pointers, aids to diagnosis, revealers of sin, guilt, distress, sham, hypocrisy, and longing. This on one level; on another, they are to be taken as expressions of the work of the Holy Spirit; Hartman has in fact entitled a two-part essay on the inspiration of Scripture "The Holy Spirit as Artist," illustrating the interplay of revelation and the artistic consciousness out of 2 Corinthians 3:6, ". . . the written code kills, but the Spirit gives life."

In the essays that make up the present volume, we see less of Hartman the narrator and dramatist, and more of the debater and Christian journalist. As I have already said, the essay is the perfect form for the expression of Hartman's theological ideas. Almost all these essays were either first delivered as lectures, or written with a view to a specific situation and a specific need. Of course, they are only a few selected out of a vast number, but I trust that they will serve to illustrate at least some of the aspects of his thought. In the first part of this collection there are essays of more specifically theological content; in the second, essays having to do with the general area of pastoral psychology and clinical theology; and in the third, essays dealing with the relationship of Christianity to culture, and especially with drama and the arts. I have also included, more or less as a postscript, Hartman's highly individual interpretation of the Apostles' Creed; this, as well as providing an excellent summary of Hartman's theology, gives a taste of a style of writing not otherwise found in this collection, though it is typical of his church dramas.

The translation is not always entirely literal. Hartman's language, in common with most modern literary Swedish, is highly compressed, allusive, and epigrammatic, and requires modification in deference to the demands of English style. I hope, however, that the urgency of the original has not been altogether lost in the process.

Eric J. Sharpe

The University of Manchester,
England.

PART ONE

CHURCH AND GOSPEL

1.

MODERN MAN IN SEARCH
OF A PHILOSOPHY

Confronted with an essay entitled "Modern Man in Search of a Philosophy," it is quite likely that the reader will react in a predictable way. He will no doubt expect to find a catalog of current philosophies or *Weltanschauungen*. He will anticipate that the writer is going to dismiss all of them in turn, except one. The remaining philosophy will then be offered to him as the only reasonable, proper, and humane attitude toward life. Should the writer, as in the present case, be known as an ordained minister of the Church of Sweden, it goes without saying that the surviving philosophy will be Christian—more precisely, Evangelical Lutheran—in character.

But if we are going to use the term "philosophy" to denote something like "a total view of human existence," then I should like to begin by raising one or two objections.

In the first place, I find it difficult to imagine having a total, or overall, view of anything that I am unable to look at from a distance. There may well be a vantage point from which life can be viewed as a whole; but that vantage point is at present inaccessible to me, for the simple reason that I am still alive. My "view" forms part of that which I am *trying* to view; and if I try to view myself in the act of viewing, that, too, is the action of a living being. In other words, I believe that I am too deeply involved in the business of living to be capable of constructing a panorama of what it is all about. I must also put on record that if I were to imagine myself capable of doing this, I should fall into a trap, since I should be ignoring a number of very important factors. No one need experience difficulty in putting together a consistent picture of life, provided that he avoids certain facts. From time to time it has been found possible to defend what has been called a "Christian view of life," and the church has had to put up with a good deal of abuse for trying to ignore people like Galileo; but modern philosophies involve the same risk as did their medieval counterparts: closed systems always shut out some witnesses and always lock some doors. I am reminded of the way the experts reacted to the first news of the discovery of Palaeolithic paintings in the caves of Altamira. They simply refused to go and see them, because it was obviously incompatible with the doctrine of evolution that paintings of such quality should have been executed in an age when men still lived in caves.

Some systems, in order to remain consistent, have to invent new facts; other systems deprive us of some part of reality. But I am convinced that we must always begin with observation and experience; whether our observations and experiences always fit one another is a matter that has to be shelved temporarily. It is, for instance, not altogether inconceivable that reality is of a greater richness and complexity than can be expressed in terms of human logic. That is why I cannot treat any philosophy or world-view as something static; for me, a world-view is something dynamic. It means observing the landscape through which I am traveling, and it means comparing experiences—without forgetting that I am still in transit. And so I should like to bring out some of these experiences (especially those which are, or can be, common to most of us) and ask, directing my question particularly to those who are tempted to close their view of life like an electric fence around a meadow, "Have you ever experienced anything like this?"

However, I must confess at once that I am a Christian believer. That means that my choice of facts (or what appear to me to be facts) is subjectively conditioned. If I consider the sun to be an important fact, that obviously means that I believe life on earth to have some degree of importance. I pass judgment on the importance of sunlight from the vantage point of a dweller on the face of the earth. But if there are such beings as angels, it is hardly likely that they would share my opinion; nor would the inhabitants of some other solar system (again, if such there be) in some other galaxy. In the same way, the experiences I cite are determined by the position I occupy at present. Therefore, what I have to say will be more of a personal confession of what I (and a few others) believe to be important than a kind of lesson for the benefit of those who want a demonstration of the real nature of human existence.

A Swedish poet, Östen Sjöstrand, has prefaced one of his books of poems with the motto *Credo aliquid esse*, a quotation from Thomas Aquinas. Now to say that something exists, is really to make a confession of faith. I believe that this book exists, but I cannot prove it. I might be dreaming that it exists. If a hundred readers write to me to say that in that case they are dreaming as well, I have to answer that I may equally well be dreaming their letters. It is often said, in the manner of an eleventh commandment, that no one should believe what he is unable to prove; but no one in fact lives this way, since in fact no one is even able to prove that he exists. If someone should think that this is hair-splitting speculation, I should have to answer that the person who is of that opinion knows very little of the nature of doubt. As Camus once put it, "No one nowadays, except the unrepentant rationalist, believes that it is possible to possess real knowledge." And if he were then to turn around and say that at any rate I cannot claim that solid matter is an illusion, my answer would have to be that I personally could make no such claim, but that there are those who live in a nightmare of fear, lest they should find that they are dreaming matter and all its qualities. There are cultures that have spent more time than we in reflecting on the nature of the world, and have come to the general conclusion that matter is an illusion—*māyā*, it is called in India.

So when I say that this book exists, and would continue to do so even if I were to cease to exist—in other words, when I say that it is a fact beyond my immediate perceptions—I have made a confession of faith, and taken sides in a religious debate. I have chosen to believe what my senses tell me, at least according to the principle of "no smoke without fire." (It is quite another matter that our senses do not "photograph" their surroundings, and that existence as such is inseparable from the attitudes of the one who sees, hears, and feels.) When I act in accordance with this stance of faith, phenomena occur that seem to me to be meaningful—as, for instance, when someone claims to have heard what I have said and, on this basis, communicates to me his anger or his pleasure.

II

Long before I was able to ask whether my surroundings really were surroundings, and not merely subjective mental phenomena produced by anonymous illusionists in hidden engine-rooms inside or outside my brain, I was profoundly concerned to know whether or not those surroundings loved me. I should not have worried very much—at least not at that early stage—if someone had come along and tried to frighten me by claiming that I had dreamed everything. My only answer would have been a howl—for the sole purpose of producing the dream I knew as my mother. This interest in love cannot be reduced to a psychical mechanism for the production of food and dry clothes. It has been proved that a child's health does not depend exclusively on such things, but also on what we might (cautiously) call "friendliness." And this hunger for love is never satisfied; all our lives we are crying out for more. Its stock question, "Do you love me?"—asked at first of parents, brothers and sisters, aunts and uncles, then of classmates and teachers, and then of one group after another—never seems to receive a satisfactory answer. Just how important this question in fact is, is seen very clearly in those who really believe themselves to be loved by everyone. In a sense, such a replete man or woman seems to be in a worse state than the person who is hungry. It is not enough that a couple of friends answer the question in the affirmative, or even that society as a whole gives a positive answer; he seeks the friendship of stones and other objects. (The expression "a heart of stone" contains a human confession: we wanted the stone to love us, and felt profoundly rejected the first time we tripped over it and hurt ourselves.) All through our lives we are asking this question of the world we live in; and even when a person no longer believes that existence loves or hates, or that objects, times, and seasons are sent as personal communications from some cosmic Father, he still gazes out into the empty silences of space and calls, "Do you love me?" In the words of Pär Lagerkvist's poem:

> Why does a creature lie down there in the darkness and cry to
>   something that does not exist?
> Why does he do it?
> There is no one to hear the voice crying in the darkness.
> But why does the cry exist?

In the long run, love is not content to remain a dream. All self-satisfaction is dissatisfaction. But if the one who is looking for tokens of love receives no answer from his surroundings, or if the answer hurts, it may be that he cannot tolerate the belief that his surroundings exist. In many of the religious and philosophical systems in which matter is regarded as an illusion, skepticism is born of disappointment. Matter is not only a lie; it is evil—a dirty mark on the soul. Therefore the only thing to be done is to seek after liberation from the bonds of matter in a purely spiritual existence, accessible through asceticism and contemplation, and frequently connected with the idea of death as a final liberation from the pollution of matter. Belief in reincarnation enters into these religions as a complication, a spoke in the wheel for those who hoped to get away from the world of time and space once and for all. It is not, as we in the West often tend to assume, a product of the desire for long life, and repeated lives, in the world of matter; it expresses instead the fear that this is what must be. The road to nirvana is a long road.

It is comparatively rare for us to look upon matter as an illusion. It is more usual to deny the reality of that which is beyond matter, which we normally call "God." In some cases this is clearly connected with the fact that the major religion of the West believes that matter has been created by this God, while many other religions hold that even if there is a God, he has nothing whatsoever to do with what happens in the world of phenomena. But there are also some religions that represent their gods as cruel; for that matter, how do we know that God (if there is a God) is not cruel or treacherous or temperamental? Bitter experience of what we call "life" is in itself no proof of the nonexistence of God. But it makes a lot of people want to disbelieve in his existence. And that is not all. If our cosmic lovesickness seems to arouse a response like that, we become tempted to deny even our own craving, and to interpret religion as a departure from normal behavior.

We are reminded in this context of Freud's characterization of religion as a universal human neurosis. If religion is really an expression of the tension between our insatiable craving for love and the cruelty of life, then it is anything but surprising that the history of religion should demonstrate so many symptoms pointing in that direction. But that these symptoms should be a decisive argument against belief in a spiritual reality is as unreasonable as to argue that the object of unrequited love should cease to exist if the unhappy lover develops a neurosis. Although this dream-world may bear witness to an incurable crisis of confidence, it does not therefore mean that we get any closer to either health or reality by lopping off one of the horns of our painful dilemma and assuring ourselves that we are created only for this world. On the contrary, this attitude often resembles the type of withdrawal from reality that so frequently threatens the healing of a neurosis.

III

It may be profitable, if we would penetrate deeper into this problem, to consider at this point a complication in our love affair with the universe—a complication that can cause even more trouble than a straightforward "no" to our longing for love. For as it reaches out to the world, our longing is brought up against a counterquestion: "What can you give me?" It seems that love, if it exists at all, exists merely as some sort of reciprocal relationship. He who has nothing to give gets nothing in return. The person who enters the world asking for love, finds himself caught up in a system of values and expectations, evidently created by the demands of other persons for different levels, different forms, and different gifts of love. The human response that is produced in answer to these expectations we call *con*-science, *respons*-ibility, or something else indicating that it is a matter of fellowship, of question and answer, of dialogue and drama. Our need for love can be measured against our willingness to have such demands made of us. Attempts have been made from time to time to cure sick people by telling them that their feelings of guilt are meaningless and pointless. This solution, however, seems to have been abandoned for the most part. And this is just as well, because we look upon it as an insult when we are told that conscience and a sense of responsibility are nothing more than the products of inward and outward circumstances. We are not satisfied to be brought before all manner of petty courts of law; nothing but final, irrevocable judgment will do. *The moral function is inextricably bound up with our need for love.*

Whether this is in fact so is perhaps best seen by observing what happens when we act as though it were not so.

If our sense of responsibility is prevented from referring itself to what it regards as transcendent authority, and is referred instead to the authority of society or the individual conscience, what often happens is that the divine authority returns incognito. We unconsciously come to look upon the Justice Department or the individual's feeling for what is right and proper as a representative of a higher world. Or else we elevate human authority to divine rank. To be sure, the terrors of condemnation are no longer experienced with reference to heavenly codes of law; but the earthly code is no less terrible. When religion is removed from public life, the words used to express moral values either keep, or in some cases increase, their metaphysical overtones. *Weltall-Erde-Mensch*, the bible of the East German youth organization *Jugendweihe*, contains denunciations that seem to be wreathed in clouds of sulfur; for instance, "When one considers all that we have said about the imperialists and monopolist capitalists, there can be only one solution: we must drive them out permanently; we must denounce them like plague bacteria, if we would live happy lives! . . . These murderers and criminals, the monopolist capitalists. . . ." Similarly the pioneers, the heroes of Communism, are not infrequently portrayed in superhuman terms. Take for example these words of the prominent French Communist Jeanette Vermeersch: "Today is Ascension Day. It is no hypothetical, invented being who has flown away by a miracle. No, it is a fresh and noble youth of 27, a young Communist who has risen higher than heaven."[1]

---

[1] Since these words were written, the Chinese "cultural revolution," with its virtual deification of Mao Tse-tung, has given us a still more striking example of the same tendency.

But it is quite possible to come to regard one's own personality and individuality as an absolute authority:

> to devalue every value,
> to discard
> what was never my property
> but bestowed from beyond:
> the genuine,
> the Archimedean point,
> the key that arises
> from the heart of being.

The author of these lines, the Swedish poet Bertil Malmberg,
has himself called in question this recipe for autosalvation.
"The nucleus of personality" might, he points out, be nothing
but "the whim of a stubborn old man." But it is rather a question of a kind of secularized pietism. For while the deification
of one individual can result in the oppression of others, it seems
to me that an illusory apotheosis of this kind can equally well
result in self-torment strangely similar to the anxieties of the
pious.

And what happens if the individual's sense of responsibility
is purged of all metaphysical elements? I make no claim to be
able to provide a formula for what happens in such cases. But
there are examples that show that the suppression of the metaphysical dimension of the sense of responsibility can give rise
to inner disturbances. Viktor Frankl tells of an atheist who
became impotent as a result of the compulsive idea that God
was going to take revenge on him. The same man was also
afraid that his mother and his sister would have a hard time
in purgatory if he were to make technical mistakes in the
adjustment of a radio. Malmberg puts it like this:

> What reason says, assumes, and knows
> has little worth and matters little
> —when the sense of an eternal judge
> passes like a shudder through our nights.

It is also worth noting that when Sartre tries to persuade
us to believe in a responsibility within ourselves—an ingrown
responsibility—he also gives an account of the distress with
which man responds to such a contradiction. Sometimes faith is

regarded as an escape from this distress; as Camus said of Kierkegaard, "What was wrong with him was that he wanted to be cured." One must, in other words, accept one's distress and be faithful to it. So there is evidently an escape into health, and not only an escape into sickness.

Let me remind you of what we were trying to prove—which may be necessary, since some reader may perhaps think that I have brought out these examples as proofs of the existence of God. I am not at all convinced that a person who is healthy and free from complexes is closer to the truth than the one who is hounded by anxiety. I am still seeking evidence of the extent to which a consciousness of responsibility has to do with the experience of transcendent authority.

A similar problem arises, in a way, when good health is made into a primary norm. Just listen to the tone of voice that the "picture of health" uses when he moralizes about what he calls "sickness," or when the man who has no complexes comments on another person's suspected symptoms: "My, you *are* aggressive today!" The tone of voice comes from the heights of mental health, from the seat of salvation. As does the indignation affected by some writers when they are attacking the idea that people might be responsible for their actions, or that their consciences might contain more than the deposits of treatment during infancy. An indignation at the belief that there is something to be indignant about.

IV

It seems, then, as though metaphysics resembles a stubborn weed: we may uproot it or try to bury it, but sooner or later it will reappear in our experience of responsibility. But if our experience of reality as a cosmic love affair can influence our sense of responsibility in this way, may it not be equally true that our sense of responsibility can in its turn influence our experience of reality? It is not inconceivable that we want to raise a barrier between ourselves and certain realities, not because God does not measure up to our expectations, but because we do not measure up to his. Perhaps there is a different form of distress than that which is born of godlessness, namely that which is born of our experience of divine love.

I should like to try to demonstrate this by giving a couple of examples of the way in which our sense of being permanently answerable has an influence on our willingness to recognize the evidences of love, which we cry after so bitterly, when we get them.

We see most clearly, perhaps, what this is all about in the case of the man or woman who becomes the object of a cosmic craving for love on the part of some other person. It is common enough in our civilization to find someone practically deifying a man or a woman, and making him or her the object of a desire as infinite as that with which deity would be approached, if it were believed that deity existed. A love story of this order often ends in terror, not least for the one who has been loved in this way and has found that he or she is wholly inadequate to meet its demands. And it may be that such a person thereafter becomes afraid to accept gifts.

Now I wonder whether the fact that so many people are afraid to acknowledge undeserved success may not have a similar background. If someone finds that his dreams are being realized to such an extent that he might justifiably be called a darling of the gods, try telling him so, and you will very likely find that he will defend himself as though you were accusing him of something dishonorable. Tell him that he is doing well, and he will regard it as an accusation. He is keeping an account of his good fortune as though it were a guilty burden that some day he will have to answer for. Our craving for love is infinite —but are we not afraid to have it satisfied?

Our incurable sense of guilt—a secret conviction that no one could ever measure up to infinite love—shows itself in the mass of counterclaims with which we defend ourselves from the danger of falling in debt to love. Counterclaims against the world around us. The uncontrollable urge to criticize our fellow men sometimes has this background. We look upon their achievements as accusations, even when they have little enough to do with us. And we know how true it is (though upon other premises) that, as Sartre said, "Hell is other people."

Similarly, the accusations we direct against our surroundings can also be interpreted as acts of self-defense. As though we

were trying to answer the hypothetical accusations of a hypothetical God by telling him that he hasn't done terribly well,
either.

In his play *The Burning Javelin* (*Det brinnande spjutet*)
Tore Zetterholm[2] has a passage of dialogue that fits the pattern
rather well. Frank, a missionary who has lost his faith, warns
David, who has been a skeptic but is now on the verge of faith,
that he had better watch out. If he has no faith, he can never
be a Judas. To which David replies that Judas might not have
been altogether guilty either. "That was the role he was given.
Perhaps we all are."

Frank answers: "Yes, that's right! And that's why I don't
want to have anything to do with Him—with the God who invented the whole business . . . . It's no excuse to say that He has
created elephants and anteaters and damned Milky Ways! It's
no excuse for Him that He lets us choose our own hell ourselves
—when He's the one who forces us to choose!"

And in Pär Lagerkvist's novel *The Sybil* (*Sibyllan*) Ahas-
uerus says of Christ: "I don't understand much of what he
teaches about love; only enough to know that it's not for me.
And is he *really* so loving?"

V

I am not now looking for a theodicy. I am not asking
whether these accusations are justified. I am saying that behind
our craving for love there is a wish that they *were* justified.
Our dream of a loving universe can become a nightmare of
guilt, and that is when we erect defensive walls of accusation
—a countermove of mistrust and bitterness. And then there
develops a whole world of accusation. This is much more than
merely an individual phenomenon. When people emerge who
seem to be charged with this sort of negative current, it proves
that the frames of reference they need to attract others are
there, ready and waiting. Realms of hatred are there, poised,
waiting only for their Führer. And the more one studies these
negative patterns, the more one has the impression of a pulsat-
ing network—a living organism, a collective ego made up of

[2] Swedish playwright, novelist and critic, born in 1915.

negativisms. As though there were a third party: not only we
and life, but something far more dead than biological death.
A contradiction of God's cosmos. And it may be worth remembering that the Bible never represents evil as the ridiculous
figure we imagine when we talk about "the devil," but as having its focus in a power called the Accuser, or Slanderer. In
Greek, *ho diábolos;* in English, the devil.

A net of accusations is spread over human existence, and I
wonder how many of the messages concerning the benevolence
or malevolence of the world around us have to pass through
this dubious system of communications in order to reach us. In
many cases it would seem that the direct link has been broken,
with the result that one has a sense of dealing with the shadows
of things, and not with the things themselves. This watering-
down of reality is reminiscent of the way the devil is introduced in Goethe's *Faust:*

> Ich bin der Geist, der stets verneint!
> Und das mit Recht; denn alles, was entsteht,
> ist wert dass es zu Grunde geht;
> drum besser wär's, dass nichts entstünde.
> So ist denn alles, was ihr Sünde,
> Zerstörung, kurz das Böse nennt,
> mein eigentliches Element.[3]

Thus through our entire system of value and judgment—with
which we try to justify our existence among men or before God
—an impression spreads of second-hand reality or unreality.
Our social status, won with such effort, defended with such
energy, is sometimes suspiciously reminiscent of a game of
charades.

But where does this world of images end? It spreads like a
pestilence. The objects reflected on my retina, the table I knock

[3] I am the Spirit of Negation:
  And justly so; for all that is created
  Deserves to be annihilated.
  'Twere better, thus, that there were no creation.
  Thus everything that you call evil,
  Destruction, ruin, death, the devil,
  Is my pure element and sphere.
                    (Act II, Sc. V, tr. J. S. Blackie)

against as I pass, the jet that roars overhead, but which I do not see—is this reality or merely an image of reality? And I: what am I? The signs tell me that I am not the only one who is seeking his identity. Cartoon heroes and brilliant writers, pop stars and politicians—they all serve as pegs on which to hang lost personalities.

We saw to begin with how faith in the evidence of our senses fell under severe strain when the world was exposed to our craving for love without being able to satisfy it. We paused for a moment to consider religion as a neurotic phenomenon, born of the unresolved conflict between an undenied hunger for love and an undenied reality. We then looked at morals, arising as the counterclaim of our surroundings on our search for love. Finally we saw how the counterdemands of life, as we experience them, influence our attitude to reality, and how afraid we are to be loved to excess. We saw how our love affair with life creates a world of accusation and bitterness—mighty collective systems of defense against complaints, real or imagined. It all ended with our faith in the evidence of our senses being shaken once more, not because we could not tolerate the cruelty of life, but because we could not tolerate being unworthy of the joy of life, and therefore we had to deny it.

VI

I shall now attempt to outline the importance of Christ for my attempts to come to grips with the complex of problems I have described. In point of fact everything that I have said so far is to be found in the problem of our Lord's suffering and death, and I cannot tell how much of it has been colored by the passion narratives. At all events, many of these attempts become fully conscious and inescapable in the light of that drama. The question of whether there is any mercy (or at least justice) in the world, the observation that it is precisely the attempt to wash one's hands of them that causes many of our worst transgressions, the impression that the evil of this world is somehow a coherent net or trap, the feeling of unreality in face of state and church dignity and righteousness—all these are recognizable in the trial and execution of Christ. That is why many people believe that our history was summed up just there. I even suspect that most of what we nowadays call doubt begins there, for it was there that we saw most clearly that our deepest craving was not for explanations. The only thing that can silence our protest is love. We saw it because it was he who had told us that in all that happens there is someone who loves us, and it was he who experienced the loving-kindness of the world when someone refuses to join its charades. If *he* had not said so much about love, our question about why there should be such a thing as war in the world would never have touched such depths of bitterness; our doubt was put into words by his executioners, just before he died. Once you have heard the sarcasm in their voices, you can never forget it: "He trusted in God!"

But we must look at the man, and not only at what happened to him. The reason why the whole demonstration of the power of religious and civil authority strikes us as nothing but a lie and a charade is the man dressed as a fool, the face beneath the ironical inscription. The fact that he is dressed up—among all the hypocrites who play their parts so "correctly" and con-vincingly—intensifies the impression of reality.

In the midst of the power game, there among all the masks, we see a naked face. Paul saw it too: "Reality is in Christ." This man is not part of the game; he is there to die.

VII

If I leaf through the documents about his life, I find that he left in his words and actions the system of arguments and merits we use in order to say (though with many paraphrases and evasions): "None of it is really my fault—won't someone love me?" And when he leaves this system, he does not emulate the Buddha, slipping away from the court in order to seek truth beyond all desire and all demands. Christ, if anyone, is involved in reality: in the joys and sorrows of his fellow men. But he was in no way involved in the art of making friends and influencing people.

To express it in negative terms, we might say with Paul that he did not insist on having his own way; and at once we recall that Paul used these words to describe a quality of love. Hav-ing reached this point in a study of the phenomenon called

Christ, one hesitates to use this word "love," devalued as it has become by the excesses of homiletical unction and poetical illumination. But there is really no alternative.

When we try to make him into an argument in a religious debate, however, this impression is endangered. For example, there is the discussion about the miracles he is said to have performed. The standard question is to ask whether natural laws can be broken in this way. But what is remarkable is not so much the miracles themselves as the involvement in human destiny out of which these narratives emerge. When it is claimed that he raised a dead boy outside the gate of Nain, it is not the miracle that impresses itself on the reader's mind, but its background: that he could not stand by and watch the woman who was the boy's mother weep. A thousand details over and above the discussion of what is scientifically possible or impossible demonstrate that the man was like that, and that his character was very largely responsible for the fate that overtook him. That is why he abandoned all securities and entrenchments: in order to be with people beyond all the superficial judgments. It has nothing to do with a give-and-take relationship; it is a matter of unconditional mercy. *It is exactly what we have been looking for all along.*

It is important that we should not lose sight of the evidence on which these claims are based. For it might otherwise be no more than wishful thinking. For example, what do we make of the observation that Christ had little enough love to spare for Pharisees and other opponents? The objection is a real one, and it must be admitted at once that we must not expect the biblical material to fit into any preconceived notion of a permanently smiling divine benevolence. At the same time, the fact that Jesus' outbursts of wrath have not been suppressed should inspire a degree of confidence. Evidently the narrative is more important than the theology of a loving God.

Furthermore, it is evident that the passion described in the Gospels is not the same thing as, say, the Buddhists' mild compassion, dealt out evenly to all created beings. Jesus takes sides —specifically, the side of the underprivileged, those despised by the moralists. His love penetrates downwards, and that is what makes it so unlike most of what the history of philosophy and religion calls love. That is why it contains anger—anger against spiritual vested interests who wanted to monopolize salvation. At times it could even be turned against his honorable disciples; when they tried to stop children from climbing onto his knee, or when they wanted to call down fire on the Samaritans. And even if his friends exaggerated his love (which was hardly likely, considering that it was not exactly popular among his, and their, leading contemporaries), his opponents did not forget it, either. They for their part tended to call him things like "the friend of tax-collectors and sinners"—an expression that had a somewhat different sound before it was varnished by preachers. The same applies to the scornful observation, "He saved others; he cannot save himself."

Today Christ still wins disciples through his opponents; one quotation from the Swedish author Lars Ahlin[4] will suffice: "I heard Nietzsche's raucous polemic against Christianity through a wall as it were. Is it really true that Christianity is an inward revolt of slaves? Even if it is, it did not repel me; instead it aroused a secret and unreasonable hope." In a way the same applies to the attempts to have Christ certified insane: both those that have left traces in the Gospels and those that crop up from time to time in the present-day debate. I shall discuss some other aspects of these arguments in due course. Here I should merely like to point out how well they fit the picture of a man who breaks out of the circle of those who set the trends, and who consider themselves spiritually rich. And anyone who has ever had to accompany people to those frontier regions in which words like "normal," "healthy," and "well-adjusted" are no longer usable, cannot avoid being confronted by his own limitations when it comes to understanding and loving these folks. May the path between the olive trees perhaps lead us into this country? That night he made a path of sorrow, while most of us were no longer capable of even watching with him.

He believed himself to have been sent by the reality that is hidden from us. He is also said to have called himself "the Life," and one of the most serious of the accusations made against him seems to have been that he regarded himself as

[4] Ahlin, born in 1915, was one of the leading Swedish novelists of the 1940s and 1950s.

God's representative. In other words, he was like that because God is like that. And you can say what you will about that claim: it is not exactly the kind of thing one normally expects of the builders of religious systems. It means that Almighty God stood there with the spit of our accusations on his face. But this is in no way contradicted by our earlier observations that we find it so hard to tolerate the encounter with reality above the level of accusation, and that we are so afraid of being loved. The gospel says that because he would not submit to our standards of judgment, we condemned him. He created, at the heart of this phantom world, a little clearing for the living; and so we killed him. And this fits exactly with what he believed his work to be—to struggle with the Accuser in order to bring about a reconciliation between ultimate reality and the world of men. Surely the Accuser was not idle.

VIII

Theologians have often used the image of a court of law in order to explain how it is that God can forgive without compromising his righteousness. When this image is forced into becoming part of a system, what often happens is that God is given the role of a chilly and impartial judge, who observes how a debt is slowly paid off by means of suffering, until the last ounce is exacted and the accused can be set free. And if we forget what the Bible says about the Accuser, God may also be made to speak his lines—and who can measure the distress caused to those who have met God playing the part of Satan? But things stand out in a new light if we accept Jesus' own testimony to his identity with God, or if we remember what Paul said: "God was in Christ reconciling the world to himself." There is insufficient distance between God and what happened on the cross for it to be the place of an impartial judgment. It is even more impossible to imagine God in the role of prosecutor. For he was the one who suffered in our midst.

If we were to attempt to express the meaning of this in forensic terms, there is a much better analogy than that of judicial guilt. Since it is a matter of love, broken fellowship, and the returning of gifts, the divorce courts would provide a much better basis of comparison than the criminal courts. Christ would then represent the one from whom we were seeking a divorce; he would not only represent, he would actually *be* the opposite party. And then we would have reason to look at the story of the passion of Christ to see how unrequited love acts, if it really is love.

It can never seek to revenge itself on the loved one, and still remain love. Nor is it capable of drawing a veil over the whole business, calling black white, and saying, "I don't care whether you are unfaithful or not." It has only one alternative, and that is to suffer together with the other person. And this is where we see the face of the one whom we have despised. The illusion is shown up; the Accuser's net is torn apart. God is love, and his love burns bright at this point in the history of mankind.

IX

I consider all this to be relevant to the experiences I spoke of to begin with: relevant to the quest for boundless love, to the possibility of accepting this kind of love instead of locking oneself up in one's own guilt and fear. But the chain of events we have been considering has not been something that we have been able to work out with the help of what we otherwise know about life; nor is it easily fitted in as the cornerstone of a philosophy. In fact I am convinced that the genuineness of the narrative is attested by its very awkwardness, since no one could possibly have thought it up as a convenient solution to the problem of life. Claiming to be a message from God, it was regarded first of all as foolishness. Of course, it is not enough to answer the person who is looking for evidence of its truth by pointing out that it does not fit into our preconceived notions of what truth should be like. How, then, are we supposed to know whether or not it is true?

He himself said: "If anyone will do the will of him who sent me, he will know whether my teaching is of God." In other words, what he is recommending is an empirical test. This may well arouse the suspicions of some of my readers. Might this not be a pious ambush? Let me only answer that it would do Christ a great injustice if one were to try to compromise one's intellectual integrity for his sake. Under his influence, the doubting mind will certainly be made to exercise its doubts, for he brings many authorities tumbling down, and not least religious authorities—if anyone should be tempted to suppose that I am trying to persuade my reader to conform to one or other of the "official" Christian types. But turn the dangerous question that has been there all along—the question of whether love exists—and direct mankind's craving like a concave mirror at this segment of history: do this, and see what happens. Then come face to face with your fellow men from within the Gospels, as it were, and see what happens. It is worth noting that long before these Gospels were put into written form, the focus of their narratives was embodied in a drama, the drama of what we now call the Eucharist. There are realities that will always remain inaccessible as long as they are merely looked at, but which are accessible to the one who is prepared to act. And in the perspective of the Eucharist it becomes impossible to speak of prayer as passive and work as active; both are transmuted on the altar into flesh and blood, and they go out into the everyday world side by side.

Must I now attempt to persuade my reader to become involved in this drama by describing the positive results that will follow? Can one expect, for instance, to become a harmonious and well-balanced person in this way? I am once more reminded of the voice from the past: "One must accept one's distress." A couple of years ago I came across this motto in rather an unexpected place: in Gertrud von le Fort's short story *Die Letzte am Schafott* (Munich, 1931). But there it refers to a nun, who found no peace just because she was consecrated to the service of Christ in Gethsemane. This much is at all events certain: that the belief in the Christian way as a smooth and trouble-free progression from life to Life is, and always has been, illusory. And it should, I think, be clear from what I have said so far that I do not regard peace of mind and satisfaction with one's lot as in any sense evidence of being in league with truth.

There are other criteria by which one may judge whether the approach to the Christ of the Gospels is an approach to reality. Experiences of a similar nature to what takes place when one decides to take seriously the evidence of one's senses. Something happens—leading us to new experiences, and thus convincing us of its importance.

One of these experiences is that hell changes places. It can
no longer be identified with "other people." As Zossima says
in *The Brothers Karamazov*, "Fathers and teachers, I think:
'What is hell?' And I argue thus: 'It is suffering, since one can
no longer love.'" And this is characteristic of the way in which
Christ encounters "other people." Let me remind you of what
I said earlier, that it is Christ who taught us to ask God what
was his purpose in doing certain things. That is no hypothetical
question: it is personal, intimate, binding. As when Petrus in
Sara Lidman's novel *Valley of Pitch* (*Tjärdalen*) talks to the
minister about the criminal Jonas, who has just died a terrible
death: "There is one thing you can't get away from; you wonder what God meant to do with someone like Jonas. He never
asked to be born, and he couldn't help being so wretchedly
equipped." The minister does his best to come to God's defense: still, it is obvious that Petrus, with all his doubts and
his sick conscience, is much more deeply influenced by Christ
than the minister is, and that it was this fact that forced him
to see. Experiences of this order are decisive for anyone who
wants to know whether he is getting closer to, or farther away
from, reality. This is the criterion we were looking for. The
most important thing is not to make everything fit, but to be
forced to observe and take to one's heart people and circumstances that spoil an equation that we hoped we might solve.
As the minister (not realizing quite what he was saying) had
to admit: "Yes, Herr Andersson, it is a great responsibility to
be someone's neighbor, and to have eyes with which to see."

It may also happen that as one approaches Christ, one comes
to see the material world in a new light. When C. S. Lewis
compares heaven and hell in *The Great Divorce*, he tells how
the ghosts who came from the great city of shades to visit the
other side had great difficulty in moving about because of their
own insubstantial nature, compared to the "matter" of heaven.
They hurt their feet on the grass, and find that they are even
unable to lift the flowers and fruit of the garden. This is in
fact entirely in line with the Christian answer to our question
about boundless love—that it is not an answer of spirituality
and ideas, but an answer of flesh and blood. We might go still
further, and say that no one who believes that God has been
a human embryo can continue to regard the physical side of

human existence as irrelevant. Karl Jaspers in his book *Nietzsche and Christianity* has compared the Greek and the Christian views of creation, pointing out that the Greeks were only interested in the reasonable and orderly aspect of the universe; matter as such was of no consequence. The Christian belief in creation, on the other hand, provides an impulse toward close examination of what is created—toward empirical reality. "This science emerges from the *Logos,* who does not shut himself up within himself (as the ancient Greeks would have claimed), but, open to the a-logical, enters into it himself by submitting to it." If this is correct, then there is a passion for empirical knowledge that has sprung from Christianity as from a root, which is not to say that it need be especially religious.

It used to be common to find Christians dividing the world into three concentric circles: the spheres of those who are believers with us, redeemed with us, and created with us. Some begin by believing in a Creator first and a creation second, instead of vice versa—"belief" understood here as a conviction about the reality of someone or something. But it is not a matter of some sort of laboratory reality, the only function of which is to be looked at and recorded. The Christian's interest in animals, plants, and objects is a family interest; they are not merely created, but created together with us. There is a dimension of respect and coinherence in this involvement.

This belief in creation, rooted in pre-Christian and even pre-biblical religions and cultures, but questioned in critical and chaotic times, was subject to a severe trial when we saw Christ crucified. But it was there that we saw unconditional love; there we were forced to take account of "other people," those who are redeemed with us. To enter into dialogue with the suffering God was to renew our dialogue with them—to recognize that they are "with us," even when they are unloved.

The circle then widens, like a ripple on the face of a pond, to the world in which the Word became flesh. Once more we can see it as "created with us." And the Johannine Prologue takes on a subjective dimension, as its description of the way in which the world came into being corresponds to the way in which it is made new *for me:* "In the beginning was the Word. . . . Without him was not anything made that was made."

Those who live in this perspective—our fellow Christians—must, of course, join in comparing what they believe with other experiences. The Scriptures promise no final and absolute explanation of the contradictions that arise in the process, at least not in this life. But they point us back to the inescapable realities of the gospel: "for he who does not love his brother whom he has seen, cannot love God whom he has not seen." So although we "suffer with him" (Rom. 8:17), we know "that the whole creation has been groaning in travail together until now" (Rom. 8:22). Fellow Christians do not merely have common opinions on various matters, they have a common cross—the distress of God and the world. The validity of what they believe is therefore tested in the fires of service rather than in the rough and tumble of debate. Whether and to what extent the individual can count himself as a "fellow Christian" is in no way determined by the number of dogmas that he can accept, but the degree in which he orients himself by the cross and the three concentric circles around it. Christ did not call this a "world-view" or a philosophy; he called it Life.

These three coinherences restore the individual's personal identity—something that was on the point of disappearing among all the masks (*personae*) and images. He has a new opportunity of existence as a person.

Here, finally, we are taken seriously. Our craving for love, our suspicion of everything that goes by the name of love, our responsibility—these things that happened to Jesus call to our innermost being, demanding an answer. Here man himself is addressed. *Addressed.* Not persuaded to abandon, mutilate, or throttle his individuality, but assured that he is a real and unique person, neither to be bought nor sold, even at the price of the whole world. He is assured of fellowship, not with one or two individuals on the level of conventional values, but with life as a whole, which he can address and by which he can be addressed. He is assured of fellowship with God.

2.

THROUGH DOUBT TO FAITH

It has been rightly said that faith always involves a belief in the truth of something. Faith must, as Luther knew, have an object; and that object must exist here in time and space, because the Christian faith knows no other God than God incarnate. The gospel itself is a piece of earthly material, and tells of something that happened at a definite time and in a definite place.

Since that time, the church has expressed a variety of opinions about what actually happened, and has attempted to make them fit one another—occasionally to some people's annoyance, as though there were anything unusual in this process, as though this were not the way in which all people work intellectually (all those, that is, that have an intellect), just like creatures building a house, adding timber to timber until it starts to look like something: like Christian doctrine, for example. And if believers do not work in this way, there is no lack of evidence to show that this is the way the devil works. If the church has no doctrine, then the others will build the house. In the last resort, doctrinal compulsion will come from outside; it is the heretic that forces the church to have a doctrine.

This essay is not to be understood as an attempt to gloss over the demand for intellectual integrity; that particular demand presses on the believer at least as much as on the unbeliever. But intellectual integrity requires that one should be able to distinguish between fact and opinion. The gospel must not be identified with doctrines about it, however well attested they may be in the traditions of the church. Making this kind of identification leads to a kind of theology of merit, in which salvation finally becomes a mental artifact. Doctrines then cease to be ways to Christ, and become instead fences, to be cleared or not. These fences are often classified by

43

degree, so that some come to be regarded as compulsory, others as optional. Should someone refuse to believe that Jesus was "conceived by the Holy Spirit," well, it is excusable, and he will not be excluded from the altar just on that account. But whatever he believes or does not believe, it is generally agreed that he ought to believe in the existence of God. If one is sufficiently "broad-minded," one can, however, show a certain amount of respect for those who believe in "spiritual reality," or at least have high ideals. The phenomenon as such is reminiscent of the well-known hierarchy of occupations sometimes affected by the religious: at the top there are bishops, priests, and ministers, then come doctors and deaconesses, then professors and others who deal with theoretical questions, finally, right at the bottom, come the manual laborers. Or take note of the kind of literature that is read in some Christian circles. It is of no account whether it is heretical, as long as it is "spiritual." It can be as biblical as Bengel,[1] but it will not meet with the approval of the pious if it deals with earth and soot and dirt and distress and devilry. All the time there is a scale of values, from the spiritual down to the material. It need hardly be said that this is not a scale of Christian values.

Atheism, however, has a clear precedence among heresies. This means that the hyperorthodox have a convenient object with which to compare their certainty. For the one who is uncertain about whether he is on the inside or on the outside, it is always a comfort to know of someone who is obviously on the outside, someone who appears to be very different. On the other side of the boundary, too, there is comfort and assurance, for the atheist need not spare a thought for Christ and his cross.

Strangely enough, the Scriptures are hardly interested in this distinction. We find that Christ went about with people who lived the most extraordinary lives and held the most unusual views, and yet he seemed seldom to question them about their opinions. Here we have a Gentile, from the morally dubious country around Tyre and Sidon. She—yes, on top of

[1] Johann Albrecht Bengel (1687-1752) was a German theologian who produced the first critical edition of the Greek New Testament (1734); his *Gnomon Novi Testamenti* (1742) was the first "modern" commentary on the text of the New Testament.

everything this Gentile was a woman, and thus utterly hopeless from the doctrinal point of view—she knows only that
Jesus is the son of David, and that means a kind of Jewish
pretender to the throne. And so she imagines that this man
might be able to help her tortured child. She is stubborn, she
is impudent, she is (perhaps) almost hysterical. And then
she is finally told that her faith is great. Faith? What faith?
The only thing she believed was that Jesus held the key to
her personal, entirely concrete, problem. The learned apostles
often had to tell stories of this kind. It cannot have been easy
for them, but they evidently had no choice, because this was
important.

A human being in distress meets Jesus—and remember that
the pietist preaching technique has not yet been invented, so
that the meeting is on an entirely unspiritual level, brought
about with the help of the legs and not the emotions. Such
meetings still take place today. Here are you, and here he is.
Your situation is characterized, not by the fact that you have
this, that, and the other; but by the fact that you are lacking
something vital. Out of this encounter, faith is born. To which
someone immediately objects that now, at any rate, I am
talking in religious and spiritual terms, for how otherwise is an
encounter to take place across an interval of two thousand
years? But it is not some spiritual or religious effort on your
part that bridges this gap; it is the gospel—the gospel in the
Bible and the Eucharist, things that are what they are whatever you may believe about them. The church teaches that
Christ is flesh and blood in these Scriptures and in this drama,
just as much as in the figure we call "the Jesus of history."
And so from the point of view of doctrine, the two thousand
years mean nothing. All that is necessary is an encounter
between a sinner—perhaps even an atheist—and the New Testament; and what is remarkable is that the atheist does not have
first of all to be convinced that there is something wrong with
his philosophy. One might even go so far as to consider that
"the God-shaped gap" unites him with a Christ who asks why
God has forsaken us.

For if we are otherwise called to be faithful to our earthly
situation, to serve our neighbor and to bear our cross even
when it all seems pointless, why do we make of our doubt an

exception to this call? We have to take disease and poverty and war seriously: that is our Christian duty, and no amount of pious emotion must be allowed to obscure these realities. But as soon as the intellect is activated and starts asking questions, it seems that we are suddenly supposed to pretend that we are in heaven already, or that all our questions have already been answered, or else that God has created us stupider than we are. Faith is not escapism; but distress (even intellectual distress) is the field in which faith grows. Doubt, too, must be part of the calling in which Christ is our brother.

Doubt that justice is built into our present world-order. Doubt that the stars are beautiful and roses friendly. Doubt that God is, or cares. These doubts must be woven into the fabric of our times, now if ever, amid the stench of rotten flesh and perfumed phrases, the defense estimates and starvation. This is the history we share with Christ.

The documents of doubt, the Holy Scriptures, in which doubt reads itself into power and protest, are like that. Unbelief, too, knows these things, but why should unbelief protest; why should unbelief rack its brains and ask questions? Unbelief is emptiness, but a replete and satisfied emptiness that has taken up residence in the "realities" of the age, and needs no other. Doubt can use the words of unbelief, but cries to heaven because of the blood of Abel. Doubt implies disappointment. Doubt demands a faith to call in question. Its darkness is like the darkness at the sixth hour, part of Good Friday. And when it meets Christ, it recognizes him. Not that it is at once dispersed in the light of the certainty that this is the Son of God. But doubt is a cross that waits for someone, and here is the one that it has been waiting for: the one who has reached the point at which contradictions meet, and is himself pierced; the one who is cursed until he becomes a curse—forgiving and blessing all the while. In his distress what doubt finds is not a curiosity of history, but its own situation. "Surely he has borne our griefs"—for we recognize them as they meet there.

Then when he says "Follow me," his words reach us as an invitation to leave the shelter of our private happiness and be with him and our fellow men in prayer and work. The Messiah of doubt calls us to watch with him and with mankind, while unbelief sleeps and the traitor lights his torches. The church, least of all, should be a bulwark against the call to live in our own age, every man with his neighbor—although the church often speaks of the present day as though she had nothing whatever to do with it. Her interest in the past, and particularly her profound reverence for the nineteenth century, has caused many a doubter to exclude Christ from the picture of what is taking place today. But of all the things that may separate us from Christ, the shock of shattered illusions is not one of them. What is there to prevent us from following in his footsteps in a situation that is ours and our neighbor's? What demand for *intellectual integrity* is supposed to exempt us from this call? If we refuse to enter into current social, political, economic, moral, and aesthetic problems with his cross before us—perhaps we refuse in the cause of science? A great deal has been said about his cross, but there is much in what Mauriac says, that in the last resort what gets us away from this subject is not his cross, but ours.

True, following Christ is one thing and faith in Christ is another—at any rate a good deal of the way. To be called is law; faith comes of the gospel. But following Christ is not merely a matter of doing certain things, it is also to be close to him. It has to do with the recognition that one's own situation has found its messiah. To enter the magnetic field of his work is to commit oneself, even without a thought of God. Whatever we may call it and however we may judge it, whoever this Jesus is and wherever he may come from, when he enters my doubt I can only say, "It is you—have mercy!"

What I mean is that the judgment we pass on him is of secondary importance. I do not know whether what happens should be called Christianity; but that, too, is of secondary importance. We must not allow Christianity to separate us from Christ. Whatever it is called, whatever it is not called—here he is, and here we are. This is seen most clearly in the Eucharist (which has been so carefully kept from those who need it the most). Suppose that on that last evening someone had said to him: "I don't understand a word of what you have been saying about God and his kingdom, but I can see that it is a dark night for us all, and I don't want to leave you; where would I go if I did?" It would have been unlike him to have shut the door on the doubter. And in any case, how much did the disciples understand about what was happening? That was the night he said to Peter, "What I am doing you do not know now, but afterward you will understand."

It is not a matter of trying to obliterate boundaries, of piling in all manner of apostles of unbelief among the faithful, of trying to publish flattering statistics of the percentage of believers in the population. It is still not a question of what things are to be called or the side of the ledger on which they are to be entered. It is a matter of an encounter between our reality and his. To be sure, no one knows what the final result will be. The doubter may come to doubt his doubt, and finally come to faith, not only in atonement and resurrection, but even faith in God the Father Almighty. For there is neither a different, nor a greater, gospel in the one affirmation than in the other. The entirety of apostolic riches is found in one single word, like the sun in a single drop of water, and once one has discovered it, one can embark on a voyage of exploration. Doubt is an uneasy bird, never still for a moment; but the impulse that makes it seek fresh fields, as though it would fly from itself, is a mystery.

But this uneasy questioning has more of the nature of faith in it than does the smug pride of possession that we confuse with faith, for faith is permanently in transit. Like the wind, "you do not know whence it comes or whither it goes." But you do not tolerate atheists in church in the hope of one day seeing them write edifying articles on the virgin birth. You are *not* looking for results. If you can repeat all twelve clauses in the Apostles' Creed with a clear conscience, that does not give you the right to look down on the doubter who can only manage half a clause and say "Who knows, some day he may believe all we believe?" If it is true that the entire gospel is contained in every fact of salvation, that means that faith is not something than can be measured by quantity. For the Gentile who only knows that Jesus is the Son of David might be more of a believer than all the apostles put together. The person who only sees him as the Messiah for our situation nevertheless sees the same Christ who was born of the Virgin Mary, and faith is a personal relationship to that Christ. Preaching and prayer and doctrine and ritual and baptism and the Eucharist are the magnetic field in which this gospel lives, this gospel that is Christ; and if it is Christ we are dealing with, then neither the church nor the unchurched have any right to set up a fence around him, with a notice to tell strangers to keep out. Let the children come. And sinners. And doubters. What happens after that is not to be recorded in the minutes, either. Let God decide who are believers and who are not. Faith is not supposed to have faith in faith, but in Christ; and it is the task of the church to bring us to him. We would see Jesus.

Let replete hyperfaith and self-satisfied unbelief play with their boundaries, anxious lest anyone should confuse them. But the hunger of faith and the desperation of doubt should know that the Christ of the church is none other than the Christ of sinners and skeptics. Whatever you may consider to be true or untrue, there is a personality like a rock in the midst of our history; and whether God exists or does not exist, *he* exists, and that is where the drama starts.

3.

MANDRAKE AND CRUCIFIX

"God is dead!" These were no empty words for those who, before history began, experienced the onset of winter as a cosmic catastrophe. They went out to look for the dead god of summer, and to take magical measures to ensure his return in the resurrection of the first green shoots of spring, which they duly celebrated. "Then he brought me to the entrance of the north gate of the house of the LORD; and behold, there sat women weeping for Tammuz" (Ezek. 8:14).

Ezekiel's horror at what he saw in his vision was understandable, for what he observed was apostasy from the law and monotheism to syncretistic fertility religion; but it need not prevent us from recognizing the reality behind the oldest of all cultic dramas—a fruitless, terrified reality, and the question, "When will the light return?"

A reality in which there is no sign of God is hardly an archaic motif. How big a gap is there really between waiting for Tammuz and belief in Progress? And where is the boundary between this ancient vegetation ritual and the kind of "life-affirmation" that was so common in the 1930s, and that, although it is gone from our literature, is not necessarily extinct. Bertil Malmberg's *Poems on the Frontier* (*Dikter vid gränsen* —1935) do not appear dated:

> In secret mankind thirsts to celebrate
> the long-abandoned feast of life's return
> —wielding again the enchanted double scepter,
> the cherubim revealed as bulls once more.

When modern biblical scholars have claimed to find traces of these ancient fertility rites in the Old Testament, there have been those who have felt extremely uneasy. "I sought him, but found him not; I called him, but he gave no answer"—to think that these words from the Song of Solomon might have something to do with a scarcely edifying vegetation rite! To think that the Bible is polluted by paganism, and the imagery of the mystics by concern for the cattle!

The continuation of this debate I leave in the hands of the exegetes. My concern is to point out the connection between a situation in pagan prehistory and the meaningless existence of modern man. A bitter contemporary doubt—"God is dead" —draws its mottoes from a primeval drama. They are woven into the fabric of different worlds of thought; nevertheless they speak of the same reality. They deal with different catastrophes; yet they originate in the same anxiety.

> They shall wander from sea to sea,
> and from north to east;
> they shall run to and fro, to seek the word of the LORD,
> but they shall not find it.
>
> (Amos 8:12)

It is widely believed that Greek tragedy, which of course also originated in a cultic drama, is woven on the same pattern as the Near Eastern vegetation rite. But there is no resurrection in Greek tragedy. It is not only a question of life and death. A new motif has been brought in: the motif of guilt. And guilt leads to death. Therefore atonement is the answer to the questions of both death and guilt.

But it is not the god who dies; nor is it the god who reconciles. God is no longer identifiable with nature; he is not humanity, and he is not suffering. God lives in his own world, and the demand for atonement comes from there. He it is who controls human destiny; but it is man who suffers and dies. So it is that Oedipus—without realizing the terrible implications of what he is saying—promises to drive away the evil from his people "for Phoebus and for Thebes." Someone has to suffer. And the chorus sings:

> Eager am I, afraid, heart-shaken with fear of thee—
> (Healer, Apollo of Delos, God of the Cry, give ear!)
> Shaken with reverent fear. Is it some new task to be set?
> Or is it some ancient debt thou wilt sweep in the fulness of
> time to the payment?
> Tell me thy secret, Oracle deathless, Daughter of golden
> Hope!
>
> (Trans. J. T. Sheppard)

But resurrection is not the only thing that has become superfluous in the tragedy. God himself, since he has become mankind's counterpart, has also become superfluous. Guilt itself is
perfectly capable of playing his role. Why else should so many
be guilty without God? No guilt is more fierce than that which
knows of no accuser; and our defense is suffering, which is
also infinite. "I'm not asking God or anybody for forgiveness,"
says Lavinia Mannon in "The Haunted," the last drama of
O'Neill's trilogy *Mourning Becomes Electra,* "I forgive myself!" But then, finally, she condemns herself to life imprisonment. "I'm the last Mannon. I've got to punish myself! . . . I'll
live alone with the dead, and keep their secrets, and let them
hound me, until the curse is paid out and the last Mannon is
let die! I know they will see to it I live for a long time! It
takes the Mannons to punish themselves for being born." The
last line of the trilogy says something about the transformation
that has come about in the ancient fertility festival now that
only man—guilty man—is left: "And tell Hannah to throw out
all the flowers."

In the world of the Bible, too, it is guilt that transforms the
festival. The Law comes to occupy the place of nature; and
God is the guardian of the Law, not its victim. Where the death
of God was once celebrated, now the King suffers death sym-
bolically for the sake of the people, in the shape of the sacrificial animal. "And the priests killed them [the he-goats] and
made a sin offering with their blood on the altar, to make
atonement for all Israel. For the king commanded that the
burnt offering and the sin offering should be made for all
Israel" (2 Chron. 29:24).

The distance between tragedy, ancient or modern, and this
animal symbolism should not be overestimated. In both cases
it is a matter of guilt requiring atonement, if all the flowers
are not to disappear from the world.

In both cases atonement is made by suffering, and the letter
to the Hebrews says, referring to this catharsis, that "almost
everything is purified with blood, and without the shedding of
blood there is no forgiveness of sins" (Heb. 9:22). Does the
drama become any more merciful when the sacrificial symbolism disappears, since obedience is better than sacrifice?
When the altar is torn down, but the thousand rules and regu-

lations still demand sacrifice and bind souls under divine wrath? Always supposing it to be divine.

Once more it seems as though God can disappear, and yet the wrath remains, as it did for Bertil Malmberg, once the Oxford Group vision had faded:[1]

> O what terrors we bring upon ourselves,
> we men.
> You too are a murderer.
> You too
> cast a murderer's shadow
> as you pass over the earth.

Sometimes we can hear similarly disconsolate tones from the Bible:

> Truly no man can ransom his brother,
>   or give to God the price of his life,
> for the ransom of his life is costly,
>   and can never suffice,
> that he should continue to live on for ever,
>   and never see the Pit.
>   (Ps. 49:7-9)

Here God is far distant. As long as there is the possibility of sacrifice to God, there remains also the thought that although God demands sacrifice, he is offering some means of escape from an untenable situation. The man who gives a sacrificial animal for his life is also God's anointed, and not merely his opponent. The lamb of God that gave its life at Passover time was once the dying god; and when in the dim and distant past this fertility rite was reinterpreted in legalistic terms and the lamb came to represent man, the people, the

---

[1] Malmberg, in common with a number of Swedish writers of his generation, was for a time in the 1930s influenced by the Oxford Group movement of Frank Buchman. The "vision" of the movement, practically expressed in the quest for the four Absolutes (Absolute Honesty, Purity, Unselfishness, and Love), has been defined as the intention "to make the world understand that spiritual common sense is of more value and use to mankind than selfish piety or blind paganism" [Anon., *What Is the Oxford Group?* (London, 1933), p. 6]. The movement, now known as Moral Re-Armament, is thus characterized by a combination of idealism and spiritual utilitarianism.

king, there remained the shadow of the humanity of God under his demands. Yet the office and function of the king is God's function among his people; and when he reascends his throne, they sing, "The Lord reigns!"

Perhaps this is why the return of life can never be obliterated from this drama. Like Joseph in the pit, Israel in the Red Sea, Jonah in the belly of the fish, the chosen one emerges triumphant from the punishment and the humiliation. And as he emerges, so the people emerge, rejoicing:

> Let the heavens be glad, and let the earth rejoice;
>   let the sea roar, and all that fills it;
>   let the field exult, and everything in it!
> Then shall all the trees of the wood sing for joy before the
>   Lord. . . .

(Ps. 96:11-13)

But it is still a long way from this cult-fellowship between God and king, between heaven and earth, to the thought of the death of God. High above such ideas there towers the mountain on which Moses meets a God who speaks out of the fire and calls himself "I am." Or the faith that speaks through Isaiah:

> To whom then will you compare me,
> that I should be like him?
> says the Holy One.
>   . . . .
>
> Have you not known? Have you not heard?
> The Lord is the everlasting God,
> the Creator of the ends of the earth.
(Isa. 40:25, 28)

One ought to bear all this in mind as one turns the page of the book of the prophet and meets God's Anointed, now not a present ruler, but an awaited king:

> For he grew up before him like a young plant,
>   and like a root out of dry ground;
> he had no form or comeliness that we should look at him,
>   and no beauty that we should desire him.

> He was despised and rejected by men;
>> a man of sorrows, and acquainted with grief;
> and as one from whom men hide their faces
>> he was despised, and we esteemed him not.
> Surely he has borne our griefs
>> and carried our sorrows;
> yet we esteemed him stricken,
>> smitten by God, and afflicted.
> But he was wounded. . . .
>
> (Isa. 53:2-5)

These words have deep roots, reaching far down into the past, to the ancient vegetation festival. The humiliation of the king, the guilt laid on the neck of the sacrificial animal, the root in the dry ground—all these are, as it were, overtones in the poem. Moreover the poem itself was brought forth in a situation in which everything that had been said during the past thousand years about death and resurrection had been given new meaning. The people who wept by the waters of Babylon and hung their harps in the willows are comforted. The desert shall blossom again.

But I must interrupt myself. There is a vision before my eyes that will not be dismissed. The mandrake, the mysterious root and reincarnation of the god of vegetation, the gallows-man in the Nordic saga, the plant that screams as it is pulled from the earth, has come to life again in a chapel in the south of France.[2]

A shoot (but a dried, shattered shoot), a martyr's stake with arms spread helplessly out, and a face that is no face, since the features are obliterated by suffering, or perhaps they have never been there other than as an ache in pith and bark, and now rigid in death. The onlooker suddenly notices that he is not alone—St. Veronica worships in Rouault's stained glass

---

[2] The mandrake root (*mandragora officinarum*) was believed in Germanic folklore to scream as it was pulled from the ground; the plant was also valued for its supposedly aphrodisiac properties, particularly if found growing near a place of execution. The name "gallows-man" (*galgmannen*) reflects both its contorted shape and its connection with the traditional Germanic method of ritual execution, namely hanging. The chapel in the South of France referred to is that at Assy, near Chamonix.

window.[3] Beside him someone has inscribed ". . . one from whom men hide their faces."

In the Lutheran confessional writings (in the Formula of Concord, to be more precise), it is stated that the expressions "God has suffered" and "God has died" are by no means *praedicatio verbalis*, "empty words." That is the great difference between the death of Christ and the innumerable symbols, sayings, poems, and rites in which the death of God is in one way or another proclaimed. One day they became reality.

The suffering Messiah. The sacrificial lamb. The ransom. The dried plant. These were no mere symbols to him. Nor did he suffer and die by accident, and thus enable us, long afterward, to express it in these symbolic terms.

That particular theory had the effect of putting distance between ourselves and what happened; we could tolerate it as we tolerate theology. But it is now shattered irreparably. He believed that he was the King who was to come. He believed that he was the lamb who was to be slaughtered. He believed that he was the ransom who was to save our brother, for surely it could not have been a ransom of silver or gold. He believed himself to be the root in condemned and cursed soil. He followed the signs like a map. He did not ask for sympathy: "Do not weep for me; weep for yourselves." What he *did* demand was guilt, suffering, distress, and death.

The cultic drama, the poems of sacrifice, the visions of atonement—suddenly the performance stops. The king is dressed for his ancient role, with his crown of thorns, his mantle, and his reed scepter. And yet it is the onlookers who are dressed up—the governor, the priests, the officers. What is taking place on the stage is real. The tragedy tears down the barriers of our security and looks at us with the eyes of reality. We were taking part in a play, a philosophy, a theology—but it is all over now. Someone is dead.

A professor in Uppsala has taken note of Christ's attitude to reality—and demanded an enquiry into his sanity. This has not

[3] According to legend, St. Veronica was the woman who gave a handkerchief to Jesus as he carried his cross to Golgotha. The image of his face became miraculously imprinted on the cloth. Some of the windows in the chapel at Assy belong to the last period of the French painter Georges Rouault (1871-1958).

gone unchallenged. During the last days of his life the whole world seems to have been insane; but where there is clarity, it is in him. We see extraordinary changes in the personalities of others; we have difficulty in placing them, but we recognize him. This man who thinks about his mother in his last extremity, surely it is the same man who helped Peter with his fishing. This man who takes time to reassure a criminal instead of sinking into an abyss of self-pity, surely the Samaritan whore would have recognized him if she had been there. But I still wonder whether the professor may not have understood more of what was happening than many a believer. I mean more of the incredible aspect of what was happening—on both levels, first in this strange man's decision and then in reality. Remember that some of his contemporaries also wondered exactly what was going on—some critics suggested that he had an evil spirit, and even his mother was not sure, at least for a time. And although I do not agree with them, I have to admit that for them what happened was neither inevitable, edifying, nor quietly poetical.

But "we esteemed him . . . smitten by God." Indeed we did. And many have since complained about the God who could act in this way. The drama does not have the effect intended by Sophocles, when he had the stricken Oedipus express his surprise that anyone should want to ask the Delphic oracle about "a pathetic man," and answered through Creon, "Well, perhaps even you believe in the god now."

For this god—call him Apollo or Yahweh or what you will— this distant god, who sends us suffering and watches from Olympus or Sinai to see that the measure is full and the debt paid, is foreign and despicable in our eyes. If he exists, we cannot prevent him from doing as he pleases; but he is a stranger to humanity. He sees from afar, and he shapes the pattern of our misery, but he remains the distant god: our door is closed.

Because Christ has been here, we have learned something about love.

Make no mistake about it, the God he proclaimed was no vegetation god. Justice derives its majesty from him. With his word he holds the universe together; he shapes the constellations. But this God is no blind force of nature; he is an open eye. Not a silent space, but a clear statement, and the fire still burns on Horeb: "the place on which you are standing is holy ground."

Yet the New Testament refuses to remove him from the place of martyrdom. "My God, my God, why hast thou forsaken me" —this verse from the cultic drama of the Old Testament, from the midst of guilt and punishment, is quoted, not *about* the one who suffers, but *by* him. But it can still be said that "God was in Christ reconciling the world to himself." The judge is in prison, without thereby ceasing to be the judge. A man suffers under the judgment of God, but it is God who suffers. The whole monotheistic development is involved, and yet the primeval message returns: God is dead.

And just as Christ took the symbols and filled them with his reality, so the Reformers assure us that it is not merely a matter of a *praedicatio verbalis*—which we suspect many *praedicationes* of being. When the divinity of Christ becomes a motto, there is every danger of an odd warping of consciences. As though it were not enough to regard God as the source of the remote majesty of the Law and the inflexible demands of justice, he is given the role that the Scriptures assign to another: the role of accuser! Suffering, guilt, condemnation—the secret of all this is that God wants to get at us. God becomes Satan.

But why does he allow it? Is he not supposed to be all-powerful?

He has answered this question from below, from the side of humanity. And his answer is not only the answer of the Son: "the entire fulness of the deity" stands like the silence of infinite space around that Word, but that silence is not the silence of one unwilling to speak. Christ is the only thing God can say. We know little enough about the ways of omnipotence, but on Good Friday, when the drama reaches its focus, infinite power becomes subject to love. The drama has planted God in our history; all things are penetrated by the roots of his love, and our distress flowers scarlet in the garden. Screaming, it is torn from the accursed earth: ". . . he was cut off out of the land of the living, stricken for the transgression of my people." For God is omnipotent, and that is why he dies a human death. None but God could be so human. God so loved . . . .

It all comes to a focus in the story of a love. Death, guilt, distress. That is what our divorce was all about. Love was life; and God was love; how could we then abandon him and live? Love was the law, and God was love; how could we then abandon him and be guiltless? Love was our peace, and God was love; how then could we abandon him and have peace?

Suffering and death are not fundamentally our punishment for having broken with God. They are what we experience as a result of having broken with God. Guilt is not written into our ledger afterwards because we have acted against love. It is the vacuum that is caused when love is shut out. The anxiety and distress of being are not sent to us as some devilish torment from a God bent on vengeance. It is the absence of God. "And *this* is the judgment, that . . . men loved darkness rather than light."

The history of religion is our evidence of a shattered love. Rites and sacrifices emerge painfully from sheer loneliness: the kind of thing one does when the loneliness becomes unbearable. The sore has been open for thousands of years; the conflict it reveals is ever being renewed.

When people talk about the righteousness of God and the love of God as though it were a kind of schizophrenia in his nature, they are forgetting the wrath of love. What should be more disturbed by faithlessness than love? Justice, weighing and measuring? Tolerance, smiling its frigid smile? But if you must love with deceit, placing it like a gift in the hands of love, the gift burns like a red-hot cinder; give it like a kiss, and the kiss is as poisonous as the bite of a snake. We threw it at God like a spear in his eye, and said, "Keep me as the apple of an eye." And now he is here. And because he is here, wrath is here —but not as revenge, as suffering, because it is the wrath of love. And this suffering is not an act of self-torment, a false martyrdom, a kind of demonstration. God does not suffer for pedagogical reasons, but because he loves in the human dimension. His suffering is nearness. And nearness answers the cry of our rites, the insanity of our sacrifices.

God enters into his absence from the earth, making our suffering his suffering, our guilt his guilt, our distress his distress, our death his death. That is what love does. Love identifies itself with someone; love cannot tolerate another's loneliness. This is not something worked out at a distance, but an art at the heart of humanity, where the king is cursed and the animal is burnt on the altar and Oedipus loses his eyes and God is dead—that is where it bears all things and shares our loneliness.

And now, when the one whom the prophecies foretold appears, carrying his reed-scepter, the question presses once more upon us, whether it was only *our* quest that expressed itself in signs and symbols. May it not all have been, as it were, a magnetic field, with patterns shaped by some unknown source of power? Our quest was "a shadow," as the letter to the Hebrews puts it, of what was to come. He cast a shadow before him, with the light of eternity at his back, and his face turned toward us for thousands upon thousands of years.

We esteemed him smitten by God. But he was God. That is why he was smitten. And that is why we peer into the tomb where it all ended. God is dead, but our distress is still alive. God has gone, but our guilt is left. For the other thing that is God—that which remained beyond the stars while he was suffering with us, that which has neither suffered nor died, since it is said that God is by his nature incapable of suffering or death—said nothing whatsoever to us. It lives in eternity but not with us. A perfect being cannot die, but the only perfection we ever knew gave his life because he was love, and if love had not done so it would not have been perfect. This is not an equation; it is a drama—the drama of one who so loved. The living return on the first day of the week and put into words what they feel: "There is no other God."

And then the paradox of the death of God is solved. One word fills the other with life, and the word that is filled with life is called "death." When death is no longer the absence of God, it is no longer death, and Christ is risen. This life pours out of the rock and into history, both that which has been and that which is still to come. The hewn gods around the altar break their silence, and the millennia bear witness, with the Man, the Ox, the Lion, and the Eagle, that the Lamb is worthy to open their seal. And coming millennia open their graves to life from the death of God, and their mouths for bread from the hunger of God.

For the gospel is no *praedicatio verbalis*, but God, who is sown and who lives thirtyfold, sixtyfold, a hundredfold. A piece of bread is broken between our teeth; it comes from the hunger of God, and we shall never more hunger. There are no survivors of this death, for it is eternal life.

And the festival does not end where the tragedy ended. The prophecy of the lost God has been fulfilled in resurrection. The King has ascended his throne.

4.

IF GOD IS ALIVE . . .

"If God is dead, everything is permissible."
—Dostoyevsky

Some of us no doubt look upon any discussion that begins by postulating the death of God as unreal. But not necessarily for the same reasons in every case. Those who have never noticed that God is alive can only have a theoretical interest in his death. And those who consider that he is close to them may think that to speak of the dead God is as sensible as to assume that the world has disappeared, leaving man on his own, uncertain as to what is permitted. It is conceivable that God was looking after more than mere morals, and that more than morals would collapse if he were to fall ill and die.

But many people regard it as a matter of vital importance to demonstrate that God is indispensable for morals. Not because they are so passionately concerned about the actual state of our morals, but because they believe that we need him as a moralist, and that this is decisive for the question of his existence. If we can live moral lives without believing in God, then he fills no further function, and therefore does not exist. The last little part-time occupation in his retirement has been taken from him. Perhaps we worry slightly about his welfare, or about "the cause of God" in our cultural life, like those who support religion generally because they think that it is good for tradition and for the country to have a cross on the national flag.

But what happens to the cause of God if they fall by the wayside? Note, however, that none of them—neither those who try to get society to support the cause, nor those who try to get the cause to support society—seem to be especially convinced that God is in fact alive. For if he exists at all, he ought to be able to look after his own affairs, as Ragnar Jändel wrote

to those who were shocked at the religious persecutions in
Russia: "if God is from eternity to eternity, surely he can stand
it."[1] And how can we be so sure that God is willing to serve as
an appendix to our patriotism? Perhaps he does not want to act
the part of cosmic bank manager to our hoarded values.

It should be clear by now that I do not regard the existence
of God as either proved or disproved by the fact that we may
possibly need him for one thing or another.

However, if we suppose that mankind can survive the death
of God, and that love, war, and professorial chairs would continue to exist, it would not, after all, seem that the question of
morals can be so profoundly influenced by his death. Gunnar
Edman has written a novel about the death of God, and I think
that he is right when he describes the reception of the startling
news like this:

> . . . Some even thought that this might mean a new break-
> through for the Church, since they could now give their entire
> attention to social work and the moral training of the people,
> which had tended to be neglected of late, due to an overdose
> of obscure and introspective sacramentalism. As an old min-
> ister put it frankly, "The Church will stand as long as the
> state stands, and that means we don't have to worry." A local
> branch of the Central Association of Humanists adopted the
> following resolution: "We express our profoundest sympathy
> with the churches in their sad bereavement. We should how-
> ever like to state that the truth we have so long maintained
> has now been unexpectedly actualized, namely that ethical
> standards and social values are *in no way* dependent upon a
> God or a belief in God. We intend, in what is perhaps a
> favorable situation for our truth, to attempt still further to
> realize in our life and work the power of our nonreligious but
> nevertheless eternal gospel of mankind."

The irony of the last sentence is instructive: it isn't easy to
purge one's values from the last traces of God. One has to take
a magnifying glass and seek out all the absolutes and eternities,
high ideals and other heavenly remnants.

[1] The events referred to by the Swedish poet Jändel (1895-1939) are
those of the 1920s.

But even when this has happened, it would still appear to be permissible for anyone to hold fast to certain values and try to get others to follow suit.

There seem to be three possibilities here. You can bring up children according to Makarenko's *Lectures to Parents.* "It is necessary," he writes, "to set up for oneself a strictly defined goal and program for the bringing up of children. One must remember that a child is not only the delight of its parents, but also a future citizen, and that the parents are responsible to their country for its upbringing. First and foremost one must be a good citizen oneself; further, one must introduce one's public spirit into the family. It is necessary to set up the strictest possible standards for one's own conduct." Although I suspect that there are yet icons in these schoolrooms (icons of moustached worthies, not bearded saints), it still seems possible to impress upon young people, replacing religious propaganda with a measure of discipline, that their citizenship is on earth and that they ought to fear and love it above all else.

It goes without saying that there are other values. Another possibility is to agree, in the best traditions of democracy, about the things we approve of, after which we make a mass of solemn rules aimed at preserving these principles. Even so it is not out of the question that we may finally arrive at the last of Makarenko's rules for the bringing up of children: "the main thing to be borne in mind when bringing up children is to organize the life of the family, paying attention to detail." Much of our present-day legislation points in this direction, and I suppose that we shall eventually all be law-abiding citizens, even in matters of detail. I don't think that many things need to be permitted.

Naturally we are also free to inflate generosity into a cardinal virtue, and twist the frequency of prohibitions by the odd art of moral antistress propaganda. Let morals look after themselves. Since there is no longer any court in the eyes of which we are all sinners, what we think and believe about one another is all the more important. Since everything has become relative, there is little left to worry about except levels of behavior; and there will surely be no lack of behavior-pattern saints. After all, who wants to find himself in outer darkness? Imagine the power of the teacher in this kind of situation. Just think of it—giving out grades, grades that really mean something! No more heaven—only scholarships. No more hell—only special classes. And so the new superego is formed. Formed for further education; for we are continually being tested.

Now we have to remember that no democratic society will protect this apparatus from observation; and that opens a third perspective to us. If I and a few others consider that people should be healthy and not sick, and that healthy people are always harmonious and sensitive, and that they have every right to wash their hands of everybody else, I have to say openly that this is only what I think. This is my overcoat; and I am the one who thinks that it is a general's uniform; perhaps quite a lot of people think so. So if you want to salute the uniform, remember that it is only me. And you are the ones who choose whether or not to salute.

So long as two and two still make four in a world without God (a moot point), we are condemned to a certain degree of clarity. That means, for our argument, that every moral authority depends on those who accept it. In other words, every individual is his own authority. And when he occupies the place of God, he assumes a responsibility of the same dimensions as his liberty. If anyone should object that there is no final authority to be responsible to, we have to answer that the individual acts as his own judge, but with the consequences—the consequences of what he does or does not do—as the jury. This insight opens a further dimension of clarity; and the question is then whether an individual can ever again dare to relax and abandon himself to sleep in exhaustion or to another person in love or to the darkness like Barabbas in Pär Lagerkvist's novel. It is as though we were held by an elastic band, constantly being pulled abruptly back into the light of full consciousness. And if we choose to sleep, we must realize that it is we who choose, so that we can answer those who come and ask where we were while someone was drowning or while someone else had happiness to share. If we forgive ourselves, then there is no atonement; all we are doing is turning our back on the universe. Or to quote Karl Vennberg:

> Even the most elementary comfort
> would cost me more
> than my estate could carry.
> I can't even afford
> my own counterfeits.

Puritanism does not allow much, but does contain an irrational factor, preventing a man from passing final judgment on himself or on others. Atonement is at least conceivable. But puritanism without God—that is the formula for a culture in which efficiency is constantly accelerating, in which immorality is itself the convention, any deviation from which is met with a raised eyebrow: "How on earth can anyone be like that?" Which is exactly the way things are with us. Since there is no God, there is no forgiveness either, and therefore no permission, least of all for the one who has seen through the machinery; for he lands in the responsibility of clarity, he is smitten with purity.

In the midst of the night in which God is condemned to death there is a special staircase, leading down toward the focus of humanity, where the lines of responsibility meet. That is the only point at which any change can come about in everyman's responsibility, the crossing at which atonement can take place. The Gospels claim that God descended to the point of judgment, and that it killed him, but that he filled very death with life, because he loved; that somewhere in heaven he ceased to be a norm and became an illegitimate love at the nadir of our humiliation. That through this event, beneath all demands and all failures, there was created a beginning in which all is brought to an end, and a new dignity for all those who are unable to cope. And whatever may be one's attitude to this view, it is nonetheless a fact that all those who loved to prohibit things were driven to desperation when it began to be practiced. They were the ones who killed God. Later, however, one of them became convinced that this death was the greatest demonstration of life ever; and even had to admit, though somewhat grudgingly, that all things are permissible. That was the old moralist Paul.

It would take far too long to point out all the consequences for morals of what he believed had happened. Some of them are however obvious.

If God is not an eye, shining red in the face of the moral traffic, but a comrade among the downtrodden and run over, there is something more important than "getting by." The ultimate fact is not that we are entered in a ledger, but that we are loved. That is why the minister in the novel by the Norwegian writer Ronald Fangen, *An Angel of Light* (*En lysets engel*), had finally to raise his chalice over the dying Nazi who was "notorious throughout Norway for his cruelty": "There lay a man who was a riddle to me. God knew him. I could not forgive him on my own behalf or on behalf of my people. But it was my sacred duty to forgive him in God's name."

Another conclusion: since we are loved from within our own failure, there is something even more important than our responsibility. There is a clarity which is not stress, but trust. St. Christopher, who has to carry so many, knows himself to be carried by the God he was about to lift onto his shoulders.

And since God is so human, the very traffic regulations are subject to a demand that seems idyllic but that is really revolutionary: be a little humane. Whatever happens to the traffic, it is rather important, even amid the secular puritanism of a Stockholm street, to pause for a moment and smile at someone. This sounds mawkish; but it is really a serious matter. Take for example the minister Bro in Jarl Hemmer's novel *A Man and his Conscience* (*En man och hans samvete*). He crawls through the barbed wire in the wrong direction and gets mixed up with the imprisoned Communists; finally he is mistaken for one of the worst of them, and dies in his place at the wall. On the one hand the barbed wire and other dividing lines become less and less important; on the other, he experiences a mysterious affinity with those inside, the condemned men. And when the soldier, the guardian of the sacred rules, hears that the minister has broken *in*, he bursts out: "If this is true, it must be hushed up, absolutely! We don't want a scandal!" To which the doctor answers, "People like that are always causing scandals here on earth."

This, too, is relevant to the chapter about the death of God and the limits of the permissible.

And if we can't manage it—if we can't manage to love—the fact remains that we were loved long before the beacons we call norms were lighted, and will be loved even after they have been extinguished for a thousand years. We were loved though we were unable to love. A continually summoning inspiration, of the kind that is never associated with moralistic rules and regulations, and a continually burning forgiveness.

In that thought there is room for more than forgiveness.

Let us admit that Christendom has seldom dared to acknowledge the Pauline consequences of the life of God. This may, perhaps, be due to the fact that it has seldom dared to believe in the *living* God, and has therefore tried to play safe and inject life into the word "God" by means of moralism and activity. And mankind has landed finally in the common paroxysm of unbelief, in which nothing is permitted, for who is there to permit it?

5.

BODY AND BLOOD

Can a modern man believe that the Eucharist is really the body and blood of Christ? Let me say first of all that in the matter of faith I do not believe that today's "modern man" is in any way different from a nineteenth-century "modern man." If there is a difference, it is perhaps that in our day we have seen more clearly the realities that the gospel speaks about.

There has been starvation before. But it must surely be a long time since the privileged classes, who know nothing at first hand of the meaning of the word, were so rudely reminded that they are in fact privileged. The wall of self-evident facts and attitudes that protects people and classes from certain dark realities so well that they need not even bother about them has been decisively breached. I believe there are very few people who do not realize that the prayer for our daily bread is more currently meaningful than the longing for all the things we think we need. The repeated reminder of the elementary requirements of existence tears through the skin of our needs. Take away the *hors d'oeuvres* and the dessert, and the bread is left. When the complex cultural equation has been simplified into its basic terms, what is left is an evening conversation over a cup. Bread and wine, body and blood. Life in the raw. But at the same time a summing up, a focus. All the other things— work, love, song, rest—are included. Our politics and our social life, our culture and our religion, come to a focus here. But it is not a dead, mechanical focus, like the focus of some optical instrument, but something living. Not merely because it has grown in the soil and ripened under the sun. The work of workers is in it, and the strength of labor grows out of it—out of bread and wine.

The bread on the altar is white, and it has been baked by deaconesses. But it comes from the same farms and the same industry as the coarse bread on our tables. It is in no way removed from the problems, struggles, and conflicts of daily life. It has also been noticed in some religious circles that the wine carries its own problems to the altar—happiness is not the only thing that grows on grapevines—and so, to be on the safe side, they have replaced the wine by fruit juice. But we are not meant to leave the realities of our daily life behind when we come to the Eucharist. What we bring to it is our thoroughly profane everyday life, with its celebrations, neither unproblematical nor sinless—life as it really is, neither spiritualized nor watered down, but flesh and blood.

And since the altar is really nothing but a table at which people eat, this is the first implication of this meal; this is its origin in the ancient customs and beliefs of Judaism—that we bring to it our life as it is, present it to God, and give thanks for the gift, in spite of everything. As the ancient Eucharist prayer puts it: "O Almighty God, thou hast created all things for thy name's sake. Thou hast given food and drink unto men, that we might thank thee."

But the prayer continues: "Thou hast bestowed upon us spiritual food and drink, and eternal life through thy servant." God has not stopped short, somewhere over our everyday life; implying that we should be able to worship him at a distance. This "servant" has eaten our bread and drunk our wine. He has lived our life. And when he broke the bread it was not somewhere at a safe distance from our devilry. The last time, when the supper was utterly transformed by his presence, treachery was there at the table. That was "in the night when the Lord Jesus was betrayed"; that was on the verge of Good Friday. He took bread, broke it, and gave it to his disciples with the words: "Take and eat; this is my body which is given for you." And then he took the cup, thanked God and gave it to his disciples, saying: "Drink this, all of you. This cup is the new covenant in my blood, which is shed for many." What does he mean? It is his body and his blood that he is talking about. While mankind betrays him, he gives us bread and wine, the simplest, the ultimate gifts. There is nothing more to give, for he has given us life. "This is my body. . . . This is my blood." He might have said, "This is myself. . . ."

John says that he wanted to give us the final proof of his love. Long before the New Testament existed, the Eucharist was celebrated. Long before we were given the story of the love of God, the sacred drama was there. For the earliest witnesses tell us that the servant who gave himself for our sakes was God of God. His story was more than human. It was the story of God on earth. The Eucharist is not merely something that represents the story. It *is* the story. Everyone who takes part is involved in the drama; and even those who refuse to take part cannot avoid being involved, because they too are body and blood. For the area of our contact with God is not especially spiritual; it is not something religious or heavenly; it is bread and wine, body and blood. Jesus Christ made it so in the night in which he was betrayed.

In Graham Greene's novel *The End of the Affair* Sarah wonders whether it is God she is touching when she touches her lover, for it was through this earthly love she had come close to God. I do not believe that there is an earthly love of this quality. But the Eucharist is like a work of art filled with personal life, a life that loves. It is more than a work of art. Here I am touching God. I can find no hiding place. Our encounter takes place in what is my own existence, in bread and wine, body and blood. I cannot hide anything, for the poverty I would hide is as dust in his hands, and the love he would hide is as dust in my hands. My story and his are interwoven, the one with the other.

This is rather terrible, but it is also rather wonderful. Nothing can ever again be a matter of indifference. Earthly life belongs to God, and my own tiny segment of life is permeated by that which is he. Everything—my entire universe, my every day, my celebration, and my eternity—is a piece of bread in his hand, and he says: "This is my body." This is the incredible story that we call the forgiveness of sins. Because he who is called "the servant" has broken through the history of all of us with the opposite of sin, that is, with love.

So I do not go to the Eucharist because my life is made up of the finely sifted flour of righteousness, because it isn't. I go because he wishes to meet me here, in this bread and this wine, in that which is my own existence, plain and unadorned. My presence at the Eucharist has nothing to do with my worthiness. There is nothing about that in the Bible; all that it says there is that it is possible to partake of the bread and wine in an unworthy manner. What, then, is meant by "in an unworthy manner"? Pretending that this meal is some sort of official or private business—as though it were not an encounter between what I am and what he is.

After which I return to the others—at home, in the factory, at the club. Their lives, too, are included in the drama. It is written that his blood was shed for "many"—the word means approximately "everybody." You cannot meet Christ without meeting everybody. And then they stop being merely "the others." Least of all can I bring up their religious opinions as an excuse for calling them "the others." The bread he broke was theirs too. He did not inquire after their opinions before beginning to love them. And since they were his concern, so they are my concern. Not merely their souls and their opinions. But bread and wine, body and blood. Their personal and social reality.

Work is unlike any celebration of the Eucharist. No breaking of bread can remove the bitterness from man's struggle for his daily bread. Even the person who has penetrated most deeply into the Eucharistic gospel must live his life in sectors in which there are barriers between some people and others. Men are divided by private interests, judgments, and traditions; and there is no one person who has the gift of universal understanding. But the drama at the altar is everybody's concern, and I run the risk of meeting them there—people from parties and classes and countries that I do not understand. No distinctions of standard of living or blood relationship can go deeper than this fellowship at the heart of life, in body and blood. And once I have seen God break into my life in the form of a servant, my own work has to be a work of service for humanity. If I fail here I deny Christ in the night in which he was betrayed.

Humanity—what a pompous word! It is easy enough to love everyone in a lump like that. Over and above the flesh and blood reality that is my contact with life. But at the heart of this reality I encounter someone who takes precedence over all the others, someone who is literally closer to me. The Bible calls him my neighbor. If I want to serve humanity I have to start with him. This is a matter of simple friendship; but it is a means, not an end. I cannot silence my conscience by claiming that I have done my share; and what happens outside my district has nothing to do with me. My marriage, my work, my circle of friends do not isolate me from humanity; they link me to humanity. The Eucharist connects my own situation with a worldwide Christian fellowship. And the Bible calls this living Christian organism "the body of Christ," which does not mean that it exists somewhere in a rarefied atmosphere high above our problems, but beneath them, for where should the body of Christ be if not beneath the sins of the world? Hence I am involved in much more than meets the eye. Anyone at all that I am linked with through Christ (and that means *anyone at all*) may at any time become my neighbor, just because our paths happen to cross. People with whom I have nothing whatsoever in common may some day enter my territory; and I shall find that it is the Eucharist that has broken down my fences.

Is it possible that the Eucharist is the body and blood of Christ? To this question I must answer that the Eucharistic perspective is the most dangerous of all for anyone who wants to avoid his human responsibility. There is no two-thousand-year buffer between the living present and what we are told about the body and blood of Christ. The distance is no greater than the distance between myself and my neighbor, for whom Christ suffered death.

6.

GOSPEL AND BEHAVIOR

Heredity and Environment

> What price the will, whining in desperation,
> Or the burst of emotion, the heart's anguish?
> Each thread in the tapestry of fate fixes
> The blind, bloody placenta.

These are the words of Bertil Malmberg, writing in *Songs of Conscience and Destiny* (*Sångerna om samvetet och ödet*). Here behavior is not a goal to be sought, something that each individual must discover for himself, but a compulsion in which the individual is caught up from the beginning. He is born with it, and there is little he can do about it. Just as no one can change the destiny that determines his sex or his physical makeup or his mental capacity, so no one, placed in a situation in which he must choose one way or another, can move the signpost of destiny even by a single degree. What then is the point of talking about responsibility? If our behavior is so completely determined in advance, what is the function of the conscience?

> Since all our deeds are utterly determined,
> What can there be to alter or to waste?
> How can we be responsible in living?
> —And what the secret of the restless heart?

However, we are going to concentrate in this essay less on the behavior that stems from heredity than on that which has to do with environment. It may appear to be as potent for the individual's destiny as are the hereditary instincts. From the very moment of our birth we come under various influences that lead us inexorably in directions we are utterly incapable of choosing for ourselves. No one who has learned to recognize the patterns in the individual's habits of thought and behavior

74

need inquire very much about a person's origins. As Professor Higgins put it in Shaw's *Pygmalion*, there are other dialects than those of language.

And then there are all those who mark our path through life like flags on a slalom course; they all stand there in their appointed places, but their influence appears to be somewhat haphazard. Bengt Nyström has described his own influence on a schoolboy. Many years after the decisive event, he received a letter from America:

> And I thought I ought to say—
> Though perhaps it doesn't matter now—
> That I never did
> What you believed I had done.

And Nyström goes on:

> What had he done, and what have I done?
> What have I trampled on?
> Was it a spell of bad temper one morning?
> A thoughtless word or two?
> It is terrible to think that I remember nothing
> Of the secrets of his heart,
> That I shaped someone's destiny
> All unknowing.

But not all the advisors who try to ensnare the individual in *their* way of looking at things are so completely unaware of what they are doing. For example there is Dr. Kilander, in Tore Zetterholm's novel *The Pigeon* (*Duvan*), the psychiatrist who has to try to cure the wife of a war criminal: "We must try to get her away from him, for her own sake," says Kilander to the girl's father. "I am sure we agree about that?"

And the father answered, "I suppose you know best, Doctor." The result of the "treatment" was eventually a divorce and an attempted suicide.

A corresponding example of ministerial advice is found in Seward Hiltner's *Pastoral Counseling*. Mrs. Thorn comes to a pastor for advice as to whether or not she should get a divorce. "I really think I'd be justified in getting a divorce, don't you?" she says, and the pastor answers—or might have answered: "Of course you've been badly treated, but divorce, Mrs. Thorn, is a very serious matter." The author comments: "The pastor thought a point had come where his moral convictions had to be asserted. Yet without realizing he was doing so, he was aiding in crystallizing Mrs. Thorn's decision around a divorce."[1]

In these two cases the counselee was forced on to the defensive, each in her own way. But defense is not easy, surrounded as we are by observers who day by day take note of whether or not we follow accepted modes of behavior among civil servants or academics, among the truly religious or the truly secularized.

The Consumer Society

It is only natural that society should exercise a more or less decisive influence on the behavior of the individual. If we are to believe David Riesman and his colleagues, writing about American behavior-patterns in *The Lonely Crowd*, the pressure is more severe now than it has ever been. The ideal of the consumer society is that people should be "others-directed," while in a previous epoch people were "inner-directed." I am not at present concerned to discuss whether or not this latter ideal was in fact an illusion. What can be discussed is the number of alternatives. Riesman's team considers that the present-day individual (at least in America) may even have fewer possibilities of choosing the way in which he is to develop than was the case in a society that was neither "others-directed" nor "inner-directed," but "tradition-directed." Fairy-tale heroes or heroines sometimes, *mirabile dictu*, act differently from the ways prescribed by official opinion. Red Riding-Hood forgets her errand to stop and pick flowers; but the stars of second-feature films are no more prone to make mistakes than are Batman or Superman. These "saint" legends leave no room for sinners; no nonconformity is tolerated.

Let us not forget that our subject is much more relevant today than half a century ago. It is no longer a matter of scorn to speak about choice of jobs or differences of taste—whether for clothes, food, or even art. Behavior is no longer shaped within such narrow economic boundaries. And yet there are innumerable possibilities for conflict between the two kinds of

---

[1] Hiltner, *Pastoral Counseling* (Nashville: Abingdon, 1952), pp. 20f.

behavior we have been speaking about: the one we are born into and the one that is thrown over us like a net in every milieu we enter. With or without financial threats. How many are teaching Swedish in our schools because they like teaching, and how many because they wanted to major in literary history at the university? There are, too, still some circles in which it is a matter of decency to go into a certain type of profession. There are working-class families in which the son who wants to be a journalist is looked upon as a black sheep; and there are still families in which the daughter of the house would cause a family scandal if she were to marry a laborer. Patterns like these are socially imposed, but so are many of our religious behavior-patterns. Why else should we have to talk about "religious geography"? Just as we can draw a map to illustrate the spread of sorrel in Scandinavia, so we can direct would-be explorers to the best areas for Baptists or Schartauans.[2] It goes without saying that some varieties occur sporadically (for example in academic centers) and never identically in two such centers in the same country.

According to Riesman, the dictatorship of the group over the individual is so self-evident in our culture that the individual tends not merely to accept it, but even to suppress his own claims altogether. Instead of an independent judgment he develops a kind of radar, with which he registers others' views as to how he ought to think and behave.

This has to do with a phenomenon observed especially by the German doctor Joachim Bodaner (in his book *Man without a Self*), that the individual is perpetually surrounded by voices, not only from his so-called "peer-group," but from all the mass media—radio, television, newspapers, periodicals, billboards, and the rest. These impulses are so many and so frequent that he finds it impossible to produce anything even remotely resembling a personal response before the next appeal washes over him. Nor does anyone really expect to hear his reactions, any more than the TV announcer expects to hear an answer when he says "Good night." Does he really exist?

[2] The followers of Henric Schartau (d. 1825), who was a preacher of strict Lutheran orthodoxy, biblically conservative, firm in his emphasis on the local congregation and its sacramental life. The Schartauan tradition is still a living factor in the churches of southwest Sweden.

The Lost Dimension

It may or may not be a matter of heredity, but we all know that the individual tends to offer a certain resistance to the attempts of his milieu to shape him after its image. Sometimes accidents happen in the (frequently unconscious) tension between individuality and group behavior. These accidents become all the more serious in those cases in which it is believed that nothing but behavior counts, in which there is no "I" within heredity and environment and no "thou" outside heredity and environment. No "I" to make a choice and no "thou" before whom to be responsible for the choice one has made. Viktor Frankl has pointed out that the denial of this ultimate "thou" can often lead to neurosis: "It is not uncommon to be able to point to a fact at the basis of neurotic modes of existence, viz. that the neurotic person shows a deficiency: his orientation towards transcendence is disturbed. His transcendent frame of reference is suppressed. But this suppressed transcendence acts together with the hidden forces of his 'transcendent unconscious' to produce a 'restless heart' . . . ." In point of fact the loss of the transcendental "thou" also means a loss of self. And the individual has no refuge, nowhere to register his protest, either in heaven or in his own heart. The final authority is public opinion, and beyond that there is no further court of appeal. As for instance in Lars Ahlin's novel *Pious Murders* (*Fromma mord*), where the ex-member of parliament bursts out: "The milieu gives and the milieu takes away; blessed be the name of the milieu." When I think about that profoundly tragic figure I am unable to accept his situation as he does in the novel. The story of his destiny gives me a sense of claustrophobia.

Biblical Variation

Riesman stresses the importance of the Bible in homes where no other literature was permitted to disturb the spiritual uniformity. He points out that the prescribed book with its wide variety of behavior-patterns provided a breathing-hole for individuality. But its greatest significance was certainly not that it provided an alternative to Red Riding-Hood and gave individualists someone to identify themselves with.

To illustrate what I mean, I shall repeat this theme in a biblical variation. I shall do it with the help of a text that is seldom preached about, and almost never willingly. I mean the passage that tells of Jesus' visit to the land of the Gadarenes, where two demoniacs that lived among the tombs came out and asked him, "What have you to do with us, O Son of God?" The demons, afraid of being homeless, asked to enter into a herd of swine feeding nearby; and this was apparently what happened: the demoniacs became normal and at the same time the swine rushed into the sea and drowned, whereupon the citizens of Gadara begged Jesus to leave their neighborhood (Matt. 8:28-34).

It may be that most people feel themselves to be at a safe distance from this text. All this talk of demoniacs is so archaic and picturesque; but we know nowadays that mental illness is not caused by demons, and we replaced exorcism with psychoanalysis long ago. And then there is the grotesque story of the swine.

Evil Spirits and an Empty House

Let me say at the outset that even if I do not identify demon-possession with mental illness (possession is much less common), I do not intend to skirt the text on this point. If we go to the original text, we find that it says that two "demoniacs" approached Jesus. And I wonder whether it is true that we in our day have never seen the signs of demon-possession. People without individuality; marionettes, as it were. "So fierce that no one could pass that way." This description, provided by the Evangelist Matthew, could well be used in an account of what happened at the heart of Europe in the 1930s and 1940s. And the protagonists were indeed surrounded by tombs before the business came to an end. Not all Christians recognized the demons; but the demons certainly recognized Christ: "What have you to do with us . . . ?"

Sometimes it can be hard to believe in God; but when people who have experienced these things claim not to be able to believe in the devil I wonder whether they are not running away from reality. Repression, as the psychoanalysts say. And I remain suspicious, even when people seem to believe that the

devilry came to an abrupt end in 1945 or was shunted off somewhere else or was drowned in the ocean. The Gadarenes had
their reasons for asking Christ to leave—we shall return to
them in a moment—but many of the people who in those days
were most afraid of the unattached demons, and who called
willingly on the name of Christ, today have a far different reason from the Gadarenes for wanting to get rid of him. In our
day and age, they claim, there is no devilry; strictly speaking,
there never has been. But the swine are still there; agriculture
and commerce are flourishing; and should there be any demons
in the world, they cannot possibly have any power over well-
nourished and contented men and women. What has God to
do with us anyway?

But there is an old and wise saying to the effect that devilry
needs somewhere to live, and is always on the lookout for
empty apartments. I don't know much about hog farming in
the country of the Gadarenes, but I do know that there is a sort
of production that exists solely for the sake of production; that
there is leisure for the sake of leisure; that there is life the
only purpose of which is to keep life going. Those who find it
frightening that young people keep four-wheeled brothels,
make deliberate trouble on New Year's Eve, or become ad-
dicted to alcohol and drugs even before their voices have
changed ought to remember the *horror vacui* that is an inex-
orable condition of life. Demons may be dangerous; but they
are at least exciting. The frightening phenomena are only
symptoms—as yet isolated symptoms—of the fact that so many
experience human behavior as devoid of drama: empty as some
prolix stage play. It is filled with nothingness like a box filled
with sawdust.

I do not mean that we should invite Christ to become our
resident expert on recreation. He is not concerned with entertainment—not even with religious entertainment. What is important is the question that has to be asked when the entertainment ends, when work ends, when life ends. What has it
all been for? What we need is not a series of amusing sketches,
but to experience the whole of life as a drama. An action that
binds together all our actions, so that life has recognizable
features. Behavior that reflects more than behavior.

A "Thou" for God

Demon possession means, strictly speaking, two evils: first, that a person or a group or a nation comes to be dominated by demoniac forces; and second, that the individual has no opportunity of making his voice heard. Personality is lost. And so it is not the demoniacs themselves that speak, but the powers that control them—a phenomenon that can occur without demons.

The Evangelist Mark tells of only one of the demoniacs. Jesus asked, "What is your name?" And the answer came, "My name is Legion; for we are many" (Mark 5:9). If it is true that we are the contemporaries of Christ, as the gospel of the resurrection teaches us, then we can see how he moves through our consumer society and asks the anonymous member of the mass, "What is your name?" A ring at the doorbell; and an indistinct murmur of voices from within: "We are many, we are many. . . ."

This chorus of contradictory voices, the voices of demons and the voices of men, speak modern languages as they once spoke Aramaic. As always, they appeal to princes, governors, presidents, and other symbols of great social units: Did the trend-setters believe in him? But most of all they appeal to their own weight of numbers: "We are many." This Gadara of the heart may be a great city, the echo of a world in which Christ is a stranger and where this strangeness is the decisive argument against him: "What have you to do with us?"

We are left in no doubt as to the way in which we are expected to behave. We know exactly how high a woman's heels should be and how short her skirts; we know exactly what make of automobile a self-respecting citizen ought to have; we know just how far sexual abstinence is to be tolerated. Our patterns of behavior are mapped out for us—our behavior, our opinions and our possessions. Meanwhile the advertising agencies push and pull, and the pattern may change tomorrow. But we know "how things are" today, and who would dare to claim that Jesus Christ has any place in it? The eccentric who tries to remind us of his existence—what does he know about "how things are nowadays"? What has he to do with us?

Just as God once called out to Adam, "Where are you?" so

the gospel confronts our modern legion with the question, "What is your name?" According to the Gadara story the demons' answer was to show their uneasiness in face of Christ. That kind of uneasiness was not limited to the demons; it can be seen equally well among the people who hide in the crowd, seen in their attempts to avoid Christ.

The biblical commentary to this phenomenon is that reservation in face of Christ reveals a secret knowledge, that it confirms the gospel. And what does the gospel say? That although Christ has become a part of our human behavior, involved in the intricacies of church and state from Caiaphas and Pontius Pilate down to our own day, in him we nevertheless encounter more than this pattern of human behavior. A voice from beyond, calling us to leave our hiding place and stand up for ourselves, to acknowledge our identity, to be responsible. Calling each of us to be a "thou" for God. And in so doing, to acknowledge that in every fiber of our being we are involved in a dialogue with him. With God. Man in the midst of his human behavior is called upon to answer—to answer across and through all the voices of demons and men, independent of their thousand opinions. An answer acknowledging that man exists; that he is more than a relay in the infinitely complex circuits of the group and society.

This interpretation of man's reservations toward the gospel has many aspects. There are atheists who, with all their denial, reveal greater sensitivity to the nearness of Christ than many "defenders of the faith" who believe that they know all there is to be known about him. And there are ministers who never find him until the day on which they discover that they do not know how to answer the atheist, when their patterns of thought and behavior no longer protect them from him.

There are many signs pointing in the same direction. Christ does not behave like a salesman, peddling a product or an opinion. He has never tried to be popular. It is written that "he shall proclaim justice to the Gentiles," but Matthew, who quotes this ancient prophecy, has not overlooked the following lines: "He will not wrangle or cry aloud, nor will any one hear his voice in the streets" (Matt. 12:18f.; cf. Isa. 42:1-4). Those who have heard his voice say that when it penetrates the cacophony, it is nothing like the politicians' blaring loudspeakers. They say that it is like the sound of waves on the rocks; or like listening to the sound of one's own heart. Experience says that it is reality calling in the midst of confusion. We have heard that the demons recognize him, but the man or woman who hears his voice experiences an uneasiness far different from theirs. For the voice does not come merely from afar— from the heavens or the depths. It comes from the heart of humanity. From a type of behavior hidden under the superficial confusion like the original writing on a palimpsest. It comes from home, and the bewildered and confused stranger in the country of the Gadarenes hears a voice that is strange and yet familiar. His brother asks, as one might ask a delirious fever patient, "Do you recognize me?"

And this is what distinguishes the gospel from all the other voices: it expects an answer. The type of behavior we were talking about just now is like the way we treat a demoniac or a madman: we look past him, speak past him, and walk past him. For so many of the forces that shape society are concerned to exploit the individual, to win his approbation; but they have no time to listen to him. The gospel is not like that. Someone is waiting for an answer.

This is the meaning of the "difference" that the witnesses speak about: the gospel listens from beneath. It would be very convenient to run away from human behavior in a dream of worlds or powers above, outside and beyond humanity. But the gospel leaves these heavens severely alone, as it leaves alone the laws of public opinion. See how Christ continually forgets the world in order to concern himself with individuals—individuals in whom he loves the world and through whom he is nailed to its patterns. A bridal pair in Cana, a widow in Nain, a Samaritan whore, a tax-collector in Jericho, and at the last a criminal on Golgotha. All this tends towards a point deep within the suffering and the imprisonment. That is where the liberty of the gospel is to be found: in a love deeper than public opinion.

There the gospel awaits the individual, with a judgment more severe than any that is to be found in a peer-group—because it really is a final judgment. And there is no way to escape from it other than by accepting it: love condescending to our human behavior, nailed fast to our situation in a cross.

Behavior is transformed by this call, reaching the individual from this place. What previously seemed to be an arbitrary point in a power struggle, a "something" between production and consumption, is now seen to be what we call a heart. The rays of human behavior that come to a focus at this point are personified.

And there are answers. Yes or no. But answers. Someone lives there.

The Church

Let us now consider how the church fits into this picture.

The question might well be asked, whether the church perhaps ought not to become one voice among others in the great legion. We are nowadays pretty well informed about ways of influencing a group. If ministers and active laymen were to study the psychology of advertising, they would probably be able to create a certain amount of goodwill for Jesus Christ; and it might well be that the question of what he has to do with us and our age would not be asked with quite so much surprise. And if the judicious use of such means would make individuals and groups think and act in accordance with Christian behavior-patterns—well, why not at least make an effort?

Because it would be unbelief. Should the church join the propaganda chorus instead of waiting for people to speak for themselves, this would demonstrate her lack of faith in the word of God as the ground of existence, and in the power of that word to speak to man's lost condition. It would demonstrate that she no longer believes in the Christ before whom even the demons are allowed to speak, or in a gospel that does not speak about "man" or "suffering" in general, but which provides an answer directed at the heart of the situation. The answer of the individual is more important than all the debates that take place about, or in, the church. If the church is to give the answer of Jesus Christ, she must listen for it. And she must not run away, even from the inhuman, the demoniac voice; for it calls out of confusion. Not even when faced by the demoniac must the gospel become a didactic lecture. God answers.

But if this means that the church, as steward of the Word of God and the sacraments, is there to restore, on behalf of Christ, man's wholeness (which the New Testament calls "plan"), she must be as concentrated and as composed as people have to be when they listen and converse. Concentrated around the gospel, in which God listens, bleeding, on Golgotha. For she is the ear of God. But in these days, instead of obeying that summons, she has to answer the one who asks after her name, "My name is Legion, for we are many." She is herself a consumer society, crisscrossed by competing propagandas. Behavior-patterns, ready to be thrown like a net over defenseless men and women. And I have no wish to deny that there are alien features in this confusion. Behind the querulous voices one can sometimes sense a distress, as though she were subject to foreign domination. As though the situation were in some way demoniac. It is therefore vital to remember that Christ is identical with his message, but not with his messengers. They, too, are subject to the summons they are commissioned to pass on; and when they speak out of the Gadarene confusion they must not pretend to be pure children of light: orderlies, as it were, in some great hospital; healthy men and women who have no need of a doctor.

Our text ends by telling how the whole city went out to meet Jesus and ask him to remove himself. It is hard to say whether it was a safety measure to prevent further loss of livestock; it was rather, I feel, a sense of insecurity that led them to ask the question that the gospel puts so politely, "What have you to do with us?" The ground under Gadara trembled, and the people longed passionately for the old days, when madmen were madmen, and Gadarenes were Gadarenes, and business was business. They wanted to see things once more under control, and their investments more or less secure. And I cannot help wondering whether this same sense of insecurity may not still be felt today when Christ becomes involved in people's lives. One way would of course be to elect him a member of the town council, or to take some other steps to make him jointly responsible with us for maintaining the status quo. We might perhaps make a good Gadarene citizen out of him. From time to time this method has been applied, with a certain degree of success, even in the church. Yes, he can be a nuisance even there, with his intense interest in madmen and the sick and sinners and the rest of the company of the wretched. For when he comes to Gadara the peace of miserable human beings becomes more important than the apparatus of ecclesiastical politics and doctrinal debates and squabbles about high and low churchmanship. This is not to say that dogmatics or church-state relations are unimportant; but when Jesus Christ is present they are so much less important than the question of how a demoniac can find peace—a peculiarly dangerous question for strategies and positions and all the other Gadarene intrigues.

A SUMMONS

But if any of "the others" should think that the church ought to listen to things like this—well, that too may be a way of protecting oneself against the influence of Jesus Christ. They say, "How fine that his question is asked by the others, the church people or the secularized. There are no demons in my country, and if there are any swineherds, they have every legal right to be there.

There is a text in the gospel that is worth remembering in this connection: "Now you say, 'We see'; therefore you are blind." Not to recognize the disease is itself a symptom, provided that other signs point to disease.

And the sign I have in mind is primarily blindness with regard to demoniacs. The gospel summons atheists and party theologians to abandon their patterns and their systems and look at the two great facts in Gadara: Christ and the demoniacs. The doctor and the suffering patients.

It is seldom that a minister of the gospel can point to devilry as something exemplary—and yet we are told that the demoniacs *came out and met Jesus*, and that *the demons spoke to him*. They *approached* the Jesus of the Gospels, as we do in the Eucharist, where we take up the conversation that the Gadarenes were so afraid of, a conversation with the Savior of demoniacs in which the words are action and involvement.

What is the significance of all this for our behavior?

It means a summons to find the place in which we can listen. It means being with God and our neighbor when life shapes itself into a cross. It means being there, like a good Samaritan, with oil and wine, being there as a "thou," an address for the random communication, a link in the dialogue between man and man.

Following the direction of the gospel into our neighbor's situation leads to conflicts with all manner of strategies and plans for the future. This acknowledgment of the existence of the individual jeopardizes all our chances of getting people to act in a "Christian" manner by the exercise of suitable means of persuasion. He and only he must choose; not even an evangelist must be allowed to make up his mind for him.

Let me illustrate this with a further reference to Hiltner's book, and to the conversation I mentioned earlier, as he believes it ought to have gone:

"I really think I'd be justified in getting a divorce, don't you?"

"You think it's right, but you still have some doubts."

"Well, yes, I do. I think I'd be justified, and yet a divorce isn't what I really want."[3]

The respect for the counselee's convictions, as this conversation shows, led in this particular case to a stopping of the divorce. So it was worth it. But haven't I in fact now recommended a method of propaganda, only a more subtle and much more effective method than most? Is this whole chapter perhaps a trap, a Christian trap camouflaged with respect for the other person?

The one who is faced with such a question must consider to what extent he is himself a thread in a net of propaganda, and to what extent he dares to be a "thou" to someone. A cross-examination of this nature shows that words like "profitable" and "efficient" compromise the entire situation when it has to do with an individual's decision. Such situations are in the most intimate sense his own, crossroads of freedom and responsibility in face of both heredity and environment. There one can tune one's behavior as one would tune an instrument. And play —in someone's honor.

[3] Hiltner, *Pastoral Counseling*, p. 20. Cf. above, p. 76.

7.

LIFE IN DEATH

Man's fear of death is something that demands analysis. I suppose that it is true that the fear of death is a complement to the will to live, and that it disappears when the individual feels that he or she has lived long enough. But the fear of death is probably intensified nowadays for many people simply because it is a fear of the unknown. Most people have never seen anyone die, and to be reminded of one's mortality is as far removed from everyday life as the cemetery from the shopping center. In an agrarian culture, on the other hand, where work is completely subject to the rhythm of nature, the cemetery is placed in the middle of the village.

However, I wish primarily to draw attention to another source of the fear of death. There is a kind of egocentricity, sometimes accompanied by neurotic tendencies, that does everything in its power to protect itself from the prospect of ultimate annihilation. It fears death as it fears every other form of personal self-abandonment—whether in sleep, in love or in worship. But the fear of death is by far the worst, just because egocentricity, whether normal or pathological, leaves no room for the thought of continuation. We know of no other substratum to the ego than an organism that disintegrates in death. The light is extinguished, and that is all. The same attitude that intensifies the fear of death tells us that death is total and final.

Others experience human life at its best in connection with moments of self-forgetfulness. I am not thinking here of mere altruism, which can of course be a source of happiness, provided that it is not used for the purpose of moralizing. There is also a degree of self-forgetfulness in love. And in a summer day, by a trout stream in the forest. There is something reminiscent of death in experiences like these. We speak of being completely absorbed in our work. The subterranean connection between love and death is a recurrent theme in literature. And the thought of disintegrating and returning to the soil is not particularly frightening for anyone who has ever learned to love birds, spiders, and grass: "you are dust, and to dust you shall return" (Gen. 3:19) is a maternal promise, warm as the sun, fresh as the rain.

Life and death are not so incompatible as myself and death. Relaxation in the face of death is a way to affirm life. The convulsive grasp is loosened, and I am left free to dare to become involved. At the same time it must be stressed that it is impossible to argue oneself out of the fear of death. The problem is not to be solved on the level of dialectics.

The same applies to the question of eternal life—as a religious question. Of course the question is one that is open to discussion. But the confession of faith in eternal life is not based on logical proof. In this connection, all our calculations concerning the probability or otherwise of the continued existence of the self are equally pointless. Whether the self continues to exist beyond death has as much (and as little) to do with religion as the question whether the self continues to exist in sleep or in ecstasy. There are, too, functions of the self that we sincerely hope will finally be obliterated: among them all those functions which stand in the way of our correspondence with God.

In the last resort, it is this correspondence that is decisive. Eternal life is not a matter of wishful thinking about the future, commanded by some doctrinal authority; nor does it begin at the moment of death. "And this is eternal life, that they know thee the only true God, and Jesus Christ whom thou hast sent" (John 17:3).

The conviction that eternal life is experienced here and now is an insight that Christianity shares with many other religions. There is a stillness in which the soul, like a radio telescope, turns towards the heavens and receives the signals of eternity. But the self must be silent first. The interior traffic has to stop. This applies equally to the actively religious self, which is so apt to drown the voice of God by its own words and works. The one whose life is oriented in this direction believes that he has at least some inkling of what eternity is. But whatever it is, it is certainly not an extension of human egocentricity.

There is an ocean surging before him in the darkness, and the more he is able to break down the resistance of the self, the clearer he hears it. In these circumstances, the question of the continued existence of the conscious self becomes irrelevant. Attention is turned elsewhere. To die—what can it be but to sink into God? And if it means the end of consciousness, what does it matter? To sink into God must be a new birth into the unspeakable.

For the Christian—especially for the Christian—the focus of attention is transferred from what takes place at the moment of death to what takes place here and now. Time is transcended. Christ, crucified, dead, and buried, is a historical fact. And yet it is possible to question this segment of history and get an answer. The Eucharist is this conversation cast in dramatic form. The personality who here breaks through the barriers of space and time is no ghost; nor is he an author, seated among the "immortals"; he is a fellow man, calling us out of our self-centeredness to a life of responsibility and service. When the self is addressed in this way, it must acknowledge its own character, but as a response, not as an egoistic affirmation. And although the voice reaches us across a vast gulf of time, it compels us to an intensive sense of the present, not least in social matters. Occasionally this dialogue can give rise to an experience described by a mystic in the words: "I felt myself to be, if possible, the less real of the two."[1] Whatever we may say or believe about life after death, *he* lives, though he was dead.

Let me add that one of the most surprising aspects of the situation is the church in which all this takes place—a church that in many ways contradicts the voice that speaks out of her texts. The phenomenon has been well described by Boccaccio in the *Decameron*. A church that "with all the care, all the intelligence and all the means at her disposal attempts to destroy the Christian religion and drive it from the face of the earth," but in vain—which prompts Abraham the Jew to draw the conclusion that "the Holy Spirit supports and maintains her, as eminently true and holy." Personally, I should

---

[1] An anonymous clergyman, quoted by William James, *The Varieties of Religious Experience* (1902), pp. 66f.

prefer to say that if it is possible to meet the living Christ in such a church, then it is certainly not the church that has invented or projected him. His life is such as to defy not merely two thousand years of history; it defies the church, too.

Although the dialogue with Christ is so profoundly concerned with earthly facts, it is difficult to escape the impression that here we encounter the power that spoke to Job out of the whirlwind. Eternity (which in the New Testament is a qualitative, not a quantitative concept) burns in his words.

Those words also penetrate to the depths of my own personality, where guilt hides. Hell is not something that Christianity has invented. We carry it within us; and it seems to be an inescapable condition of human life to project its imagery onto the knowledge that we must die. The primary cause of the fear of death, among believers and atheists alike, is the sense of guilt, particularly if it is not acknowledged. What is remarkable about Christianity is not the fact that the sense of guilt is there recognized and acknowledged, but the fact that it is overcome: the fact that words from the other side can extinguish the fires of hell.

To anticipate death on a basis of these premises is to anticipate that the dialogue will continue. The imagery in which men have clothed this conviction has varied greatly from age to age. Many of these images are now worn out, and no longer have anything to say to us. What we need is a renewal of symbols. But it may also be a positive advantage if we can avoid such narrow concepts as "I," "personality," "consciousness," and "corporeal." Paul knew this, and reminded his readers that there is a difference between the seed that falls into the ground and dies and the plant that bursts into flower a few months later.

What is it like, a consciousness that reflects God with perfect clarity? Or an "I" who is a "thou" to God through all eternity? Of one thing we can be fairly sure: that it is unlike what we now know as "consciousness" and "I." The same applies to the continuity between what now is and what will be: despite the difficulty I experience in trying to imagine a situation in which "I" am not actively thinking, there is continuity in the person of the one who loves, "for all live to him," as Christ says. That is the level of continuity between what has been, what is, and what is yet to be. We can sleep without being afraid of our dreams. We can love in perfect self-abandonment, completely absorbed by the face of the beloved. We can stop worrying about the precious self. All our questions are directed to another—a "thou." Hope reaches out to the goal in which we "see God."

Is there such a thing as an eternal life? I repeat: the question has nothing whatever to do with the problem of what happens when consciousness is extinguished. The one who believes in eternal life believes that he is in touch with it here and now, when he prays. The real question is whether he is right, or whether he is merely deluded.

PART TWO

THE HEALING TEAM

8.

LOVE UNLIMITED

If someone were to ask me to define the kind of situation or the kind of relationship that leads to neurosis, I should be unable to provide a satisfactory answer, unless I were able to limit myself to a small segment of experience. It is, however, possible to discern a number of primary conflicts, which may later branch out into very many areas of life, and I should like to draw attention to one of these. What I have in mind is a certain kind of demand that is normally made of the younger generation in our culture.

It has become something of a truism to say that most neuroses can be traced back to childhood experiences, and it might be wise to be a little skeptical at this point. But although this attitude has sometimes been exaggerated by psychologists, it has received surprisingly little attention from theologians. And yet the conflict I have in mind has to do with the very heart of Evangelical theology, the doctrine of justification by faith.

In school, the boy or girl is assessed on the basis of his or her achievements, first and foremost on the basis of knowledge. The young person who is not especially gifted can be commended for energy and industry, provided that he does his best. But what of the boy or girl who is neither gifted nor industrious?

A school that expected nothing whatsoever of its pupils and made no effort to assess their progress would be inhuman as an institution. And the teacher who allows personal considerations to determine the grades he gives his pupils, so that he raises or lowers them according to his personal sympathies or antipathies, has no business in the teaching profession. We might say the same of the teacher who uses the grade list as a form of psychotherapy. But it is an equally serious matter when a teacher permits his sympathies to be influenced by the kind of work his pupils do. And it becomes all the more serious

when grades, awarded for knowledge or industry, are able to
determine whether the young person is allowed to remain in a
certain class or in a certain school.

We are still far from an educational system in which the
teacher is able to be the personal friend of all the members
of his classes. As a rule, there are simply too many of them.
And it is also hard to imagine what a school would look like
that had no form of course or class differentiation based on
achievements of one kind or another.

It is a dreadful responsibility to be a teacher. It is common
knowledge that success and failure in later life are seldom
experienced so profoundly as an unjust grade, or even a sar-
castic remark from the teacher. But for many children and
young people the teacher is less important and less far-reaching
in his influence than the other members of the class. They also
have their requirements and their standards of judgment; but
these are often utterly different from those applied by the
members of the faculty. In extreme cases it may be that the
individual is not permitted to be on too good terms with the
teachers, at the price of ostracism by his classmates. But what
he loses in the one situation, he can regain in the other, and
so retain a measure of self-respect. If he does not happen to
belong to the chosen group who have no difficulty in winning
the confidence of his classmates, he may have to work hard to
be accepted; for instance, he may have to buy popularity in one
or other form of currency, from actual bribes to practical jokes.
Most of all he must take care not to jeopardize his good conduct grade—not the one he has on his report, but the one his
class gives him. He must wear the correct clothes, use the correct slang, and keep a straight face.

But this brings me to the heart of the problem. Most children and teen-agers seem to be able to stand a good deal at
the hands of both teachers and classmates, provided that somewhere in their lives they are able to experience love that is not
hedged about by limitations and conditions: love unlimited,
in other words. And where should they be able to find love of
this order if not from their parents?

What I was saying just now about the educational situation
in which nothing is expected of the child applies equally well
to the relationship between parents and children. The parent-

child relationship in which no demands are made is interpreted by the child as something other than love; for instance, as evidence of a lack of interest, or nonchalance: "Mom thinks I'm no good." It all depends on which impulse is decisive: whether the expectations are a result of love, or the love a result of fulfilled expectations. The second of these phenomena is by no means as uncommon as one might imagine. Parents often judge the success or otherwise of their children on a basis of a wrong and not infrequently fatal identification. Instead of experiencing the situation with the joy or distress of the child, they view it in terms of their own prestige. When the son or daughter comes home with a bad grade, it is not he or she who has to be comforted but Father. The grade is an insult to his parental prestige.

This sense of prestige observes and registers the child's conduct with a constant sense of worry. The result is constant nagging. And if, to add insult to injury, the child is not "good" (as the saying goes), then he or she may well have to put up with lectures on his or her rank ingratitude in face of the parents' goodness, generosity, and the rest.

Whereupon the child reacts by developing an intense desire for independence. And this struggle may well last for as long as the protagonists are living. This desire on the part of the parents to shape their children according to an image of their own choosing is intensified when it comes to the point of choosing a career. It would be instructive (if not particularly enlightening) to know exactly how many young men have entered the ministry or become farmers or insurance agents for no better reason than to avoid giving father another heart attack or to try to ease mother's migraine. And then when another young person of the opposite sex comes on the scene, the struggle enters a new phase. The children have to show consideration. What will they say if we tell them we want to get married? What will they say if we have too many (or too few) children? What will they say if we both go out to work? Or if only one of us goes out to work? And so on. . . .

It is unlikely that the average parent will recognize himself or herself in this kind of situation. But some of the worst accidents are caused by parents who are unable to tell the difference between their passionate private concerns and love. If

they try to make up their children's minds for them, it is only
because they have their best interests at heart. So they say. But
in the final reckoning, this attitude is nothing but a disguised
lust for power.

And the result? Perhaps a lifelong echo of mother and father.
An obedient and weak-willed person who all his life never
does anything of which he feels his parents would not have
approved. A complete triumph of parental authority. But the
woman who marries such a man is marrying nothing but an
echo—not to mention all the other troubles she is likely to
inherit.

But the result may be diametrically opposite: a person who
never does anything that he feels his parents would have
wanted him to do, so great is his intense desire for independence. A conflict situation of this order may lead to a variety of
results in respect of the individual's career. I am thinking now
of the man who has absolutely no self-confidence, who is condemned to work all his days on a level in no way comparable
to his capacity, ever and always so burdened by the judgment
passed on him by his school, his classmates, and his home that
he is a worthless nonentity. I am thinking too of the careerist,
permanently preoccupied with the task of proving his own
worth, continuing to collect laurels for the sake of winning his
parents' approval, even when they are dead and buried. Many
so-called "brilliant careers" are nothing more than neurotic
repetitions of the question, "What will Dad say?"

There are vast numbers of variations on this theme. There
is the nervous model of propriety, who is permanently afraid
of being late for school, or of getting dirty marks on her pin-
afore. Or the obstreperous old lady who all her life has to do
something different from what people expect—in order to assert
her integrity against an overbearing parent.

The experience that nothing is ever free—least of all love—
is thus transferred to all manner of relationships. Many an incurable womanizer is basically uninterested in the women he
chases; he is actually looking for his mother the whole time.
Many a star of the social scene is in fact going about among the
grown-ups he or she remembers from childhood, making a
good impression, to the delight of mother and father.

The individual's relationship to God may also be copied from this pattern. Many a child experiences God as a final guarantee of his or her integrity, a refuge from all injustices, even those inflicted by parents. But in many cases the image of God is never entirely freed from the image of father; God becomes a kind of Superfather, but with vastly increased authority. Parents may in their turn use God as an ultimate support for their own authority over their children: "Now remember, God is watching you!" Here, too, love is offered on conditions. To be sure, God loves us, but if you are naughty. . . . I well remember hearing, some thirty years ago, a sermon in which we were all assured that "Jesus doesn't like naughty children." It is impossible to run away from an authority like that: nothing can ever be hidden and nothing is ever forgotten. The watchword is obedience: unconditional obedience and self-effacement.

This is not the gospel. The gospel has a different message, but the message is often proclaimed so tentatively that it is powerless to break through the ideas inherited from home. If the minister says, "God loves you, but take care that you don't . . . ," the seeker notices only that he has to take care that he doesn't. . . . That is one of the reasons why, in the context of individual pastoral counseling, when someone is confronted with a boundless gospel, offered unconditionally, he is often utterly astounded, and remarks that he has never heard anything like that before.

Psychiatric help may be necessary in order to free the individual from this particular kind of burden. But what can the gospel do?

The gospel is not medicine. And yet it is the gospel that opens a perspective that is missing from the experience of the seeker who has never known unconditional and unlimited love. The majesty of divine love speaks to us not only from above, from the heights of parental authority, but also from below, through our Brother, the friend of sinners. Divine love is not the same as mere tolerance, which takes nothing seriously; nowhere do we see our shortcomings in face of God and our fellow men as clearly as in the light of the gospel. But because it is unconditional and because it does not seek its own, it takes the individual seriously, respects his decision, and brings about a rebirth of personal responsibility. At the heart of the gospel there is what the neurotic is seeking: security.

9.

THE GOSPEL, THE PASTOR
AND PSYCHOTHERAPY

> And I feel I must . . . *atone*—is that the word?
> Can you treat a patient for such a state of mind?

These words, from the second act of T. S. Eliot's *The Cocktail Party* (from Celia Coplestone's conversation with Dr. Reilly, to be more precise), sum up in two lines what I should call a "classical" view of the relationship between psychotherapy and Christian pastoral care; I mean the view that Christian pastoral care spreads out a net of guilt and responsibility before our feet, while psychotherapy helps the individual to free himself at least from demands that he has no chance of meeting.

Take for example this quotation from an article by Poul Bjerre:

> The patient's mother was a believer. She was not formally a member of any Free Church congregation, but attended various chapels regularly. She had a powerful personality and persuaded her husband to turn to God. In this way their home was strictly Christian in spirit. Although it *need* not be so, the result is that life becomes in these circumstances permeated by a constant and enervating sense of guilt—particularly in a milieu in which there is no counterbalance of culture and common humanity to be taken into account. . . .

This quotation may be supplemented by these few lines from Arvid Runestam's book *Love, Faith, Discipleship* (*Kärlek, tro, efterföljd*):

> It is claimed that morals and upbringing, with their rules and regulations, should pay more attention than they do to the demand that instincts should be satisfied in the cause of general health; it is also claimed that the demands of morals should be lowered accordingly. An excellent example of such

a naturalistic ethic is provided by the new science which, under the name of psychoanalysis, has formulated both a distinctive theory of the life of the psyche and a distinctive technique for the curing of certain of its ills. . . . Its aim, by and large, is to break down the claims of the moral consciousness. And it is claimed that its advocates have the right to this attitude by explaining and trying to prove that without it, health is endangered. This psychoanalysis also speaks of *the problem of adaptation* as the great practical problem of life. . . .

True, the debate nowadays is carried on in different terms. But the problems raised here are not irrelevant. There are still many who collapse under the weight of a legalistic Christianity or (and this is perhaps more usual) under the weight of a tyrannical upbringing with certain Christian elements introduced. The New Testament expression "the nurture and admonition of the Lord" (Eph. 6:4, KJV) still has overtones of violence and implacable judgment, despite the fact that in its context it stands in contrast to methods of upbringing that "provoke your children to wrath"; in other words, it is quite different to be admonished by the Lord, that is, by Jesus, than by a nagging father or mother. Parents, teachers, ministers, authorities, opinions—all assume frequently the burden of final judgment, with or without reference to God. And since they cannot see everything, they rely on the eye of God to keep watch while their attention is otherwise occupied: "Remember that God is watching you." It is not at all surprising that doctors and others should look for the source of many a guilty conscience in a religion that supplies its authorities with such powerful symbols.

But law and judgment are by no means confined to the church. She shares both the use and the misuse of laws and requirements with the world, and the tender conscience does not need to feel the eye of God watching its every move in order to feel condemned: the thought "Imagine if people knew . . ." is usually enough. For example, "Imagine if people knew that I said my prayers at night" (for atheistic opinion, like so many others, has cat's eyes, and can see in the dark). Like the state's TV eye in some totalitarian fantasy of the future, enabling the police to judge even people's thoughts.

But the judgment of thoughts can do without the police, and it need not use a truth serum; all it needs is an honest person's self-imposed goal of being what he or she seems to be.

In point of fact we are the perpetual bearers of the expectations, exhortations, and pressures of both God and our fellow men. Our achievement-oriented society demands that the conscientious civil servant should get ahead, and it is a moot point whether all ten commandments, singly or collectively, could annihilate a failure so completely as the innocent question, "Daddy, why didn't they make you a director?" Other sections of our society have different demands and different expectations. Like the office-worker Unoson in Curt Salomonsson's novel *The Man Outside* (*Mannen utanför*), who tried to join a gang of building workers. One of his mistakes was to bring his lunch to work in a paper bag instead of a box. He was promptly saddled with the nickname "Baggy," and his chances of being accepted came to an abrupt end. The author's *alter ego* comments: "You broke a sacred law . . . the law that everyone must be alike."

Psychotherapy can influence the attitude of the patient in face of all these demands and expectations. And yet this does not prevent it from creating new ones. Mental health itself becomes a new law, yet another "must," and behind the psychoanalytical jargon that floats around in the general chatter there are wakeful eyes—watching, judging, sorting. Theologically this is hardly surprising, for psychotherapy belongs in the context of creation and law. It can twist and turn the problem of guilt in many ways: some healthy and some not so healthy. But it is incapable of twisting a single human life out of the vice of responsibility and demands that grips the whole of mankind, because it is not exempt from these same laws.

But if this means that both the church and psychotherapy must work under the assumption of the laws of God and man, it does not mean that the individual can be left at the mercy of every demand and expectation. Christ speaks of the legalists who place heavy burdens on men, but who refuse to lift a finger to touch those burdens themselves. Legalists of that sort are the common enemies of both pastors and psychotherapists: whether they are religious or not is irrelevant. It is a matter of common concern in William Faulkner's novel *Light in August* to protect Christmas from his foster-father, who is trying to beat the law of God into him. Similarly it is a matter of common concern to build up the inner resistance of the civil servant who was not promoted, or the laborer they called "Baggy."

But supposing the pastor quotes the book of Revelation and claims that we are set free from the demands of mankind, the psychotherapist may object that although the church is right in trying to save the individual from being judged and condemned by the collective, it only succeeds in subjecting him to an even stricter judgment; and we are right back where we started. Poul Bjerre tried to tell his patient that she should not demand more of herself than God demands. But the patient objected, and supported her objections with texts from the Bible. And if he had told her that she would have to break away from these texts *if she were to be healthy*, she might well have answered that she would have to believe in these texts *if she were to be saved*.

Goals differ. The goal of pastoral care is beyond health and sickness in the heavenly world. The goal of psychotherapy is on this side, in the possibility of men and women to accept, here and now, themselves and others. And it is written that these goals are not always reconcilable. The Sermon on the Mount says that one may have to cut off one's right hand in order to become a whole man—a treatment of which no doctor would be likely to approve as a doctor (whatever his private convictions may be). If in deference to the commandments of God someone wishes to hold on to a shattered marriage, at the risk of a breakdown in mental health; or if a pregnant woman wishes to have her baby for the same reason and at the same price, is not the doctor forced, in face of such a situation, to require certain modifications in the Christian faith?

Not to mention the situation that classical pastoralia calls "poverty of spirit," in which every motive is seen through, in which the individual despairs of his own righteousness, perhaps in utter desolation or in the gray, implacable certainty that judgment has been passed and that there is nothing left to hope for. Human laws, nevertheless, operate largely in the area of attitudes, and can be obeyed a good part of the way by means of the actions of which we are all capable. But how are we supposed to be able to command ourselves to love our enemies? What are we supposed to do about lechery in look and thought? How are we supposed to deal with envy? In the state of poverty of spirit the knowledge that God sees the heart is anything but a comfort. Once more we sense the eye of judgment, and this time there is no doubt whose eye it is.

> You can conceal your wickedness
>   From summer sun's bright rays,
> But never from the face of him
>   Who measures all our days.

These words are in the *Swedish Hymnal.* Are they genuinely part of the Christian message? They most certainly are. Christian pastoral care may not delete a single dot or comma from "the perfect law." There is no way of salvation that leads away from the truth—and the church is convinced that the truth about the human heart is a terrible truth, and is so experienced under the hand of God.

Does that mean that all that the doctor can do is to resign himself or try to build up his patient's defenses, this time against pastoral care? And say, as Poul Bjerre said about the patient we met earlier: "She could do nothing but dedicate her life to dragging around the cross of duty, and hope for grace."

This tone of resignation is characteristic of a view that was common among psychotherapists twenty or so years ago. I am not quite sure how common it is today, but I do know that it is still there. I mean the view that this business of "grace" is as it were an insignificant appendix to pastoral care, an emergency exit for hopeless cases.

In point of fact we are here faced with the most distinctive feature of Christian pastoral care. It is true that the Christian pastor cannot help people by relativizing the Law of God. The faith has no illusions about how we are situated *if* right is to be right. But at this point there comes the about-face. Gospel. The forgiveness of sins. "The comfortable absolution," Luther called it. The distinctiveness of Christian pastoral care is not to be found on the level of law. Whatever functions the law may have retained in the sphere of pastoral care, it has finally and irrevocably lost its power to condemn. It can no longer penetrate to the profoundest levels of life with its "must": must do, must be, must believe—for in this dimension not even faith is a demand; it does not say, "You *must* believe," but "You *may* believe." Human worth is based, not on some kind of health certificate, but on the fact that the sinner is loved. And this is what he may believe.

From the point of view of psychotherapy this is a positive step forward. I am reminded of what one of Viktor Frankl's patients said when the doctor actually listened to what she had to say about her need for God: "Every kind of treatment up to now has been an eternal condescension (*Danebenreden*)." It is certain that the conflict with God—conscious or unconscious— is no less prodigal of one's strength than erotic or financial troubles, and there is no lack of empirical evidence that this is the fundamental human injury. Once it is repaired, power is released.

Vilgot Sjöman has described what happens when the conflict is resolved, in his novel *Image of Woman* (*Kvinnobild*):

> He knew that something had happened, at some time in her life; something that had shattered her confidence and broken down her sense of security. She said that on that day she had behaved badly toward another person; that she had been cruel because she had been desperate. But in that case it was excusable, he thought. But she shook her head and said that it wasn't: she couldn't be excused just because of that. She said that something happened, finally, to resolve the conflict and set her free. What was it that had happened? He did not want to ask; and she only said: Inside me; without words.
>
> "You think that people ought to forget, Verner. But if you can't forget? The thing that was most important . . . ," she said. "I don't know why, but I think there's always a shadow of guilt in the most important things. You're shaking your head, Verner. Don't you understand?"
>
> "No, I don't understand. How a person could *bear* to go around and remember what she has done."
>
> When he saw her eyes, he thought they seemed surprised.
>
> "But I have been forgiven," she said.

This is the level on which pastoral care proceeds. Nothing is smoothed over, nothing is "forgotten." But a reconciliation takes place. An atonement, as Eliot says in *The Cocktail Party*.

But this atonement has consequences in the area of psychotherapy. Of particular importance is the fact that atonement in the Christian sense is not merely a matter of the wiping out of guilt; it is much more the lifting of the whole of existence—even sin, weakness, and disease—into a meaningful context. Not only a theoretical context, but an organic participation, discerned most clearly in the fellowship of the broken bread.

This is what cures "the neurosis of emptiness" (the term coined by Boss and used by Arvid Möller). There is no more meaninglessness. Often the subject is so happy that his friends wonder what is the matter with him; and this state can last for a considerable time. Joy of this kind is not limited to a narrow sector of life called religion: it stretches out into work, friendship, human love. The fragmentation of life into tiny areas, each of which was meaningful only in and for itself, now gives place to a centripetal movement which lasts even when the first intoxication has passed off. In the newfound wholeness, "in Christ," as the New Testament puts it, the fragments of existence gain new life. Often the signs of fragmentation disappear altogether. As a former alcoholic, now a member of the Salvation Army, put it: "I have moved to a new eating place." I have myself observed that the Eucharist can bring married couples closer to God—and to each other, with a renewed sexual life as a result.

Both the achievement of such results as these, and their absence in the case of many who have experienced forgiveness, demand an explanation. I think that it must be sought in the fact that the fundamental conflict I have been speaking about is most painful, as well as being difficult of access. Freud said of Christianity that it is the only religion that dares to admit that we have killed the Father. The implications of that acknowledgment—and the gospel that atonement has been made for the murder—often clarify slowly, and amid hard opposition from the self-righteous ego. But the first glimpse of a context is at least a beginning, a first rolling pebble; wait and you may perhaps see the avalanche.

At this point it might be thought that pastoral care and psychotherapy can "rejoice together." But there are new conflicts hidden here.

First, that forgiveness is beyond the reach of psychotherapy: "Can you treat a patient for such a state of mind?" Had Eliot's Dr. Reilly been a psychoanalyst he might perhaps have answered that there are methods, but that forgiveness is not a method. You cannot use it as you would use medicine. The one who takes God like a medicine—who uses him, in other words —shuts the door to the gospel (however noble his intentions, for instance, as a means of moral rehabilitation). The therapist who sends his patient to a pastor for treatment (or tries it himself) is wasting his time, unless there is an entirely different perspective, personal and irrational, involved. This procedure is as pointless as it would be to propose marriage to a woman on the grounds that she would be good for the nerves. God is not a method; he *is*. The gospel is not medicine; it is love.

But this means new difficulties for therapy. For when the law of God in the New Testament is made into an absolute, this is because in the story of Jesus Christ it has ceased to be merely a *modus vivendi*, and has been brought into the extraordinary love affair the bloody seal of which is the cross. The law that previously threatened and crushed men was at least something with which one could discuss; but love does not discuss. Right up to the instant at which the relationship between God and man is drawn into this magnetic field there remains a possibility of setting up boundaries, of compromising, of saving something or other—like Ananias and Sapphira saving what they thought they would need for their old age. But love makes its sacrifice unconditionally, even when it involves mental health, or life itself. It is significant that when *The Cocktail Party* was first performed in Sweden, it aroused a storm of protest. Why? Because Celia Coplestone's story ended in martyrdom.

> Everyone makes a choice, of one kind or other,
> And then must take the consequences. Celia chose
> A way of which the consequence was crucifixion. . . .

Those who reacted sharply against this cruel consummation did so, often enough, in the name of mental health. Perhaps the medical profession ought to watch out for the gospel? Human love has its risks, and yet it is no more than a pale reflection of the reality that Paul tells us is to be found in Christ.

But we ought not to forget that this love story, too, has its healing aspect. Celia Coplestone gave her life in the service of mission, and that way was not infrequently a healing way.

Certainly it would be a mistake to believe that physical health is the only thing that may suffer in the process. Crucifixion is never merely a matter of physical suffering. We might, then, go so far as to suggest that psychotherapy might demand, in the name of Christ, the individual's—i.e. the doctor's—mental health as a deposit and guarantee.

No one can prophesy the direction of another's *via dolorosa;* but the history of the church, and especially of its saints, is not calculated to prove much of a comfort. Particularly since sanctity most resembles a stream in winter, disappearing for long periods at a time under the snow—and it would seem that the disappearance is due, not to any lack of fellowship with Christ, but to faithfulness in the face of an insurmountable task. Scriver once said that "lazy Christians are never troubled by the devil"; serious Christians are not so fortunate. In this respect, modern novels are often more true to life than the devotional literature of the past. The whiskey priest in Graham Greene's *The Power and the Glory,* who had to drink himself into a stupor in order to dare to become a martyr; the pastor in Georges Bernanos' *Sous le soleil de Satan,* who had no peace because he had offered it all to his "souls"; the vicar in Birgitta Trotzig's *The Victims (De utsatta),* who ends his life in a straitjacket, dying slowly into the death of Christ. Everywhere a seemingly hopeless struggle against devilry, desolation, disease, depravity. And yet—everywhere the Power and the Glory.

It is remarkable how often this struggle is against other people's devilry, desolation, disease, and death. In other words, the gospel can give a person back his mental health, and then demand that he lay it down for the sake of another person's mental health. Sometimes it seems to go even further. The love of God in a human being poses problems both for pastoral care and for therapy; the powers that are active here are not to be manipulated. One might just as soon try to manipulate a raging ocean.

And yet the love that draws men and women to itself shows a passionate interest in ordinary, common health. The same man who said that it might be necessary to tear out one's eye or cut off one's hand risked his life to cure a blind man or a cripple. And he was not using this as a method of winning men for God. It is as impossible to use therapy as a method of pastoral care as to use the gospel as a method of therapy. The catch is too obvious. But apart from this, the gospel does not lend itself to such calculations. Calculations are a waste of time when love is involved.

And when atonement is involved. The wholeness I was talking about, in which the fragments of life are incorporated into an organic fellowship, is by no means irrelevant for pastoral care and psychotherapy. They meet in the goal of love for the individual, a goal that might be expressed as "the whole man, consecrated in the service of healing." But they also meet in a collective, called the church. Doctors, ministers, social workers, building laborers, chauffeurs, housewives, scholars—a vast conglomeration of competing attitudes, swollen egos, ingrown personalities; but when the gospel blesses our daily bread and wine, the hidden unity becomes manifest. In that perspective the functions are coordinated. Therapy, pastoral care, industry —all these areas of life are subject to the summons of the broken bread to lose one's life in order to find it. This is atonement.

But when I refer in this way to pastoral care as an "area" among other areas, and to the minister as its particular occupant, I do so as a concession to a mode of thought that is in fact abolished by pastoral care. For it is not a sector of human experience, but the proclamation of the word of God to the whole of human experience: the word of atonement in which all things are comprehended. Individual pastoral counseling, it has been said, is the word of God to the individual. But where is the common denominator for this form of dialogue and all the other elements (such as the giving of advice) that occur in pastoral counseling? As Asmussen has pointed out, this is not *Seelsorge* (pastoral care), but *Seelenführung* (pastoral guidance). One factor is missing; and as long as it is missing, even atonement becomes just another fragment of human existence. The factor is the worshiping congregation. And that is why Protestantism has been uncertain as to the number of sacraments: sometimes two, sometimes three (as in the Augsburg Confession). In the former case an attempt has been made to connect oral confession on the one hand, and baptism and the Eucharist on the other—confession not as a third sacrament but as a way back to baptism. Strictly speaking, there is

no such thing as private confession, since all confession points
to the totality, to the congregation.

It is this congregation that is the subject of Christian care.
Within it, no one aspect is more sacred than another. In his
pastoral letter, Bishop Olof Herrlin (Bishop of Visby) issued
a warning against giving people "stones of psychological
knowledge instead of bread and sustenance for the soul."[1] It
would be equally cogent to warn the deaconess training col-
leges against giving them social and medical knowledge "instead of." But there is no such thing as "instead of" where the
church is concerned; in the church bread is literally "sustenance
for the soul." The profession of baker, like that of doctor, takes
its place alongside pastoral care as an aspect of atonement.
The one serves the other. And Christ says to the sick man:
"Which is easier, to say . . . 'Your sins are forgiven,' or to say,
'Rise, take up your pallet and walk'?"

Pastoral care must therefore rejoice—and weep—with psychotherapy. But this is not all; in the perspective of the altar it
can be seen that the latter is indispensable to the former. Bread
is an indispensable part of the gospel. Like the body, which
hears the gospel and eats bread: the body, with ears, eyes, and
other members, with reason and senses. To deny this in the
interests of some imagined pastoral self-sufficiency is tantamount to denying the incarnation and with it the possibility
of atonement. And the church.

The indispensability of therapy to the work of pastoral care
is confirmed by experience. However, I shall deal with this
subject at greater length in a subsequent essay ("The Minister
as Pastor"), where I shall also discuss the question of cooperation between the ministry and the medical profession as a
necessary consequence of what I have been saying so far.

If the Christian congregation is the subject of Christian care,
we cannot limit ourselves to ministers and doctors. We must
extend our scope to embrace the whole of the therapeutic
milieu. This in its turn involves the risk that individual confession and absolution will vanish in the welter of activities

---

[1] In the Church of Sweden it is customary for a bishop, upon election,
to publish a pastoral letter (*Herdabrev*) addressed to the clergy and
laity of his new diocese, but sold to the general public. Olof Herrlin
became Bishop of Visby in 1960.

that are carried out in the name of the church. If that risk is to be avoided, due emphasis must be placed on the dynamic aspect of the word "congregation," which comes from the sacramental focus of the church: the congregation comes into being, and the church is, where the Word is proclaimed and the sacraments administered. This has the effect of holding the pastoral care of the individual to its sacramental origins—and we escape the necessity for adding the word "church" to all our thousand and one activities in order to legitimize them: "church study circle in Spanish," "church athletic clubs," "church family advice bureau," and the like. Therapy or teaching or trading does not become part of the organism of atonement either, because they are incorporated into the organization of the church; but only by acknowledging that their fulfilment is only to be found at the altar and in the service of mankind.

It may seem that this argument has led us away from our subject; but this divergence is more apparent than real. In point of fact we have been setting our sights on the distress situation in which therapy and pastoral care encounter their common problem in its clearest and most dreadful form. For neuroses and mental illness take place, not in some hidden corner of human existence, but in its mainstream; they are not as it were accidents, having nothing whatever to do with "normal" life, but reports—blown up and exaggerated, in the manner of some artists, but reports nevertheless—concerning conditions in precisely this "normal" life. To heal a mentally ill person and then send him back to the milieu against which his mental illness was a reaction (incidentally, in some ways a more "normal" reaction to the distortions of life than that which we find among the more insensitive, those whom we call healthy) is only fifty per cent therapy; it is like curing the symptom and ignoring the actual disease. In other words, the problems of fragmented personalities express a situation in a fragmented society—and in a fragmented church.

The opposite of fragmentation is congregation: and the answer to fragmentation should be the congregation—a form of cooperation for the sake of atonement, in which pastoral care and therapy are everyone's concern and everyone's responsibility. This is not to say that all its members should pronounce absolution or practice psychoanalysis. But they should all know what the Scripture says to the one who is tormented by guilt or fear. And they should all know which features of our everyday life tend towards fragmentation, and which towards healing. They should know in order to practice: in order to qualify as members of "the healing team."

This dynamic view of the church is not calculated on a basis of present-day Swedish ecclesiastical organization, but I firmly believe that the organization of the church could be, and should be, reformed in this direction. This means, among other things, that the church's organization should be as inconspicuous as the state in a genuinely democratic society. Only the gospel should stand out. When the gospel is given free rein, it impels men and women to serve, and blesses their service; but this must take place in an unselfconscious fashion, without necessarily calling itself "Christian" or "church" work. No one need know how far such service is service of the altar; like prayer, as the Swedish theologian Gustaf Wingren has pointed out, it should be carried out in secret. Special Christianity and party Christianity shatter the bond of peace. The kind of exhibition congregation whose members set out deliberately to show the world what it means to live a Christian life and be a healing team very often succeeds in demonstrating the exact opposite. In fact there are no worse wasps' nests. In the schizoid intensity of their superspirituality they provide only a variation on the old theme of the Tower of Babel.

Nevertheless some form of organization is necessary in order that the dynamic movement around the altar should reach out into the world. The healing team must meet, not in order to "form" an organization called, say, "The Healing Team," but to coordinate their activities, in much the same way as ministers and doctors meet to discuss pastoral care and therapy. Similarly, when architects and artists, or employees and employers, meet to coordinate their views and their objectives, they too are a healing team. There is no need to call conferences of this type "Christian"; they should provide an impulse, not towards religious practices, but towards the service of our neighbor in some specific situation—and this is the right form of religious activity.

But now that I have extended the common responsibility of

ministers and doctors and made it the responsibility of the congregation and of society, it may be objected that this is utterly unrealistic, the present situation of the church being what it is. I am convinced, though, that this is an adequate answer to the situation. It provides a program for teaching, in the church and in the schools. Above all, it provides a way of praying and working in the face of "the dividing wall of hostility"—which the Scriptures assure us that Christ has broken down.

10.

GUILT AND FORGIVENESS
IN CONFESSION

The debate about pastoral care is at present suffering from something that would be a deadly poison for pastoral care itself, and which is having a serious effect on the debate: abstraction, language that is pious but vague, a perspective of noninvolvement in which the real situation of the individual disappears.

The real reason for this is undoubtedly the fact that theology, and particularly the debate about "the nature of the church," has turned its back on people—not on man as a concept, but on real people, singly and collectively, tangible people. Theologians seem to regard it as a guarantee of their scientific objectivity if they can avoid answering practical questions—questions about the situation in the marketplace, or in court, or at the conference table. And when ecclesiastical factions come into conflict, we hear the clash of exegetical, hermeneutical, and dogmatic weapons; seldom do we hear anything about the people whose fate may be decided in this tactical war. We can discuss the remarriage of divorced persons for months on end without anyone sparing a thought for the remarried divorcee who is trying to live a Christian life: is he really married to the person he is living with, or was the minister lying when he pronounced them "man and wife"?

But the debate suffers from a further hindrance to concretion, that is, the pastor's vow of silence. Confessors do not keep journals, and cannot discuss their "cases," even if they alter names and addresses. To be sure, there is need in Sweden for "clinical theology," but ministerial candidates in Sweden are not permitted to be taught in the same way as their colleagues in the Augustana Hospital, where pastoral conversations are recorded, and later criticized by a team of ministers and doctors. Swedish pastoral psychology teaching has to use other methods—either role-playing or the discussion of purely imaginary conversations.

This essay is an attempt to use this method to bring the discussion down to ground level. I shall be working with three fictitious episodes. I am not making use of actual situations but the situations I describe might very well come about. Further, I make a certain amount of reference to characters in literature to illustrate my points. In other words, there are innumerable parallels to the three persons I shall be talking about. Their problems are well known to every moderately experienced pastor the world over. But there is no Celia Coplestone, no Jeppson, and no Loman. Nor are the problems I describe more characteristic of the social classes or professions in which I happen to have placed the three subjects than of others. I have, however, permitted myself to draw on my own day-to-day situation as a minister of the gospel.

What I have to say is indebted to at least two influences. The first is perhaps most noticeable in the way in which the minister's answers are formulated. These answers are not calculated to be original or profound. They are simply repetitions of the subject's own statements. Reflections. In these answers I have used a conversational method first worked out by Carl R. Rogers, and later developed in different areas of personal counseling. It has been adapted in the field of pastoral psychology by Seward Hiltner and others.[1] The aim of the method is to assist the subject to discover for himself and verbalize his conflicts, and it is known as Client Centered Therapy.

One of the advantages of this method is that it compels the minister who is consulted, first to listen to what the subject is saying, and secondly to wait for the real conflicts to reveal themselves, instead of being satisfied with the more peripheral (and tolerable) problems around which the discussion often circles. It proves to be the case that (to use theological language) the minister seldom need preach the law to the subject; if he only has patience to wait, the laws of God and man will find expression soon enough in the words of the subject himself. And when the right moment for the gospel arrives, the

---

[1] Hiltner, *Pastoral Counseling.*

proclamation can penetrate at once into the heart of the situation. (I ought perhaps to mention that when I say that the minister ought to proclaim the gospel to the subject, I am departing from Rogers' rule that nothing new should be introduced into the conversation, but that it should keep strictly to the material brought out by the subject. The influence of Lutheran theology is here noticeable—a therapy that says that the law, but not the gospel, is present in the human heart, and that the gospel is a message from outside, from God.)

In this way a minister can, without being a depth psychologist, penetrate far enough beneath the surface of things to be sure that he is not speaking—or preaching—over the head of the person he is talking to, always provided that there are no morbid complications.

As far as content is concerned, particularly in the last conversation, I no doubt reveal the extent of my indebtedness to the classical pastoral tradition of the Church of Sweden, and at the same time to two seventeenth-century continental authors, Johann Arndt and Christian Scriver. Although I am unable to identify myself with them theologically—any more than I can feel any particular theological affinity with Rogers or Hiltner—I have a profound respect for the cumulative experience of this tradition, particularly in respect of the reactions of the individual to the church's preaching.

After this summary account of some of my presuppositions, I should like my reader to recall Celia Coplestone, as she is described by T. S. Eliot. A lady reminding me of her once stayed for a week at the Sigtuna Foundation guest house. The day before she was due to leave, she asked me after morning prayers whether she might have a short conversation with me. I took out my diary.

"The day after tomorrow?" I asked.

"Oh, I leave tomorrow."

I recognized the situation. She wanted to—and yet she didn't want to. She hoped to have an appointment—and hoped that I wouldn't be able to fit her in. So I proposed that she should come on the following day after morning prayers.

At 10:15 she comes in through the little door on the north side of the chapel, and looks around a little uneasily while I put up the notice to keep inquisitive tourists out. We go together a little nearer the altar, and sit down beside the arch. At once she sees the crucifix on the opposite wall; I see in her face the look of the traveler in a strange country, critical and yet without prejudice. And then I lose sight of her face; I am sitting beside her, conscious or half-conscious that she is as it were resting in herself, one hand in the other—open like a cup.

"I am an atheist," she begins—evidently to avoid misunderstanding. "The people I go about with are like that. We think it's a matter of intellectual honesty."

I say nothing, wait out the pause. Any word, and particularly any apologetical word, would be a risk.

"But I have to talk to somebody," she goes on, "to get my thoughts in order."

Then comes the story. Divorce. Her former husband has married his former mistress.

"I don't blame him for having a mistress," she says. "I've paid in the same coin, you might say. But divorce. All that bargaining about the child, about the house, about money. There we sit; expressionless faces; we talk politely and factually—after all, we are modern adults. And all the time my heart is howling its protest like an animal in a trap."

"You have to shut in your protest."

"Yes—and face all those friends of mine, with their questioning eyes, and their ready-made psychoanalytical clichés—'My, you *are* aggressive today!'"

"They refuse you the right to be disturbed."

"The right to admit that it hurts."

"You don't feel that they take you seriously."

She sits a moment in silence; and I remember some words of one of Viktor Frankl's patients, which he quotes in *The Unknown God* (*Der unbewusste Gott*): "I was always afraid, when I spoke of my need for God, that they would put me in a straitjacket." There are so many models of straitjacket. The one my subject is afraid of seems to be of academic cut.

"I know what you are thinking" she says. "You are thinking that without God nothing can be taken seriously. But God is unreasonable. For me."

"And the trapped animal is unreasonable to your friends."

"If there were a God to notice our protests, the world would look different."

I manage to avoid the temptation to indulge in apologetics. If I have anything to say, it will be like the other medicines: it will do good only when the sore is open. I answer:

"And if married couples heard each other's shut-in protests . . . ?"

"It might have meant a reconciliation."

"Reconciliation," I repeat, thinking at the same time that reconciliation is another word for atonement, and recalling the words from *The Cocktail Party:*

> "And I feel I must . . . *atone*—is that the word?
> Can you treat a patient for such a state of mind?"

Here the conversation was broken off. But the themes of love, responsibility, and guilt—as well as the question of being taken seriously—came up again in our conversations (for she came back to Sigtuna, and to the chapel) and developed in a definite direction, though without ever breaking through the barrier that was keeping her from faith in God. And then one day:

"What is the use of my seeing and admitting my own part in wrecking our marriage? I am accusing myself to myself, and judging myself by laws I have made myself, or at least laws I have decided apply in my case. But it doesn't change anything."

"No, it doesn't mend your marriage."

"All my life I am going to feel guilty before my child."

"You don't know how you would bear it."

"Anyway, forgiveness can never be anything but an escape. And who is going to do the forgiving?"

"You mean that no one can forgive without ignoring reality."

"Not forgive *oneself*."

"But someone else."

"Yes, if there is love."

"And you doubt it."

"You know that I can't believe in God."

"Not in God."

"And there is no other love big enough for such a reconciliation," she adds.

"You mean a love that doesn't take revenge and yet doesn't pretend that everything is perfect. That sees through things and takes seriously. That must mean suffering."

She looks at the crucifix.

"I can't believe in him the way you do—you know that."

"Not in the way I do."

We are both silent, and she bends over, as though I had placed something in her open hands.

"The fact that he has lived only judges me."

"He judged no one."

"And that is what judges me."

Involuntarily I look towards the altar. This would have been the moment for an absolution, if there had been any absolution for her. How do you absolve an atheist?

Finally, I say, "I have a message from him for you."

"For me?"

"I didn't exactly get your name and address; I was only given a description, but it fits."

"What description?"

"Those who hunger and thirst."

"Yes, I know; 'after righteousness.' But I'm quite sure that I don't belong among the blessed."

"To those he loved."

"A message from a dead man, then."

"From a dead man."

Once more there is silence, and then she says, after a while:

"Are atheists allowed to take Communion?"

This particular Celia Coplestone did not become a missionary, at least not in the same sense as T. S. Eliot's. She still lives in the same town as her former husband and his new wife, as her lover and her friends. Nor has she run away from them and hidden in a conventicle. Our conversations continue, and new problems are brought into the complex of guilt and forgiveness. For example, what is one supposed to do with a lover, when one has come to live in guilt and forgiveness? Send him packing?

"It's all very well to suggest that," says Celia, "when you are a married man and a minister. Don't you ministers know that it is always hunting season for divorcees?"

I can see that she is saying this to challenge me, and so I

wait to hear her real motive. And sure enough: "Incidentally . . . have I no responsibility at all towards a lover?"

I recognize the crisis of conscience that in many cases has come to take the place of that which Christians tend to take for granted: the primary cause of the sense of guilt is not that the subject is having an illicit affair, but that the affair is over, that someone has been left high and dry. "The lonely crowd" seems to have an eleventh commandment: "Thou shalt not abandon." It is like a lost echo of the Sermon on the Mount.

I know that every attempt to convince Celia of the rightness of the church's view of marriage has to start with that commandment; and I know that if she is to understand what I am trying to say, she must learn to *live* in the mystery that is called the love of Christ for an abandoned world. Not until she realizes that the relationship in which she lived long before the abandonment was hedged about with reservations—so that she was in point of fact loving too little, not too much—not until then will her conscience react on this point. And I must beware of anticipating events, not only out of respect for Celia, but out of respect for the Holy Spirit, who does not always take matters in the order most acceptable to an impatient pastor.

I suppose someone is bound to want to know what happened next. Whether Celia was converted. Whether she left her lover. But that was not what I have been trying to illustrate—whether or not I succeed in converting people, and what kind of ethical progress I can talk them into. What the pastor has to do is to listen, and to create some point of contact between human problems and the gospel of God. What happens after that is the concern of the Word, according to Luther's exposition of the third article of the Apostles' Creed. I do not believe in techniques of conversion, whether in preaching or in pastoral counseling. I only believe in the Holy Spirit.

And what shall I call my second example? The man I want to tell about reminds me of the end of G. K. Chesterton's short story "The Invisible Man": "But Father Brown walked those snow-covered hills under the stars for many hours with a murderer, and what they said to each other will never be known." But this man is no Flambeau. And should he tell the story of his life to the police, it would not only mean prison for him; it would kill his elderly father. He is an artist, and we met at

an exhibition, where a number of our mutual friends had assembled. We came to a corner, and stopped in front of a painting by Dubuffet (who so often has a drop of gospel on his
brush when he paints the things we trample on); suddenly he
caught my arm.

"You must pray for me."

"Gladly," I answered.

"Now—at once!"

We stood as though we were having an ordinary conversation, and only my friend alongside me could hear that I was
praying. Later we went out together, and wandered around for
hours in that part of Stockholm, until we stopped, late at night,
before a church. It was locked. He was not satisfied, but
banged on the door. Then he knelt by the west door, in the
flickering shadow of a tree that fought in the wind with the
light of a street lamp beyond the churchyard.

"Do you ask the forgiveness of your sins for the sake of
Jesus Christ?"

His "yes" dropped like a heavy burden on the step where he
knelt, and I pronounced the absolution.

At this point, I might begin an edifying homily on the salu-
tary ethical effect of learning to distinguish between guilt and
forgiveness in the eyes of God on the one hand, and in the
eyes of society on the other—if I could only provide the story
with a happy end. But my friend is an alcoholic, and seems
likely to remain so.

As far as he is concerned, psychoanalysis is useless. Once
I managed to persuade him to go to a doctor I often work with,
who is also a psychotherapist. Together we were able to get
him to undergo a cure. But he could not stand the psychoanalytical treatment.

Nor have any of the women who have tried to save him by
love had any success.

But confession? Sometimes he comes to me, radiant, and
shows me a couple of paintings. He tells me that with the help
of God he has been sober for two weeks, that he has sold one
picture and is working on new ideas. And then, a few days
later, a friend calls and tells me that Jeppson is lying dead
drunk in a Gothenburg hotel room with no money to pay the
bill.

Soon enough Jeppson is back at Sigtuna, in the chapel. New confession, new remorse, new absolution, new. . . . I think of a few words from Graham Greene's *The Heart of the Matter:* "Go to Confession and start over again." The words are directed at Scobie, who was, you might say, one of Jeppson's many relatives here in the world. Scobie saw only one way out of the situation: he freed the world from Scobie. But Jeppson will never take that step. His life will never be grand enough to deserve the name of tragedy; all his days he will remain one of society's failures—not even material for the stage. Nor will pastoral care change matters unless (and we ought not to discount the possibility) God himself is pleased to intervene, against all the laws of psychology.

But what I can do is, as it were, to hold Jeppson's hand until he dies. Give him the comfort of absolution again and again, so that despair, desolation, and all the sins that follow in their train do not persuade him that he is lost eternally. I can do no more than save him from desolation for new desolation. And yet I cannot help wondering whether Jeppson may not be my greatest responsibility. I am not sure that when, one day, I stand before my judge, he will ask about my conferences or my novels. But he will ask about Jeppson: "Where is your brother Jeppson?" And all the more since in this case what has to be confessed is not only Jeppson's guilt, but also my guilt and the guilt of a great many other people. Our situation has, as it were, broken out in this man, and if we have no time for him, believing that we have so many other more important things to do, then that, too, is a sign of our guilt. If there is no forgiveness for Jeppson, then there is no forgiveness for us either.

The danger of blunting the seriousness of the confession of sins, with the result that we go and commit exactly the same sins again, is common to all forms of confession and evangelical forgiveness. We all know how easy it is to go out and commit a certain sin directly after having confessed it to God in secret. Whereupon we confess once more, not treating it with the seriousness it deserves. But it is much more difficult in oral confession to avoid taking one's sins seriously, since there one spreads them out before another person.

But it is *the gospel* that is hardest to avoid in this situation, since it is spoken so personally and so emphatically that one must answer yes or no to it. If Jeppson is allowed to receive the gospel and the forgiveness of sins without first becoming a respectable (and healthy!) man in the eyes of the world, then it would seem that absolution is, so far, the only way of convincing him that he is included in the offer of the gospel. Particularly since many Christians would be stunned to meet Jeppson in heaven, and might think that they had arrived at the wrong place. (And they might not be so far wrong, at that.)

The difficulty in distinguishing between the judgment of God and the judgment of society distresses many people, and not only Jeppson. There is for example Willy Loman in Arthur Miller's *Death of a Salesman*. The man I shall call by this name is a company treasurer, not a traveling salesman. He has never had a mistress; always, as far as I know, he has been an exemplary husband, and his two boys are proud of him. But he has one thing in common with Miller's Willy Loman—he simply does not measure up to modern standards of working efficiency. There is nothing wrong with his brain, and I am sure that he is an excellent treasurer. But he is a slow and deliberate worker, and this is especially disastrous when he is entrusted by his firm with matters involving organization. Sometimes he has to give way to younger colleagues, and now he is starting to be afraid of dismissal—just like Willy Loman. A couple of years ago he had a nervous breakdown and came to Sigtuna for a complete rest. One morning he sat on my left (I am nearly deaf in my right ear) behind the arch in the chapel. He is a diffident person; his movements are slow, and yet deliberate. But there in the chapel his bearing was dignified and at the same time relaxed, as though he were at home here. I could see that he was no stranger to the church.

"Can you tell me how I can possibly go back to work next week?" was his question.

His anxiety is fully justified, and is a sign neither of neurasthenia nor of psychotic depression. The dismal possibilities unfold: even if he is allowed to keep his place, he is condemned to a rhythm and pace of life that is altogether alien to his nature. The difference between his working pace and that of his firm makes the necessary reciprocity utterly impossible. And if he is dismissed—well, firms are not exactly falling over themselves to engage men of his age.

"When my wife read in the firm's paper that Andersson had been made a director, she said, 'Haven't you been there longer than he has?'"

I understood. Even if Willy Loman had not had any particular personal ambition, he could hardly avoid feeling for the hurt pride of his family. Once again there was a resemblance between the traveling salesman and the treasurer: failure complicates things at home.

"I feel like a reject, just waiting to be eliminated."

He smiled—a smile half serious, half ironical—as though he were begging my pardon for using such strong words about himself. I paraphrased:

"As though you had been rejected."

"Do you know, there is a verse of a hymn that I am always mumbling—or groaning—to myself when I think about all the things I ought to have done, but haven't had the time or the energy for: 'Heavy is the guilt that presses/When the sinner breaks thy word.'"

"You make the demands of your work into a divine commandment."

We both realized the truth. The laws of a mercilessly competitive society had condemned this man and given his failure the dimension of unforgivable sin. In other words, this society had assumed the role of God. But this insight was the beginning of a slow liberation. Failure remained failure, troubles remained troubles—but they lost their power to condemn. Together we searched the Scriptures and found that Christ became neither a bishop nor a company director, and that on Good Friday, according to the norms of competitive society, his life-work was a complete failure. We tried to understand that God can even create in the midst of failure.

Thus there was no absolution from the sin of failure, but there was a liberation from hostile powers. When I pronounced that absolution before the altar, the kneeling Willy Loman straightened his back and looked at me. And I remembered that a couple of days previously we had read Revelation 14:4 together: "these have been redeemed from mankind. . . ."

This did not mean an end of Willy Loman's wrestling with the problem of guilt. The clearest difference between pastoral care and psychotherapy is perhaps that psychotherapeutic treatment aims at rendering itself unnecessary, while pastoral care attempts to make the subject more and more dependent on the gospel.

No miracles happened in respect of Willy Loman's attitude to his work, but he began gradually to conquer his paralyzing fear of failure. It is perhaps too much to say that he made the best of the situation—but he did manage somewhat better than he had done previously. He found a kind of *modus vivendi* with his work, and at the same time found the time and the interest to deal with other problems. He says that the pressure of his work had made him neglect his family. Not only that he had spent too little time with them. It was more important that he had been so afraid of personal failure that he had not been able to take a reasonable interest in his wife's everyday worries. There were also tendencies in his behavior at home that might be interpreted as compensations. And this meant that new guilts began to emerge from the shadows: new confessions, new absolutions, new attempts to regain lost ground.

One day he had discovered that while he was so afraid of making his family accept a lower standard of living, this was really not because of love. It was caused by fear. Fear for the loss of face that he might suffer in his wife's eyes. Soon he was back again in the chapel.

"What is there in my life that hasn't been a matter of prestige?"

"You thought it unimportant, and now you are afraid you have deceived yourself."

"Deceived myself and others."

"You feel like a fraud."

"Particularly where Christianity is concerned. All that nobility I tried to cultivate at home and at work—all those friendly smiles, polite questions, understanding looks—it was all lies and play-acting, just a beautiful mask."

"And behind the mask. . . ."

"Behind the mask—the real me; me, me, me! I feel such a wretched hypocrite, especially in church, because underneath the pious pretense I am nothing like a Christian."

"You mean that you should only go to church when you are a genuine Christian through and through."

"Oh, what's the use? When I pray, it's like talking to a blanket. There's no echo. As though there were no God. It feels exactly as though he had abandoned me. Doesn't that happen sometimes—I mean, that God abandons an unworthy person? And what does it matter anyway? What does it matter to me whether there's a God or not? Going to church is only going through the motions. I'm frozen inside, just an empty, frozen space."

He was as helpless as Jeppson. Was it a depressive phase in a manic-depressive psychosis? There was no other evidence to show it—nothing but this desolation, riddled with guilt. Nor was it a question of neurotic scrupulosity; what he was suffering under was not the memory of things he had done, but his own nature. The trouble was not what he had done, but what he was. He had experienced guilt. Not a collection of separate guilts, but the guilt of the world, the guilt of the universe, reflected first of all in his nature and then in his conscience. He was drawing up accounts quite apart from his work as treasurer, and he had identified, beyond all recall, the guilt of the world with the guilt of the individual.

It was no easier to save Loman from desperation than it had been in the case of Jeppson. We did our best to find out who had given him this painful insight into the truth, and we found that the Holy Spirit had probably been at work somewhere. So God had not abandoned him! Then we undertook a new journey of exploration into the gospel, and saw that Christ had been crucified in the hell into which Loman had looked. But Loman was not convinced by theological expositions, by heavenly visions, or by shattering experiences. Just as a child sees, hears, tastes, and touches the world, and in that way comes to know the world, so Loman found his eyes, ears, tongue, and nerves to be the gates of faith, through which he could leave his own affairs and his own guilt and see instead his salvation. Evidently God knew in advance how hard it would be for Loman to believe in such a forgiveness, for the fact that the gospel is repeated in so many different symbols—baptism, Scripture, the Eucharist, absolution—all of which seem so unnecessary to the self-satisfied, was Loman's incredible salvation. An incomparable medicine.

This time, when he came to the altar to receive absolution, he threw himself on his knees, and knelt there heavy as a stone, unable to avoid the words he had just heard.

When we parted, I thought of what Lars Ahlin had said about a communicant in one of his novels: "He heard someone tell him that he had entered into the peace of his Lord."[2]

---

[2] The reference here is to the words of dismissal spoken from the altar in the Swedish Eucharistic liturgy: "Go in the peace of the Lord."

11.

THE MINISTER AS PASTOR

The kind of demands that are made of the minister in his pastoral capacity depends on what we mean by a minister and what we mean by pastoral care. Twenty years or so ago the Swedish Institute of Clinical Psychology and Psychotherapy published a book called *Själavård-Själsvård* (*The Cure of Souls —The Cure of the Soul*), in which a contributor attacked the view that "the minister as the representative of the Christian religion has the task of bringing the individual to God," but not that of "carrying out some kind of therapy or the like." What he meant was that the only reasonable point of departure for pastoral care is the spiritual conflict-situation, whether its roots are to be found in religious or secular problems, in "healthy" or "sick" states.

In these circumstances it is difficult to assign any limit to the demands made on the minister as pastor. When the same author quotes with approval Archbishop Yngve Brilioth's statement that "the innermost secret of the ministerial office is to be found in pastoral care," this has the effect of robbing the ministerial office of its contours, and one is tempted to apply the suggestion once made to congregations, that in choosing a new minister they ought to decide whether they want a therapist, an administrator, or a representative of the traditional office.

An entirely different view is to be found, for example, in Thurneysen's book *Die Lehre von der Seelsorge* (Zürich, 1948), which stresses that pastoral care is the Word of God addressed to the individual. Psychology can help the pastor to make his diagnosis, but healing comes from another source entirely. "Pastoral consultation, like the church's proclamation in general, contains only one thing: the assurance of the forgiveness of sins," states Thurneysen. Between psychology and this concern there is a gulf fixed, which can be crossed only by a leap.

128

This would seem to imply the placing of severe restrictions on the minister's task in individual pastoral care—indeed, on the minister's task in all its aspects. It is his business to forgive. As an instrument of forgiveness he baptizes children, administers the body and blood of Christ to sinners, cares for individuals committed to his charge, and preaches—for in the Evangelical tradition, gospel, preaching, and absolution are one and the same: *absolutio nihil aliud est, quam praedicatio evangelii*, "absolution is nothing other than the proclamation of the gospel," says Luther.

But if this limitation of the demands made on the minister has the effect of relativizing many of his concerns, it is because it believes that his primary concern is of incomparable importance. What is to be forgiven is not some departure from the normal, some little weakness troubling the tender conscience, some isolated crime committed by an abnormal individual. What needs to be forgiven is what all people do and what they are; without forgiveness even the saints are lost. It is a cosmic sore that requires to be healed:

> Myself, I question rather where to find
> A cure to rouse the Mima's shattered soul:
> Afresh the torn celestial membrane bind
> Where waves from dark lands took their toll.

These lines, from Harry Martinson's *Aniara*,[1] describe the problem that arises as a result of man's sin against matter. He has also invented a Norn of goodness,[2] who weaves healing into the course of human affairs and succeeds in creating something

---

[1] Harry Martinson (b. 1910), one of the outstanding Swedish poets of the century, published his space fantasy *Aniara* in 1956. "Aniara" is a spaceship in which some eight thousand people are being evacuated to Mars from a world in the throes of the final atomic war. But the ship goes off course; its central TV-computer, "the Mima," to which the passengers have learned to look up as almost a god, breaks down, and the passengers are doomed to isolation and ultimately to annihilation in space. *Aniara* has been made into a highly successful opera, with music by Karl-Birger Blomdahl, and it has been translated (though less successfully) into English (*Aniara: A Review of Man in Time and Space*, adopted from Swedish by Hugh Macdiarmid and Elspeth Harley Schubert [London: Hutchinson, 1963]).

[2] In ancient Scandinavian mythology the three Norns were the female arbiters of fate.

like scar-tissue over a wound. But the poet would presumably never have had the idea, had the healing not already been in existence. This cosmic power of healing is placed in the minister's hands: he is *Verbi Divini Minister*. He has Christ in his mouth and in his hands.

Remarkably enough, "the office of the proclamation of the Gospel and the administration of the sacraments" (to use the words of the Augsburg Confession) arouses entirely different associations in the public mind. The minister is a sort of congregational director, convener of innumerable boards, committees, and societies. On top of that he is a professional talker, speechmaker, and master of ceremonies. In virtue of this he is called to be dignity and decorum incarnate. It is expected that he should be allergic to everything that conflicts with good manners, and since our society believes tolerance to be an essential part of good manners, he is a friendly, understanding man. And yet this can never quite dispel the image of something black having to do with judgment and death, as he passes by with his measured tread, in his elegant black suit and his white silk scarf.

Public opinion concerning what a minister is and does cannot help affecting the individual minister in some way. It makes demands: all the stronger since we live in a society in which everybody studies his or her reflection in somebody else's expectations, afraid to be a nonconformist. This means that the minister is torn between being what people expect him to be and being what his office, the office of reconciliation, demands that he should be. He must choose between what has been called "the gospel of harmlessness" and the gospel of the forgiveness of sins in the blood of Christ.

When he was ordained, he was faced with this choice and promised to proclaim the Word of God. But *he has to know what the Word of God is.* His ordination vow presupposes that he knows not only the Bible from A to Z but also the witness borne to the biblical Word in the early Christian and Reformation traditions of the church. The word of reconciliation is the apostolic word. Pastoral care that has no roots in the early church may be therapy; it may be advice; it may be more or less brilliant. But it is not forgiveness. Forgiveness springs from a definite point in our history. The sacraments and the Scriptures flow from that source, and it is there that the minister must draw the water of life for those who thirst.

But the well is deep, and the pastor must not imagine that he can ignore the chain of experience that stretches down through the ages to the source of pure water. Without reference to the spiritual distress and certainty of salvation that we find in the Reformation, the study of the Bible is mere history, geography, semantics, or what you will, but nothing for the thirsty. Without the witness of the early church to the facts of salvation, our talk of justification by faith is history of ideas or motive debate; but neither ideas nor motives can forgive sinners.

It is thus only reasonable to demand of the pastor that he know the pastoral tradition of the church. We often hear the complaint that it is difficult for the modern pastor to apply the words of Scripture, across a two-thousand-year gulf, to situations the nature of which the biblical writers could never have envisaged. Anyone would think that we were separated from the Scriptures by a total vacuum. The two thousand years are in fact filled with the questions the church has asked of the gospel—and has had answered. "Modern man" is no Melchizedek, without father, without mother, without genealogy. Our situation is not so void of points of comparison as we imagine. And if a present-day pastor should equip himself with experience from all the psychiatrists in the world, and yet ignore the church's pastoral tradition, he has confused pastoral care with one of its auxiliaries. He will know a great deal about mental illness, guilt, and neurosis, but very little about the medicine that no psychotherapy can prepare—or about how it is to be used.

The minister is *the final link* in a chain of forgiveness, in a succession of reconciliation that stretches from Genesis to the absolution he is pronouncing this very day. We must be quite clear about this: that tradition must not become a hiding place from the pressures of his current situation. If tradition is not used and applied, it ceases to be tradition and becomes a fossil. In the same way, the gospel cannot be locked up in a book and remain gospel. Nor can the consecrated bread be shown in a monstrance and at the same time feed someone. "Always be prepared to make a defense to any one who calls

you to account for the hope that is in you" (1 Pet. 3:15). When
the minister meets a desperate man or woman in the street he
should not need to run home and take out his Bible in order to
find out what the gospel has to say to that particular person.
The Word has to be in his mouth and in his heart. He must
know many passages from the Word of reconciliation by heart.
He should also be prepared to pronounce absolution. The possibility that someone he meets might perhaps need it should
not be a mere eventuality, peeping out of some hidden corner
of his mind after the person in question has left. This means,
further, that for the minister the distance between any given
situation and the liturgy of forgiveness should never be more
than one step. The Eucharist and the pastoral conversation. It
is not enough for him to have an open church and some form
of confessional. He must be able to turn a park bench into an
altar, and a crumb of hard bread into the body of Christ. He
must know how to use the seat in a corner of a ballroom as a
confessional, and he must know the way from the news of the
day to Isaiah 53.

But it is still not enough for the minister to know the ways
of forgiveness in Scripture, in tradition, in the existential moment. He must know where forgiveness is needed, and he must
speak forgiveness into the situation. For the gospel is determined by the situation. The forgiveness of sins is not a doctrine; it is a message, an answer. That is why the Scriptures
are so full of dialogue. Forgiveness is not something that hovers
over the biblical figures like an atmospheric cloud; it is given
to concrete people in concrete situations of need; it strikes
them.

This means that the minister must know something of the
Law, and not only of the gospel. He must know why forgiveness is necessary. Above all he must know what the Law says
about the thing that is worse than the thousand and one over-
sights, the "great" crimes, and the "petty" failures—the state of
being turned away from God and one's neighbor, the state in
which the ego (even the religious ego) is turned in upon itself.
His awareness of the convolutions of pride, reaching deep
down to the roots of human personality, can be sharpened in
many ways, not the least of them by his knowledge of the
"order of grace" proclaimed by the old-fashioned pietists. But

he can learn from the same tradition to see the work of the Holy Spirit in the helplessness of the one in need of help.

The minister must never think that he is dealing with people who know nothing of the workings of the Law. He can, however, frighten away this knowledge, or he can silence it. One way of doing so is to minimize or otherwise ignore the seriousness of the situation: "We are all sinners, you know. . . . But you meant well. . . ." It is surprising how often this minimizing attitude arouses a sharp protest. The moralizing attitude is much more effective. A superficial and unjust judgment can for a moment transfer a person's attention from his own foolishness to that of the minister, while a just judgment may even succeed in preventing the same person from passing an identical judgment on himself. The judgment from without silences the judgment from within.

It is common enough for people to regard the task of the minister as pastor in terms of the man with the accusing finger, ready and bound by duty to point it at transgression wherever he may catch a glimpse of it. How can he be a forgiver if he does not first of all point out that there is something that needs to be forgiven?

All well and good, but it is much better if the person in need of help points the finger at himself. And he will do so if the minister gives him the chance. Then the minister can give him back his own words as in a mirror. This opens the situation, and the minister can answer with the gospel. This is absolutely necessary, for the Law is in the hearts of all men, but faith comes from the proclamation of the Word of God. Faith that there is such a thing as forgiveness, in the very situation in which the individual finds himself.

When I say that the subject as a rule "knows" a fair amount about his own situation, I do not mean only surface knowledge. If the pastoral conversation is carried on in the right way, he may well reveal things that he had had no intention of saying, simply because he did not "know" they were there.

It is of the utmost importance that the pastor should not confuse the situation as it appears to be with the situation as it really is. Here again the Scriptures are his best textbook. Christ comes to a man who has been ill for 38 years, and the man complains bitterly; but the Lord asks, "Do you want to be

cured?" They come to him with a difficult case of moral theology: "Now in the law Moses commanded us to stone such.
What do you say about her?" To which he answers: "Let him
who is without sin among you be the first to throw a stone at
her." And the real situation of the moral theologians stands
revealed.

The church has always known that neither the religious nor
the irreligious person is quite what he seems, or quite what he
thinks he is. And it was a sign of the decadence of pastoral
knowledge that when the psychoanalysts, followed by a host of
novelists, made the same observation, it was received as a
piece of news, of particular danger to the church. Since then,
a great deal has happened that ought to have persuaded the
protagonists to recognize one another's traditions. Psychologists
and psychiatrists have investigated a mass of behavioral symptoms that reveal the individual's knowledge (though not his
admission) of his true situation. Fiction, too, when it is at its
best, recognizes the game of charades in which everyone tries
to hide his own identity, not least from himself. The pastor
cannot afford to be without this kind of help.

It is true that the Word of God, as the Scripture says, "penetrates" and reveals to the individual things that he did not know
about himself. But the defense mechanism that hides the real
situation is not always merely a matter of pride and love of
sin. There is the scrupulous individual, who has been attempt-
ing all his life to satisfy a father-image from his childhood,
and who has consequently come to confuse the commandments
of God with the rules and regulations of men. There is the
potential suicide, who believes that he hates himself, although
it is his mother he hates. There is the atheist, who believes that
Hedenius[3] or Bertrand Russell took away his faith, although
it was in fact a careless minister or Sunday school teacher who
was to blame.

[3] Ingemar Hedenius (b. 1908) has been Professor of Practical Philosophy in the University of Uppsala since 1947. He is known less for his
purely philosophical work than for his constant polemic against Christianity and the Church. His best-known book, *Tro och vetande* ("Faith
and Knowledge"), was published in 1949. He is an old-fashioned rationalist, very similar in his general outlook to Bertrand Russell, and is no
longer taken very seriously by theologians.

If the minister is to proclaim the Word of God in situations like these, he needs the help of psychological methods to uncover inner realities. Otherwise he is in danger of providing answers to irrelevant questions. He comforts the man who has been ill for 38 years, instead of apprehending him at the point of his retreat into illness. He discusses the water in Jacob's well with the Samaritan woman, and it may even be a theological discussion—ministers are rather apt to believe that they have been engaged in pastoral discussion every time they have an opportunity of expounding their own theology without interruption—but he never penetrates the shaft of distress that is her life. And the fact that psychology is able to help in cases like these is due, theologically speaking, to the fact we discussed in our essay on "Guilt and Forgiveness in Confession," that therapy and law belong on the same level. The distress of the human conscience cannot be cured by all the psychology in the world; but it can be laid bare.

It is important to be aware of the dangers lurking in language. "They have healed the wound of my people lightly, saying, 'Peace, peace,' when there is no peace" (Jer. 8:11). Or we produce a reason why things are not as they should be, when the real reason is far different. Like the atheist in Viktor Frankl's *Der unbewusste Gott*, who came to the doctor with the compulsive idea that his mechanical errors might worsen the pains of purgatory for his relatives, but whose real trouble was atheism, not the compulsive idea itself. The man was bilingual; in one language he complained of the compulsive idea, and in the other, using the same symbolism, he revealed to the doctor the real situation.

If the linguistic situation can make it hard for the minister to penetrate behind words to reality, it makes it no less difficult for the subject to penetrate the minister's words. The man or woman whose childhood was a nightmare of fear of his or her father may be horrified to hear the minister say that God is to man as a father is to his children. Or, to take another example, the mind set on the Law finds it difficult to see anything in the Bible but demands and judgment. In certain states of depression the same difficulty recurs, but swollen out of all proportion. Should the minister say to the patient that if we confess our sins, God is faithful and just to forgive us our sins, the patient may well answer that he is therefore damned, since he cannot produce a confession.

That the pastor, in situations like these, needs the help of psychiatry in order to be able, at a later stage, to proclaim his message is as self-evident as the fact that we go to a doctor to have our ears examined. Psychiatry never competes with the Word; it does say, "*Ephphatha*—be opened."

The last example we gave emphasizes the importance to the pastor of being able to distinguish between a genuine sense of sin and a morbid sense of guilt, between joy in God and manic exaltation. Confusion at this point may lead to the death of the patient. The minister must know enough psychiatry to avoid trying to act in the place of the doctor, and to avoid sending someone to a doctor when only the pastor can help (always supposing that the doctor is not himself a pastor, which fortunately is not altogether unknown).

Naturally, there are innumerable other ways of bypassing the real cause of distress. It goes without saying that the minister must also know a great deal about the situation before his eyes. For instance, if someone comes to him for help who seldom comes to church, he ought to know whether the person in question is a shift-worker or works in one of the public services. Without a thorough knowledge of working life and home life in his own area, the minister runs the risk of giving advice and encouragement on a level with that so effectively satirized by James: "If a brother or sister is ill-clad and in lack of daily food, and one of you says to them, 'Go in peace, be warmed and filled,' without giving them the things needful for the body . . ." (Jas. 2:15-16).

All these points are important in order that the pastor can speak the word of forgiveness into the situation as it really is; they are no less important in order that he can free people from guilt where there is no guilt. For it is not only through morbid guilt complexes that some people can experience tortures of conscience over things that have nothing of sin in them. Many a conscience remains all its life chained to some human authority, for example that of parents (a situation that not infrequently has a neurotic background). It is not the Law of God, but the rules, conventions, and behavior-patterns of men that decide for such a person what is guilt and what not. The immature conscience needs forgiveness, to be sure; but not for what it thinks needs to be forgiven. The same applies to innumerable individuals who, although they are not chained to parental authority, are instead concerned to be "with it," in tune with the times; for instance, the girl who was asked if she would like to be able to fly like Superman, and answered, "I would like to be able to fly if everybody else did, but otherwise it would be kind of conspicuous." Many wings have been clipped in this way. And it is not unusual for the one who separates himself from the masses to feel guilty about it—even when it is a matter of study, promotion, or going to church.

It is the nonconformist who comes off worst in our uniform society. He may well experience his own conduct, his opinions, or perhaps his appearance as asocial, and hence a source of guilt. And the fact that he does not happen to have the word "sin" in his vocabulary does not improve matters.

There are other levels of society—"achievement society," as Joachim Bodamer has aptly labeled it—in which it is a source of guilt *not* to separate oneself from the masses, *not* to be promoted, *not* to achieve recognition as an out-of-the-ordinary person. There are circles in which it is shameful not to have been to college, and a handicap not to have a doctorate; while in industry, and especially in the executive class, the "achievement conscience" flourishes freely. (Consider the story of Willy Loman in the previous essay.)

It is in situations like this that Paul's words can be applied most cogently: "For freedom Christ has set us free; stand fast therefore, and do not submit again to a yoke of slavery" (Gal. 5:1).

But when the minister tries to set someone free from his (or her) subjection to all manner of authorities, and teach him that he is "delivered from mankind," he must not subject him afresh, either to himself or to a new group, however pious and sound. It is of no benefit to the kingdom of God if the immature person is set free from his conformity to the world, only to be chained once more somewhere else, in the church: "Do not become slaves of men" (1 Cor. 7:23).

And yet there are many who *want* to be chained: those who

are afraid to assume responsibility for their own actions, and want someone to blame if and when things go wrong. As Sartre pointed out in *L'existentialisme est un humanisme*, the person who lets a minister or priest decide for him has in fact made a decision. Freedom of responsibility is a fiction. But in this way the precious ego escapes (or so it is thought) the unbearable humiliation of groping in uncertainty or, worst of all, of making a mistake. In this way it is possible to run away from doubt—although Jesus has been there before us—and to preserve the belief in one's own relative innocence that so many maintain (desperately) while at the same time talking piously about the sufficiency of grace.

However, in many cases the entire equation can be reinterpreted in terms of immaturity. The subject is looking for his father or his mother, and the minister must avoid becoming a surrogate for either. He must remember the words of Christ: ". . . call no man your father on earth" (Matt. 23:9). The task of the minister is to help the subject to attain full independence in the gospel.

It goes without saying that the pastor, like the psychiatrist, has to take account of the problem of transference, especially since he is "God's doormat" (Bruce Marshall), and must accept the fact that anything is liable to rub off on him—bitterness, hate, love, gratitude. Therefore he must not be horrified if the subject accuses him of being responsible for the dullness or pain or injustice of his home, his work, or "life" in general. Nor must he be overwhelmed when gratitude for a newfound liberty is directed towards his own person, perhaps with unmistakable erotic overtones, instead of towards God. Both phenomena are transistory, if the minister does his job properly.

But what does he do next? In the first place, he carries on listening, to give the problem a chance of crystallizing and the right recipient of bitterness and gratitude a chance to emerge from the depths of memory and motive. Second, he must turn the attention of the subject toward God and his neighbor. The altar is of immeasurable help in this connection, and so is the ministerial office. In this perspective the minister's personal qualifications recede, while Another's grow. Guilt, bitterness, and love reach their true destination in the mercy of God.

Third, it is of the utmost importance that the subject be allowed to decide for himself. The minister must not precipitate a decision either by suggestion or persuasion. This applies to even the most vital of all decisions. The Word of God does not demand of a minister that he should be successful in converting a single individual; merely that he should communicate what the Word actually says. The Holy Spirit takes care of the rest, and should be left in peace to get on with it in his own way. The result is, at all events, that the individual says "Yes" or "No." Both answers are respected in the Scriptures. God is nowhere represented as a dictator, with a department of propaganda, or as a specialist in brainwashing. Hell is nothing but God's respect for man's right to decide for himself: if he wants to say "No" and go on saying "No" for all eternity, he has the right to do so.

Certain American pastoral psychologists have incorporated respect for the integrity of the individual into their method: a good example is Seward Hiltner, in his book *Pastoral Counseling.* The most important thing there is to be learned from the application of these methods is respect, in which active listening is so much more important than talking.

If the minister gives any advice at all, it ought to concern such things as are inseparable from penitence: "Let him who steals, steal no more"; "Go and sin no more"; "Be indebted to no one"—all biblical examples. Or, as Laurentius Petri has it in the Swedish Church Order of 1571, the act of penitence should cancel out and make restitution for the sin.

Everything over and above this, for instance, the sharing of the minister's own personal experience, must be presented as having no other authority than that belonging to common sense, whatever its source.

The same applies to his teaching on the subject of Christian faith and behavior: the minister must distinguish between the doctrine of the church and his own personal opinion. In doubtful cases, admit the doubt. Above all, never use the name of God as a cloak for purely human interests—for example, in the interests of ecclesiastical party politics.

If the minister, armed with these resolutions, is to be successful in furthering the subject's independence, and his own personal decision whether to accept or reject the gospel, he must—and this is my fourth point—avoid being drawn into his problems. He must not become a close friend or an enemy, a debtor, a creditor, or a guarantor. If there arises a relationship as between employer and employee, or superior and inferior, the relationship, which should be determined by the attitude of confession, will be placed in jeopardy.

It is of the utmost importance to avoid countertransference; in other words, the minister must on no account do what the minister dreamed he did in Ingmar Bergman's film *Winter Light* (*Nattvardsgästerna*)—confess to the person he is confessing. That is to open a forbidden door.

But it is even worse when the minister involves the counselee in his own personal problems by giving him a role to play. No method aimed at bringing him personal maturity is going to be of the slightest use if the minister secretly *needs* him as a dependent, so as to be able, for once, to act the father, to exert a little authority. Ministers of this type give advice in categorical terms, in a tone of voice the firmness of which stands in inverse proportion to their experience. It may be, too, that he longs for authority among his fellow ministers, or in his congregation. Now and again he drops discreet hints about his pastoral experience; or he uses cases for sermon illustrations: "A man came to me the other day, wondering what he ought to do. . . ."

Or the counselee may be given a role in the minister's love life. As a rule, this happens in subtle ways, much subtler than in Pär Lagerkvist's novel *Pilgrim at Sea* (*Pilgrim på havet*), in which the minister—an incredibly helpless and ignorant man, incidentally—proves the point of the book of Proverbs, when describing this kind of seduction: "All at once he follows her, as an ox goes to the slaughter" (Prov. 7:22). The train of events is usually more complex and more banal. The minister finds a woman who is willing to listen, however much he talks. Now he knows what it is to be understood. Soon he begins to count the days between conversations. But it might be better if there were no more conversations. If the minister has become erotically involved with his counselee, it is as well that he should consider carefully the role that she, as a person and as a Christian, ought to play in his life. But one thing is certain:

she cannot remain his counselee. The situation has become impossible.

The minister should always be aware of his high calling. The reason why I say this is not out of any wish to moralize, but because he must not overvalue his own person. It is not the minister who needs to be understood, but the counselee. The drama is not about these two, but about Christ and the sinner. The minister does not stand in the center of affairs; he represents Another. He has no need, therefore, to underline his authority by the tone of voice he uses. If it is true that he represents God, it is of no consequence whether he does so as archbishop or as junior assistant, stammering or with heavenly eloquence, as a saint or as a publican. These things may have their importance: but not here, not for his authority. God has no need of his desperate attempts to create an atmosphere of goodwill on his behalf.

But no theology of the ministry can set the minister free from his own heart. And that is the direction from which the greatest dangers come. He must have his own self under control. No one can be a psychoanalyst who has not himself been analyzed. But unconfessed confessors are plentiful: a kind of senior executive among the poor people of God, themselves immune from the petty problems of their clients. When trouble strikes, these "experts" in the things of the Spirit are the first to go under. And when they do so, they pull others down with them willy-nilly.

The pastor has to be gazing constantly into the abyss. His very calling is a challenge to the evil around him—and within him. If he makes no use of the means of grace he offers to others, his situation is extremely precarious. Without personal experience of the situation of confession; without the insight into oneself that comes only in the presence of another person; without access to the comfort of absolution—he is, to say the least, poorly equipped. And what is much worse, he is running the risk of being a humbug.

Finally, a fifth consequence of the minister's attitude of respect for the seeker. As a pastor, he ought not to limit himself to some partial insight in the Christian tradition, but represent the Christian heritage in its entirety: "For all things are yours, whether Paul or Apollos or Cephas or the world or life or

death or the present or the future, all are yours" (1 Cor.
3:21f.). As a minister in the Evangelical tradition he has the
keys to the entire storehouse, and need not direct his people
to the crumbs they can pick up in a corner. As he helps them
to live in the forgiveness of sins, he should unlock one room
after another in God's house, so that they may see for themselves "what are the riches of his glorious inheritance in the
saints" (Eph. 1:18). Sanctity is not something restricted to
certain types of person, certain professions, certain family
backgrounds; nor is there any stereotyped way of reaching it.
There are many helps along the way, not the least of them
being the Bible: "All scripture is inspired by God and profitable for teaching, for reproof, for correction, and for training
in righteousness, that the man of God may be complete,
equipped for every good work" (2 Tim. 3:16f.). The respect
for each person's individuality that should govern the minister's attitude to every pastoral problem thus finds its correspondence in the use of the means of grace. Life in the forgiveness of sins is a continual conversation with God, and in
that conversation no one is ever silenced or forced to conform
to a stereotype. In this, as in all his labors, the minister is required to cooperate with the Holy Spirit.

Returning to the question with which I began this discussion,
I have followed Thurneysen in gathering the whole question
of pastoral counseling around the forgiveness of sins, in which
the minister is acting on God's behalf. Should there arise conflicts in which the minister is unable to act in this way, then
he is unable to act at all. Does this then mean that he should
remain totally indifferent in face of questions of health, finance,
the family, or friendship? By no means. But his attitude to
these matters should be similar to his attitude to psychiatry—
it can help him to find an open situation for his proclamation,
prevent him from dabbling in the doctor's profession, remind
him that each person he meets is an individual. But the particular form of distress with which the psychiatrist is concerned
is outside the minister's province.

We must not forget that in matters of pastoral care, the subject is not the minister but the church—the congregation. The
sufferings of the world and the individual are an exhortation,
in the name of Christ, to cooperation between members of the

church—ministers, doctors, engineers, economists. The minister should be constantly in touch with laymen whose judgment he respects, and who can help him when he reaches the limits of his task, or his knowledge, It is especially important that there should be close contact between pastors and psychiatrists.

But it is necessary to have a certain degree of knowledge in order to be able to direct a serious case to the appropriate specialist. As far as the minister himself is concerned, he ought to be able to administer first aid, that is, in areas where he is himself not an expert. Should he happen to be familiar with problems of finance, he can hardly listen to someone's money worries without offering such advice as he is able to give; this may not have anything to do with the forgiveness of sins, but may well help someone weather a crisis. This is not pastoral care; it is Christian service. But it is often the case that the one must fill in for the other. The Good Samaritan did the work of a doctor, while the priest and the Levite, keeping strictly within the bounds of their respective ministries, passed by on the other side. All suffering is the minister's concern, and, although he is not ordained to solve every problem, he is ordained to be a neighbor (in the Christian sense) to all; here the only limit is the limit of his capacity to help.

Most of what I have said here is counterbalanced by what may appear to be a negative factor in the minister's pastoral function: his silence. This leads to difficulties for research into the history of pastoral care, for discussion of the methods of pastoral psychology, and for teaching this and related subjects. It also means that it is strictly forbidden to use sermon illustrations of the kind I mentioned just now—these are weeds that must be uprooted from Christian proclamation. It forbids, too, hints between ministers; the only permissible excuse for discussing a case is if the counselee expressly requests it. Even obtaining medical advice is complicated by this rigorous duty of keeping silent. But I must emphasize that there is no excuse whatsoever for breaking the seal. In time, the pastor will find that when he meets the counselee in other situations, their relationship will no longer be determined by what has passed between them. He will simply forget it. And this may serve as a symbol for what happens in absolution: "I, I am he who blots out your transgressions . . . , and I will not remember your sins" (Isa. 43:25). This silence, in which the counselee is shielded even from civil justice, affirms a higher law, the law of forgiveness. It is a reminder that the counselee is redeemed from mankind, that his integrity is guaranteed by God himself.

The silence is turned toward God. It is the silence of prayer, of intercession. It speaks into the sacred darkness, into the divine secret.

Intercession is not a reserve to fall back on when everything else has failed; it is the very life-breath of pastoral care. It is not often that the minister can keep track of its "results," and for that reason he may be tempted to undervalue and neglect it in the rush. But the effect of intercession is no less for being outside the scope of our measurements. Gradually, the minister comes to realize how much he himself needs the intercession of others, and what it means for his own growth in grace that he should constantly be praying for others.

In time, he realizes that he shares secrets with God.

12.

THE PASTORAL ASPECT OF PREACHING

Is it really possible to speak of a pastoral *aspect* of preaching? It has been pointed out by the Swedish scholar Henrik Ivarsson that for Luther preaching is entirely pastoral. It is the forgiveness of sins, just like individual absolution and the holy Eucharist. The difference is that in these means of grace, the Word is directed to each person individually. Ivarsson also reminds us that the Swedish Church Order of 1571 speaks of "the universal ministry of preaching, in which our Lord Jesus Christ is proclaimed as an Atoner and as a sacrifice for our sins" as "a true and perfect Absolution," and that absolution is likewise characterized as an act of proclamation: "Therefore the act of preaching, which is otherwise commonly known as *Absolutionem privatam*, shall also continue in accordance with present practice."

Following this tradition, it is impossible to point to some special part of preaching as pastoral, and to another as having no pastoral significance. What I want to try to do here is also to distinguish a dimension of preaching, an attitude on the part of the preacher that corresponds to that of the confessor. Assuming for our present purposes that every sermon should contain the two elements of biblical exposition and general application, it follows that the biblical exposition has to contain points of information that are not in themselves pastoral. For instance, if the preacher points out that the three wise men in the Epiphany Gospel are not called "wise" in the text, that particular point is hardly likely to convict or convert anyone. But on the other hand, points like these, if they do not fill some direct or indirect pastoral function, have no place in an Evangelical sermon. It is not enough to claim that they are motivated by the text, still less that they are interesting, curious, or calculated to arouse the congregation's respect for the preacher's scholarship—they remain what one American pastoral tradition calls "distracting."

In point of fact there is no more central exposition than that which prefaces the Gospels: "The Gospel according to. . . ." Not even the scholar can understand these texts unless he understands them as a message. And unlike the scholar, the preacher must not only understand them in this way—as he might grasp the meaning of a letter from Gustav Vasa to the peasants of Dalecarlia[1]—he must realize that his sermon is an integral part of the text. Not until the text becomes a gospel, "good news," does it become genuine. Unless it is proclaimed as such, the text remains lifeless—like a pressed and dried flower.

The gospel, then, simply does not exist as a so-called objective fact under any circumstances. It is always a communication from one person to another. It is often said that the difficulty of preaching is the tension that exists between the text and the situation in which the ministry of preaching is exercised. What is meant is the distance between the original situation of the text and the present-day situation of the person to whom it is addressed.

This distance must not be taken lightly; it is reprehensible to treat texts as though they were rooted in thin air. The fact that the texts have their roots firmly fixed in history is an essential part of the gospel. The gospel is no myth (in fact, it becomes mythologized when the message is separated from history); it is incarnation. So we have to admit that it is not the easiest thing in the world to pretend that all these peasants and serfs with their tools—grindstones, cattle yokes, fishing nets, leather bottles, and the like—belong to our own day and age.

But I suspect that the difficulty has been put in the wrong place. Ours is by no means the first social pattern to differ from that reflected in the Bible. The social situation in which

[1] Gustavus Eriksson Vasa (d. 1560), a Swedish nobleman, became King Gustav I of Sweden in 1523, having in 1520 headed an insurrection against King Christian II of Denmark, who then ruled the two countries. His main support came from the peasantry of the central Swedish province of Dalecarlia (Dalarna), where he raised his first army. Many of his letters are preserved.

St. Sigfrid—or for that matter Olaus Petri or Henric Schartau
—preached was in many respects just as remote from the biblical history as ours is.

The real difficulty is, I believe, twofold.

In the first place, it is difficult to use words that are rooted
in another historical situation *because many people do not
recognize that any historical situation exists.* The struggle to
be modern and up-to-date leaves no room for the idea that it
is even possible to be different than people are nowadays. In
fact it is part of the spiritual distress of the present day that
modern man accepts his modernity not merely as a destiny,
but as a norm. Like Melchizedek, he has no father, no mother,
and no family tree. Biblical pastoral care demands, not that we
should confuse him with Esau or Manasseh or Bartholomew or
Alexander the silversmith, but that we should free him from
his self-imposed isolation and place him on the same level as
all manner of men from the obscure past. By this means, the
individual may possibly be helped to be a real individual person in the mass society, and not merely a cipher in the production of goods and ideas.

But if this is to succeed, it will not do to approach modern
man as though he were a native of some exotic country to
which the missionary comes, bearing the blessings of civilization. Preachers sometimes speak in a disparaging manner that
inevitably—and rightly—arouses resentment in the hearer—not
least when they try to speak what they believe to be the local
dialect. And this brings us to another aspect of the problem of
ancient texts in the modern world. For this problem is not only
one of two temporal situations; it also has to do with eternal
mercy brought into a situation that is common to all men. As
Martin Niemöller once expressed it in his attack on the myth
of the noble Aryan race: "All men, from Adam to Adolf Hitler,
are sinners and can be saved by grace alone, for the sake of
Jesus Christ." *It is from this basic human situation that man
attempts to escape, by taking refuge in the myths of his own
day*—and democratic myths are as good as any to hide in, especially with the help of the clergy.

There are two special aspects of modern life that are of importance in this context. First, that we live in what might be
called a consumers' society, that is, a society in which adver-

tising and propaganda are of the utmost importance. Living in this kind of society, one has no chance to test the truth of everything that is said—or shouted—about goods of various kinds. Victory goes to the best advertisement. And there is a danger that preaching may be regarded as just another voice, another advertisement in the midst of a thousand advertisements.

And then we would do well to remember that there is in our day a widespread distrust of authorities. This is a feature of the type of society we live in, but in some cases may be a result of an unresolved father-fixation, dating back to some forgotten crisis of puberty. But since it is unpleasant to have to admit an old hatred of one's father, some substitute authority has to be found, and the church provides a very convenient patriarchal symbol. So it does not pay the preacher to speak with the voice of paternal authority. He may think that it is his right and his duty to speak in this way, however, since he speaks on God's behalf, and thus represents the supreme authority. The danger in this situation is that the hearer may not notice the voice of God in the resonant tones of the preacher. He hears another paternal voice.

Dressing oneself up in "contemporary" clothes is always a welcome disguise when faced by the Word of God seeking sinners. Preaching is never modern. It is particularly difficult to hide this at the present time, for should the preacher enter into competition with all the other things that are supposed to be modern—things that everyone has to have, to do, to believe, to think—he is not likely to convince many. The historical heritage is all too apparent. And should he try to speak with the voice of authority, it is not enough that he represents a situation dating back two thousand years; worse than that: he represents a situation dating back to the end of the nineteenth century.

What I mean is that the particular difficulty facing the preacher today has to do with much more than the text and its remoteness from the present day. It has to do with a situation that is strikingly unfavorable for *every* form of address, and especially for a paternal form of address. And man—who always uses his particular situation as an excuse for turning away the Word of God—gives the key of his locked door an extra turn.

In a situation like this, it is particularly vital that the preacher should realize what is happening. Not merely in order for him to be able to break through the shell, but because the shell bears witness to what it hides. As at the time of the first fall, man gives himself away by his disguise. And it is all the more important that the preacher should recognize, and be able to interpret, this charade. He ought for example to know that some people indulge in free sexual relations, not because they want to, but because it is demanded of them. In other words, it is not a matter of sexual liberty at all. And if the church then turns to the individual and tells him that he ought to observe the fifth commandment, he answers, "There you are. That shows you how little the church knows about the way things are nowadays." He cannot even imagine the kind of liberty within a group that the church without more ado assumes. But if he can see through a situation, the preacher can attack the lack of freedom, and not the freedom, it reveals: because he can hear the strained tones in which the declaration of liberty and other proud claims are made, and can translate them.

This applies, too, to the common objections that are made to the Christian faith. Try to defend God against the implications of the indignant question of how he can see all the world's suffering without interfering, and the questioner turns away contemptuously. But make a point out of his argument, and try to see—as it were on a plain white surface—what kind of a picture the instruments of his doubt create. The suffering God.

Individual pastoral care has of course far greater possibilities than the sermon when it comes to uncovering the real meaning behind human attitudes. Often enough, all one has to do is to listen long enough, and the speaker will reveal, to his own surprise, things that he scarcely even suspected of being hidden under his patterns of behavior and speech. And in most cases what he reveals is not merely guilt, but above all a feeling of guilt. Offer the least trace of criticism, and the counselee will very likely withdraw into his shell like a frightened snail. For what he needs is not to feel guilty; he is already swollen, poisoned with guilt. But it does not help him, either, to pretend that everything is all right; such "understanding" is equally worthless. What he needs is to admit that he feels what he in fact feels—and to interpret his inner voices when they, as the Scripture says, "accuse or defend" him.

If the pastor can allow free expression to his counselee's feelings of guilt, without damning them by his own superficial judgments, the conversation will gradually penetrate to other levels of the experience of guilt. When some modern Jacob can be induced to speak freely of his feelings of guilt over his brother Esau and his heritage, it may well prove to be the case that it is not Esau who occupies the forefront of his story, but his father (it was his father's God who appeared to Jacob at Bethel—and at Jabbok). He has not only cheated Esau; he has cheated Isaac, and that particular deception is not one that he has dreamed up for himself. Jacob is his mother's son, and it takes time for him to become mature enough to look his father's God and his brother full in the face.

This entire pilgrimage into the labyrinth of guilt presupposes, on the one hand, that the pastor should be prepared to hold his peace and listen, and, on the other, that he should help the counselee to interpret his own language.

It is also a relief to the counselee that someone will listen to him without making irrelevant observations. Otherwise he is surrounded by salesmen who take a friendly interest in him, but only in the hope of being able to persuade him to accept their goods or their pamphlets. At last someone is taking him seriously. There is someone who is waiting for him, not to use him in some way or other, but simply in order to find out who he really is. Nor, when the gospel can finally be proclaimed in the new and open situation, is it a matter of persuasion. Not until he has met the God who speaks at the focus of all our guilt does the seeker finally become a real person. The New Testament waits for his answer to the gospel, his Yes or No, with an entirely different kind of respect than one finds in the kind of preaching that competes with pop singers and politicians for the acclamation of the people.

If we now look for the corresponding features in that type of public pastoral care that we call preaching, at once we run up against a number of signs pointing in precisely the opposite direction. First and foremost, the sermon cannot begin with silence or reflection. The congregation has nothing to say, since the preacher himself is talking the whole time.

Nevertheless this is not the whole truth if the preacher is a real pastor. Assuming that he preaches every Sunday, that gives him six days in the week for listening—listening to the text, but also to the voices around him. The great example here is Paul and his sermon on the Areopagus in Athens (Acts 17:23): ". . . as I passed along, and observed the objects of your worship, I found also an altar with this inscription. 'To an unknown god.' What therefore you worship as unknown this I proclaim to you." What Paul learned from Greek altars the present-day minister can learn from contemporary life and literature (which he should read not merely in order to inject a little color into his sermons)—but above all in individual conversation. Without this kind of listening, all preaching is flying blind.

There are, however, many ways of making use of the things one gets to know during the six days. It is a common enough idea that the preacher ought to give back to his congregation what he has observed—but this is entirely different from the way in which the listening pastor reflects the confidences that are made to him. I have no wish to deny that the preacher ought to make his voice heard against all manner of abuses; and this kind of preaching is indirectly pastoral—corresponding to Moses' action in going up to Pharaoh and demanding, "Let my people go!" But in that case, the message also has to be directed to those in authority. The Scripture tells us how it is received by the masses when it is turned in *their* direction: "This crowd, who do not know the law, are accursed" (John 7:49).

But does not judgment precede grace? Let me give you a quotation from a collection of sermons:

> What is preached may contain wise words, appropriate words, remarkable and original words, but it does not contain "the word of reconciliation." In that case it is not strange when the sermon is not received. But even when the message is rightly proclaimed, very few receive it and allow themselves to be comforted by it. Why is this? Because only the broken heart can receive the message of comfort. To be sure, there is distress in these days, but very little of "that distress which

> is in accordance with the mind of God," distress over sin. And
> when there is nothing of that distress, the Word of God can
> never be received with joy. Only the broken and contrite
> heart understands that "the word of reconciliation" is a gospel,
> a glorious message. . . . Therefore, you must listen to the
> word of judgment before you can receive the word of comfort.

This argument is often heard. First and foremost because
people imagine the order of grace to be as the preacher I have
just quoted described it: the Law comes before the gospel—
though the catechism says that the Holy Spirit calls men by the
gospel. But also because it is imagined that the so-called
modern man is extraordinarily shallow and thick-skinned, indifferent to laws and norms of every kind. But in point of fact
our contemporaries are very much on the defensive—surprisingly so. This can be deduced from our present-day morality
debates: nothing gives away the true state of a sick conscience
like the effort to shape norms to fit behavior, instead of *vice
versa*.

In a situation like this, should the preacher attempt to increase the feelings of guilt of his hearers, he will run up against
a compact defense. He touches a very sore spot. And I have
already mentioned a couple of the best excuses that the listener can make when he wants to ward off these accusations:
the sermon is only one voice among others, and it speaks in
paternal tones.

A still more effective way of preventing one's hearers from
opening themselves to the Word of God is to introduce the
divided state of the church into one's sermon and use it as a
platform for attacks on churchmen of other traditions and other
opinions. Then, as Gunnar Edman has said in a sermon entitled
"The Capsized Message," flint enters the spoken word: "Even
the word 'God' can contain flint," he says, "and so we pass
judgment, and stone and kill one another with God and His
Word."[2]

But how, it may be asked, is God's Law to have its way and
compel people to turn to Christ if we are not to be allowed to

---

[2] Gunnar Edman (b. 1915) is a Swedish journalist, novelist, poet,
essayist, and "lay preacher."

throw the Law in their faces? Must not the power to bind also have its rightful place in pastoral preaching?

The power to bind should be used against unwarranted security. At all events, it should not be used at a time when so many people have excommunicated themselves, to place further bonds upon those who are already bound.

The really difficult task is *to put into words a half-conscious or wholly unconscious feeling of guilt, and to transform it into prayer*—so that it becomes a confession of sin. The penitential liturgy of the early church contains one element that might help here. When the penitent was to be received back into the fellowship of the church, in the presence of the assembled community, he fell on his face before the altar; but not on his own: the bishop lay beside him. The bishop also had to share the penitent's preparation in a period of fasting. In every sermon there should be an element of that kind of identification. I do not mean that the sermon should be preached in a tame and conventional first person plural, in which all the "dear people" are lumped together into one bleating flock, loaded onto a raft, and ferried over into eternal life. There is a kind of gentle sermon that smoothly avoids giving any possible offense connected with either sin or doubt, and that acts together with its apparent opposite—the throwing of stones from the pulpit—to create the infinitely distressing spectacle of a church in which most people believe that doubt and distress have no right to exist. "Here, more than in any other place, people were encouraged to put aside all that business of faithlessness, lovelessness, and self-justification—and consequently they had very little to confess in the General Confession, which became an irrelevant preliminary that people just had to sit through."

What I am trying to say is that in our preaching we need the kind of identification we find in Ezra's prayer (Ezra 9). We need not preach in the first person plural, but our preparation must be made in the first person plural: "O my God, I am ashamed and blush to lift my face to thee, my God, for our iniquities have risen higher than our heads, and our guilt has mounted up to the heavens . . . . But now for a brief moment favor has been shown by the Lord our God . . . ."

This identification should not stop short at the point of

doubt. Of course the preacher has to defend and establish the gospel—but not against his hearers. It is hard to say which is the more effective in shutting off the gospel from them, the refusal to come to grips with the great facts of salvation or the overeager and insensitive defense of these facts. God does not need defending. To do so is really a mark of the lack of faith. The preacher should pray for faith in the presence of God in the Eucharist and, like the bishop beside the penitent, face the altar in all that he says. He should inquire of God on behalf of his fellow men, just as Ahimelech inquired of God on David's behalf when David was a refugee. Not merely as a rhetorical question; the preacher should turn to the gospel of incarnation and resurrection. "I am the questioner. I have been wandering through the world, wondering; and a little while ago I began this calling into the darkness. I have to call. They tell me that at the heart of the silence there is someone listening."

Answers come—answers to even the questions we ask, in our universe, in our society. As Gunnar Edman found (long before J. A. T. Robinson was even thought of in this country)[3] when he turned to the Lord's Prayer and discovered the dwelling place of God: He is "at one and the same time incomprehensible—incapable of being localized—and nearer to us than we are ourselves: He is supreme Majesty and intimate Friend."

Above all there is an answer to the cry of guilt. An answer from the one who became a curse for our sake. His help overlooks nothing. Peter's sense of guilt overflowed three times. I am not thinking of the time Paul had to pull him up and lecture him, but of three episodes in his life with Jesus: when Jesus helped him with his fishing, when he denied all knowledge of Jesus, and was given nothing but a look in return, and when Jesus asked, "Do you love me?" It is the gospel that calls, and it is the gospel that enables the sinner to enter more deeply into the truth through the Law.

[3] *Honest to God* was translated into Swedish, and an energetic attempt was made to start a debate similar to that which had followed the first publication of the book in England. Although a good many unfavorable comments—and a few favorable ones—were forthcoming, the debate, for a variety of reasons, remained insignificant.

It is important that the gospel should not be rationed. This applies supremely to the great facts of salvation. The hearer has a right to know whether it is true that Jesus is the Christ, come in the flesh; that he died for our sins; that his resurrection was a reality cutting through the dimensions of spirit and matter. Do not believe that the people only notice what the minister says; they also hear what he does not say—as a result of which some go back to sleep in their undemanding and well-organized universe, others reject in disappointment and perhaps desperation the entire lukewarm business, and others again despise the preacher, not without bitterness. It may be that it was this third group that the preacher thought he was obliging by his smiling caution.

Equally dangerous is conditional absolution in the form in which I once heard it, as a famous preacher expounded the parable of the Prodigal Son, ending with the reminder that it was a son *who came home* who was forgiven. This son has certainly received a great deal of attention—time and time again it has been described as something out of the ordinary how he came to his senses, how he arose, how he set off, how he approached his home, how he arrived. But is it so strange that an underpaid swineherd should act in this way, if he thought he would be better off at home? What was really remarkable was not that he went home, but that he was made welcome. But preachers surround this remarkable fact with a host of reservations, and transform the gospel into something conditional, an *evangelium in conditionalis.*

Our modern world is riddled through and through with guilt, and the stumbling block in the church's message is not the claim that guilt should be measured according to other norms than those which happen to be modern just now. The stumbling block is that guilt can be forgiven. This is so incredible that it has to be proclaimed at the very heart of guilt, as a full and unconditional gospel, bloodstained and soiled with the filth of blasphemy, filled with the fullness of God and all his angels surrounding the throne.

The preacher, then, finds his answers standing down there with the tax-collector; and then he turns, in a manner of speaking, and offers them as bread to the hungry.

Afterwards he does the same thing literally. In our time the

sacrament of the altar has become a transitional means of
grace, like the bread taken by Israel on its journey out of
Egypt. Often enough secular man "understands" what God is
doing in the Eucharist long before he notices that God does
anything in the sermon. It is all the more important that the
sermon should be turned toward the altar, in such a way that
it "comes" to the bread and wine; as the confession expresses it:
accedat verbum ad elementum et fit sacramentum. It is not a
little address that, for no particular reason, is delivered somewhere or other in the action of the Eucharist. It is part of the
communio sanctorum, and is never isolated, even when it appears to belong in a different context. It belongs together with
the Kyrie and the Gloria, the Sursum Corda, the Sanctus and
the Agnus Dei. An army of holy spirit and fire—like the army
Elisha's servant saw: "and behold, the mountain was full of
horses and chariots of fire round about Elisha." And the
preacher, who may well ask the servant's question, "Alas, my
master! What shall we do?" can take as his own the prophet's
answer, "Fear not, for those who are with us are more than
those who are with them."

With whom? Not the congregation! The angels of heaven
and the gospel are not a Wartburg in which the preacher is
imprisoned, far away from his listeners. A real pastor would
immediately demand his release, leave the security of his castle
and go out to be with his congregation. He is on the side of the
defense. The prosecution is facing him. And it may be a necessary part of pastoral care to point out to his people—not least
the secularized among them—that God and the prosecuting
authority are not one and the same; the gospel has something
to say about the devil, too.

It is also vital that the line of demarcation should not be
drawn between regular churchgoers, the little group of the
faithful, and the so-called worldly people, as though no shadow
of accusation ever fell on the believer. A bishop is said once
to have asked a Finnish lay preacher of the school of Paavo
Ruotsalainen,[4] "Well, and what of the secularized children of

---

[4] Paavo Ruotsalainen (d. 1852) was a Finnish revivalist preacher
whose influence was widespread in the 1820s and 1830s. His type of re-
vivalism is characterized as "penitential pietism," as opposed to the
"holiness" movements.

the world?" "We are the secularized children of the world," answered the preacher.

It is part of the pastoral aspect of preaching to attack the accuser, even when he functions under the disguise of faith. Just as some people join other groups in order to find security, and comfort their sick conscience with the fact that they are in good company, so the fellowship of the faithful can provide the individual with a good hiding place from both the Law and the gospel. There is such a thing as a pious fear of man!

We should pay special attention to the fact that it is not only the worldly who confuse the church with their childhood home. Some, as I have said, use the church as an excuse for working off old and long-forgotten hatreds; others find in her a convenient shelter from the demands of maturity and independence, and so remain—in some sense at least—on the level of childhood. The inner circle of the faithful, or the minister, or the youth leader, makes the individual's decisions for him, although this in no way prevents him from imagining that he is actually deciding for himself. And when the question of responsibility (leading to the question of guilt) forces itself upon him, he has a double alibi: for he has really been in the thick of things, and has not kept away from the action; and in the last analysis he has not made the decisions, they have been made for him by the group. People like this would much prefer to have a sermon *between* them and the Word of God, rather than a sermon that leads them *into* the Word. As the writer to the Hebrews put it, "every one who lives on milk is unskilled in the word of righteousness, for he is a child. But solid food is for the mature, for those who have their faculties trained by practice to distinguish good from evil."

The hope of being able to remain in a state of spiritual immaturity is naturally often connected with a certain degree of laziness. Food must be homogenized. Everything has to be said at least three times, so that there is no need to exert oneself unduly. The preacher who is also a pastor must on no account encourage these tendencies. In his preaching he must transmit inspired Scripture in such a way "that the man of God may be complete, equipped for every good work."

There are preachers who have the power of suggestion, especially when they happen to be in the midst of a crowd of

like-minded listeners—in which case their gift takes wings and
becomes mass suggestion. I am sure the devil is only too glad
to see the individual swallowed up in such a witches' cauldron.
But note how often the words of the New Testament are addressed to individuals: "You lack one thing." "Go, call your
husband." "Follow me, and leave the dead to bury their own
dead." In the innumerable pastoral situations of the Bible the
individual is represented as being unique. He is pulled out of
the crowd—even the pious crowd—and brought face to face
with God. Black and white angels call up their armies for his
sake, and heaven rings with joy when a single sinner repents.

The Christian life is by no means as calm and pleasant as
some preachers paint it, in those sermons in which the children
of God wander round in green pastures, their noble features set
in a fixed expression of sheeplike peace. The peace of God does
not look quite like that. Those who have experienced it are
not strangers to temptation, suffering, and distress. Christian
Scriver once wrote that "you will never find a converted person
who is unacquainted with distress of the conscience and the
heart." And anyone who listens week by week to true pastoral
preaching often recognizes himself in what is said; not because
he and the sermon are cast in the same mold, but because a
battle is being fought, and a new creation can be dimly seen
through the mist—a new creation as vast and as varied as the
first.

But all this presupposes that the various parts of the sermon
are all filled with the true life that breathes through the Scriptures. Whatever the pastoral sermon may contain of modern
psychology and literature, whatever it may reveal of the
preacher's gifts (or lack of them)—in the last analysis what
lifts it above the level of candy or cold oatmeal is its biblical
content. The passage about the man of God who is to be
equipped for every good work also says that this end is to be
attained through the Scriptures, for "all scripture is inspired
by God and profitable for reproof, for correction, and for
training in righteousness" (2 Tim. 3:16).

13.

THE CHURCH AND THE PROBLEM
OF ANONYMOUS GUILT

Anonymous guilt is a guilt that is neither seen nor recognized, but which makes its presence felt on a different level from that on which guilt is normally seen and recognized. That such a guilt exists is attested both by the tradition of the church and by modern psychology.

One such guilt is original guilt, the barren ground of society and the life of the individual. It is not hard to polemize against Freud's well-known myth of some primeval parricide, but this apocryphal hypothesis about the origin of religion fits in with Christianity on at least one important point: there is no denial of original sin. Freud himself realized this, pointing out that Christianity is the only religion that admits that we have murdered the Father. And this is not merely a matter of a chasm appearing in the past, but of deep spiritual places in which the past has, as it were, accumulated. In both cases it is a matter of original sin. However, I do not intend here to concentrate on the theological implications of the idea of original sin, but on the shadows it throws across the spiritual life of the individual.

The Father we have murdered (according to Freud) symbolizes the conscience in which our parents or guardians still speak, and this entire symbolism corresponds to a stage in our moral development. In order to reach maturity, the individual must come to grips with this early authority, presupposing in most cases a critical period in which paternal authority is seriously called in question. Some never leave this stage, and remain in a state of permanent rebellion against their parents, either because a father or mother has tried to prevent a child from developing into an independent person, or because the child has gained such a warped and distorted picture of parental authority that he has to reject it, and does so throughout his life. But a negativism of this kind is no real independence. An independent man or woman is strong enough to love, and even to honor, without ceasing to criticize.

The process of emancipation is always attended by feelings of guilt, and if the final result is spite or even hate, the sense of guilt can be overwhelming. One convenient form of defense against this kind of guilt is to try to eliminate it by means of constant argument aimed at silencing one's opponent. But measures of this kind lead to new feelings of guilt, which are repressed in their turn.

Another possible way of defending one's innocence is to deny to oneself that such negative feelings as these exist. Or to admit them, but deny that they have anything whatever to do with parental authority. In which case they may be turned against substitute authorities, such as the government, society in general, the church, or God. In this context it is interesting to note the suggestion made several years ago in a Swedish conference for psychiatrists and theologians, that some of the anti-Christian voices in our present culture debate are to be explained less as the products of genuine doubt than as resulting from difficulties in the process of coming to maturity. These persons attack the church as a convenient substitute for their parents.

The personal crisis behind a substitution of this nature is not made any the easier to master for being a crisis within a crisis—the crisis of authority that is currently affecting our entire culture. Perhaps this latter crisis has to do with the collapse of older, authoritarian methods of upbringing; but we must not oversimplify this development, or its causes. The inability of an older generation to maintain world peace, violent popular reaction against the authoritarian regimes of the 1930s and 1940s, the influence of adolescents on trade (as independent, fairly affluent consumers)—these are just some of the background factors in the crisis of authority. Very often in these days we hear talk of a new confidence, a new maturity, a new sense of power; and all against a technological background. Bishop Robinson tells us that he no longer asks for God's help when he travels by airplane; he prefers to trust the pilot. An eloquent testimony.

Dietrich Bonhoeffer was right when he not only observed, but welcomed the liberation of modern man from the guardianship of the religious authorities. The only question is whether the world has really come of age. I am not thinking merely of the fear that follows, consciously or unconsciously, hard on the heels of all our arrogant declarations of the divine power of man; "terrified and unprepared, we have gained the mastery over the whole world and over the life and death of all living creatures," said John Steinbeck at the giving of the Nobel Prize in 1962. I am thinking still more of the sense of guilt concealed behind so many of our declarations of independence, guilt that makes our voices strangely shrill. It is another matter whether the fear I mentioned a moment ago comes as a result of the responsibility that man has brought upon himself as a result of his technological progress, or *whether it is an unconscious fear of punishment.* The literature of centuries bears witness to the fact that power, arrogance, and the sense of guilt are links in one and the same chain. Time and time again modern arrogance has shaped itself into what the ancient Greeks called *hybris.* We might once more take as an example Steinbeck's Nobel Prize speech, which ended in a travesty of the prologue to John: "In the end is the word, and the word is man, and the word is with men." It is hardly surprising, then, that everywhere in these days we should find traces of guilt, suppressed, to be sure, but no less real.

To return to the theme of power and responsibility. The Swedish author Göran Palm, in his book *An Unjust Homily* (*En orättvis betraktelse*) has reminded us that today, for the first time in 5,000 years, anyone on earth can be called our neighbor, "for we, who enjoy the blessings of civilization, have in our mass media the daily means of seeing those who 'have paid for civilization, without sharing its benefits.'" He adds:

> But when everyone is our neighbor, no one is our neighbor, and when we see the distress of the world every day, distress becomes banal, and we see it without seeing it. . . . We sympathize ostentatiously with all the suffering in the world as never before, but when it comes to the push we refuse to do without any of our privileges. I do not want to do without my salary, and you do not want to do without your home.

If, in a situation like this, the sense of guilt seems conspicuous by its absence, it is certainly because it has gone into hiding somewhere. The guilt is there, but it is anonymous. Petitions and collections make us feel a little better; we have an opportunity to feel generous, like the ladies of the aristocracy, taking little baskets of food to "the people" at Christmas. But the hidden conscience is not to be bribed by indulgences.

The problem of authority and power, then, reappears when one exercises authority and power oneself. How much of our modern unwillingness to forbid children to do or have things is really a symptom of our fear to exercise authority? And how many divorces are caused basically by the uncertainty that has replaced the traditional roles of men and women in marriage? Here, too, the question of power is shot through and through with guilt—a guilt that is often hidden beneath a confident "modern," "radical," "emancipated" surface role.

Authority as an anonymous problem of conscience also makes its presence felt in industry. The same people who would tolerate no other authority than that of democratic decisions in politics, observe an entirely different set of rules in their work. The leaders of industry often say that it is impossible to run a firm on a basis of majority decisions, but sometimes the emphatic way in which this is said hints at an inner conflict. For whose benefit are they saying this? For the labor organizations, discussing "Democracy and Management" at their annual conference? Or perhaps—and this is more likely—for an unrecognized inner opponent?

I have tried to sketch the outlines of a genealogy of anonymous guilt. There are also other symptoms of guilt that have to do in part with this system but which gather around other primary questions. I believe, though, that those stresses and strains that can be traced to questions of authority, power, and responsibility are of extraordinary importance in our present-day pastoral situation.

Let us now pass on to consider how the pastoral function of the church is to be exercised in this situation, beginning by making clear how it is *not* to be exercised.

In the first place, the church must on no account attempt, by means of commandments and prohibitions, to increase the burden of human guilt. Ministers and others commonly believe that it is necessary to begin by arousing secular man's sense of guilt; only when this has been done can we proceed to preach the gospel to him, since when it is not done, he has no chance of understanding what the gospel is. But this same secular man spends his entire waking life trying to obey the ten thousand commandments imposed on him by society, by his in-group, by his family. For he finds himself (perhaps as a result of his revolt against parental authority) placed consciously or unconsciously under a vast number of authorities. Teen-agers find in their gangs an alternative to the authority of their parents, and so-called "mature" adults often seem to shift authorities in a similar way. Adults gladly accept the norms imposed by others; as Riesman says, they are "others-directed." Man is "free"—for man *has* to be free in this day and age—but there are laws directing how a free or emancipated person ought to behave. These laws are often contradictory, and however hard the individual tries to obey them all, he is never fully convinced of his right to exist. (That, incidentally, is the modern formula for justification. We pay for our indulgences in a different way, but the equation is the same as in the sixteenth century.)

Man, burdened down by his sense of guilt at being unable to satisfy these demands, quite naturally turns in hatred against the stranger who wants to pile a still heavier burden on him by telling him to follow Christ. But a diametrically opposite situation may arise: he may find in the rules and regulations of the church a new hiding place from anonymous guilt. He may become an exceedingly respectable, exemplary "religious" person, insulated from all accusations, whether internal or external. He may also confess that he is a sinner—for we must not be conceited—and his confession patches the final gap in his protective fence. Presumably his spiritual adviser is perfectly satisfied as well. But the real situation can perhaps be described in some words from Bertil Malmberg's *Songs of Conscience and Destiny:* ". . . the sense of an eternal judge passes like a shudder through our nights."

The church's moralizing is often closely linked with an authoritarian message. And words like "father-confessor" may assume overtones that are anything but beneficial to genuine pastoral care. The father-confessor comes to represent paternal

authority, which ever since the childhood of humanity and of
the individual has pontificated: "Do this . . . . don't do that."
And since he in a sense recalls an archaic mode of living, it
becomes all the easier to link him with the voice of authority
and the experience of imposed immaturity. One naturally does
one's best to avoid him—particularly as long as one's own conflict with authority remains unresolved. In fact we might look
upon the church as a useful institution from the point of view
of mental hygiene; after all, she annoys a great many people
and gives them a chance to let off steam. But her real task is
somewhat different.

However, there is an alternative to this reaction. Just as some
people need all manner of rules and regulations (as a surrogate
for a proper solution of their conflicts), so there are others
who are *seeking* an authority. Instead of resolving their conflict with authority by advancing towards maturity, they fall
back into a kind of childhood. The minister becomes the
father-figure they have been looking for. And in cases like this
it becomes a question not so much of commandments from
Sinai as of petty regulations for use in the conflicts of day-to-
day existence—regulations that release the "child" from the
need for making his own decisions and assuming his own
responsibilities.

What, then, should the pastor do? First of all he has to be
there and listen. There are different ways of listening; for
example Carl Rogers' "Client Centered Therapy": instead of
doing all the talking himself, the pastor should reflect what is
being said to him, by putting some of it in different words, and
by repeating the most emotionally loaded of the counselee's
expressions. If all goes well, sooner or later a way will open,
cutting through apparent conflicts and surrogate solutions to
the heart of the real conflict, provided that the conversation
does not run off the rails somewhere. There are four ways of
sabotaging a conversation of this kind: by moralizing, by gen-
eralizing, by forcing and by distracting, that is, by losing
the thread of the subject.

But the most important thing is not the method as such, but
the attitude it expresses: an attitude of respect for the other
person and for God's Law at work in him. Instead of a judge
the counselee finds a sympathetic listener—and may therefore

allow his suppressed conscience to speak out. Instead of a superimposed, imperious authority he finds a servant; and he may for that reason dare to express his conflict of authority.

In other words, what comes to the surface is anonymous guilt, guilt that has been near the surface, but which has been unable to break through. Of course, it is possible to go far deeper; but not without adequate knowledge and experience of the presuppositions, methods, and dangers of depth psychology. Where these prior qualifications are lacking, I should certainly advise to let well enough alone. This means that pastoral care is not the sole responsibility of the minister or priest; it is also the responsibility of the doctor. (I mean the *qualified* doctor, since most doctors know very little more about depth psychology than do ministers.) Ministers and doctors must be prepared to complement one another at this point.

But there are also depths of the human soul that no psychologist can penetrate—and here I am speaking of the secret behind the shadow I mentioned in the beginning. I am passing across the frontier to theology and mystical experience. There is only one who knows the levels at which *that* anonymous guilt lives: the Holy Spirit. When someone has spent years of self-examination and thanksgiving in the company of the gospel, it can bring him to the gates of his own inner hell. When he passes through, that is *Angst*—the distress and desolation of the soul. The pastor must not attempt to muster his forces and his techniques to prevent or precipitate this development. He may point the way into the Bible and the literature of prayer; he may call out the words of absolution into this blank darkness; but the rest is Someone Else's business.

We have now come into the area reserved for the ministry. The task of listening and understanding is the task of everyone who is concerned with helping others in times of trial and distress. And on this level the minister is only one among many helpers who go to make up "the healing team." His special task is to speak the words of the gospel, that is, to forgive sins in the name of Christ. That is his office. He is not a peripatetic moralist, an incarnation of middle-class decency. He is a forgiver.

Part of this special service is to release people from the false demands that play upon and beneath the surface of the soul.

The pastor must be able to say: "You are not the slave of your
parents, or of your group. The world and the church are not
your guardians. You are free; and your only responsibility is
to crucified love. You are not meant to be an echo of all manner
of traditions or passing modernisms; you are meant to acknowledge the identity into which you were baptized. You are
ransomed from mankind. Stand up and decide for yourself in
the name of Christ what you are going to do with your life
and what kind of a person you are going to be."

But at this point there emerge feelings of guilt more profound than those on the immediate surface, and behind them
a formless mass of ghosts from the past.

One characteristic of Evangelical confession is that it recognizes that there is such a thing as forgiveness of unconscious
sins—this is in fact stressed especially by the confessional
writings. This means that Evangelical confession takes account
of anonymous guilt. However, the assurance in the absolution
and in sermons that the forgiveness of sins is a forgiveness
of *all* sins does not always penetrate beneath the surface of
the individual consciousness. When we talk about the universal grace of God it means for many people just as little as the
confession that we are all sinners. For that reason the gospel
must be spelled out in all its biblical offensiveness, without
the conditions and reservations (*if* you are converted, *if* you
believe, *if* you obey) with which we are normally in the habit
of dampening the Evangelical impact. It has in fact happened
in my own experience that a counselee has said to me after a
conversation of this type: "Really? I have never heard that
before."

Of special importance in this connection is that the word
of unconditional fellowship should come from a brother, that
is, from Christ. God does not love the sinner from above, but
from below. God's authority is the authority of the cross, which
means that man has really come of age, since he has the power
to accept—or reject—God.

Elsewhere I have written that Ingmar Bergman in his film
Winter Light (*Nattvardsgästerna*) has tried to solve the problem of parental authority through the image of the Gothic
crucifix. It is beneath that image that Märta prays for Tomas:
"If I could only lead him out of the emptiness, away from his

false god; if we could only find security enough to show each other tenderness. If we could only believe in a truth . . . . If we could only believe . . . ."

Close to this gospel even the utterly desolate can dismiss the guards from the door to his anonymous guilt—just as Ingmar Bergman has done in this film. But we must not forget that if the crucified Christ is a way to faith, as is so often the case in our day, his own words apply: "No man comes to the Father but by me." Christ is the way, not the terminus. The believer in Christ is not meant to live on with his unresolved father-conflict. Christ is the way to the Father. In fellowship with him the process of maturing can proceed, so that the believer is not left thrashing about in a perpetual crisis of puberty, but can in time approach the Father, a free man.

When it is connected with confession, the act of listening that I was talking about can be an understandable expression of the Christian message. If listening opens the gates of anonymous guilt, it also makes possible the proclamation of the gospel in open situations. In the New Testament the gospel is not some watery fluid spread over human existence. It is one side of a dialogue carried on in open situations. And the fact that there are "open situations" means that confession must reveal genuine conflicts. It is true enough that absolution applies to sins of which the individual is unaware, but the gospel is not satisfied with anonymity of guilt; it beats at the door of the soul's private hell and demands to meet the lost souls there. The words of absolution are constantly being pronounced over vicarious sins; but not until it is allowed to be an answer to genuine conflicts can it overpower desolation. Realities meet: the revealed gospel and the repressed guilt.

PART THREE

CHURCH AND CULTURE

14.

CHRISTIAN CULTURE?

Let spiritual culture continue to develop; let science widen and deepen, and the spirit of man expand as much as it likes; nevertheless, "it will never reach higher than the heights and the ethical culture of Christianity, as it glitters and shines in the gospels."

These words are taken from Goethe, and were quoted by Thomas Mann a few years ago in a lecture in Sweden. Mann went on to comment: "Christianity's 'ethical culture,' its humanity, its civilizing, antibarbaric tendency were what he [Goethe] acknowledged, for these were his own ideals, and there is no doubt that he delivered this eulogy out of a sense of affinity, from the conviction that the task of Christianity among the Teutonic peoples was closely related to his own."

I do not relate this episode to start a debate about the beneficial influence of Christianity on cultural life. There are some who would advertise Christianity by taking Christ from the cross and sitting him down among the members of the Swedish Academy: "He is so human, so refined, so good for morals." There is something in Thomas Mann's tone that is calculated to attract that kind of impresario. Swedish theology has been quite correct, for some years past, in regarding such efforts with suspicion. In the last analysis, we are not likely to find conclusive proof of the truth of Christianity until all cultures have gone the way of all flesh. When even church art lies in ruins—"there will not be left here one stone upon another . . ." —there will remain the ultimate reason why we are Christians: the essentials will be left, and there is something essential in Christianity. Expressions like "the culture of Christianity," or "Christian culture" (which is more complicated), contain a good measure of obscurity, and have played their part in softening the impact of faith; the result has been that some have missed completely the essentials of Christianity—a fatal omission, since it is the essentials that save.

Basically, the word "culture" can as well refer to a field of potatoes or a laboratory tray of bacteria as to painting or poetry. And this is no mere semantic coincidence. Art and literature grow out of social realities, and those realities depend in many ways on factors like that potato field. Even a highly subtle philosophy grows out of the earth, just like a tree, though its roots are more complex. This situation may perhaps horrify the Platonist, but the Christian has no need to feel insulted in the name of culture by such a connection. He if anyone ought to know that God has made the soil. The poem has not been written that is more divinely inspired than an ear of barley.

If, then, the connection between the potato field and poetry is based on fact and is legitimate from the Christian point of view, the next step is to ask whether we can talk about "the potato field of Christianity," or "a Christian potato field"—which appears dubious. But the farmer who grows potatoes may be a Christian, and so we might perhaps speak in his case of *indirect* Christian culture, but only if it can be shown that there is some connection between his Christian faith and his farming. This has (as a rule) nothing to do with the quantity or quality of his crop, for a rich landowner may be a good farmer but an indifferent Christian. Nor can we judge the degree of Christianity by what grows in his fields. Potatoes are no more Christian than poppies: potatoes can be distilled into spirits, while poppies can be used to make medicine. And it is only natural that farming, in common with other forms of culture, should reflect the attitudes of a people concerning the nature and the needs of man. If a country decides that there is no need to grow crops having to do with medicine, or to do anything else to supply its people with drugs for medicinal purposes, it would be a reasonable conclusion that that culture was influenced by a form of Christian Science, or something similar. Again, if the Secretary of Agriculture encouraged every farmer to concentrate on growing nothing but medicinal herbs, one might conclude that his view of human destiny was somewhat pessimistic.

In the same way it is possible to talk about Christian culture in the sense that the culture in question reflects a Christian view of the nature and destiny of man. It would be useful to know what such a culture looks like; and while I do not claim to be able to provide any definitive answer, I can at least attempt to sketch the outlines of what I feel to be Christian culture.

The connection between the spiritual and the earthly, the sacred and the secular, is the unconditional presupposition of a genuinely Christian view of culture. If God has created the world, and if he expects our bodies to be temples of the Holy Spirit, it is blasphemy to build churches and schools and not hospitals and old people's homes. A culture in which science, art, and religion flourish, but which lacks the apparatus of social care, appears to me to be decidedly un-Christian; and if the church can observe a situation of this kind without protest, then she is unfaithful to the gospel. When the World Council of Churches met for the first time in 1948 at Amsterdam, there was revealed a good deal of this acquiescence in what is nothing but spiritualized paganism, and it was not least this that gave point to the Assembly's message about Christianity as "a church that has largely lost touch with the dominant realities of modern life."

Another consequence of the doctrine of creation is the dominant role of marriage in any Christian view of culture: "male and female he created them." Any culture having a rich tradition of hymn writing but without love poetry must be a field for Christian mission. If its leaders can preach like angels and prophesy like John, but do not have the gift of playing with children, then we must pray for their conversion, since it would seem that this is what has *not* happened. And when it happens, I am sure that it will be noticed far beyond the nursery, for in Christianity, a child is more than a creature to be trained: the child is rather an influential personality. Shut in or shut out the naive and the spontaneous, the unpredictability, the inventiveness, and the improvisation that characterize these personalities; make laws and petty regulations to neutralize the child's love of the unexpected; and you have sabotaged the whole of art, whether it is expressed in hymns or in love songs. People in jail do not sing. But more than this: you have attacked the Christian view of man. For the Christian ideal of life is not to be compared to a machine or railroad schedule: "The wind blows where it wills, and you hear the sound of it, but you do not know whence it comes or whither it goes; so it is with every one who is born of the Spirit" (John 3:8).

We must beware, however, of using art in an un-Christian way; culture is not meant to be some kind of heavenly fish-hook. If we feed the hungry merely in order to make them listen to a Christian sermon, our benevolence is un-Christian. Christ often omitted to preach to ears he had made to hear. So too a novelist ought to write about the secrets of human life in order to try to reveal them, not in order to provide preachers with sermon illustrations. Ears and apple trees do not have to look like religious symbols in order to praise God. If God really has created life, and if he has given mankind the privilege of sharing, however slightly, in his work of creation, we do not have to justify such things by pointing out their conceivable uses "in a higher cause." From the Christian point of view, culture is in no sense a missionary method.

But suppose all men are really sinners? Suppose that the heart of man is evil from his youth? People sometimes seem to believe that one consequence of sin is that we should live as little as possible—except in our prayer-life. In politics this is called dictatorship. In art and poetry it is called censorship. In fact, the exact opposite is true. If man is *totally* depraved, then prayer is as sinful as dancing. Censorship, too, is sinful. And the idea that it is possible to purge politics of its sinfulness by leaving the whole business in the hands of a megalomaniac is not only mistaken; it is stupid.

We ought also to remember that "sin" is more than a word describing human depravity. It also has to do with human destiny, because it has to do with man's relation to God. The doctrine of total depravity is a doctrine of man's total relation to God. The word "sin" embraces at one and the same time the highest and lowest in our life. It is a word charged with powerful tensions.

In a Christian culture these tensions can be felt everywhere. A criminal has to answer for his crimes, but we have to love him. Evil is called evil, and is not defended—and yet it is surely only in a Christian culture that the hero of a novel can be a priest of the God of justice, and still react to a crowd of convicts as did the priest in Graham Greene's *The Power and the Glory:* "He was moved by an enormous and irrational affection for the inhabitants of this prison. A phrase came to him: 'God so loved the world. . . .'"

This is not what Thomas Mann calls humanity. The tension revealed in this situation cannot be expressed by such a polite and civilized word. Here the life of man is lifted into a heaven-shaking drama. Humanity talks about maladjustment; Christianity talks about sin. And while both might be permissible in some antibarbaric treaty, the difference between them stands out just as soon as we attempt to make a drama out of some kind of transgression and have to decide what to call it.

T. S. Eliot has pointed out how important it is for literature that there should be an orthodoxy to act as a sounding board for divergent opinions. There must be a living and yet firm tradition in culture if the debate is to have any quality at all. If this applies to orthodoxy in general (and Eliot uses the word in a very broad sense), it applies in a very special sense to the Christian doctrine of sin. Sigrid Undset suspects that modern legislation in sexual questions is in fact, for all of its laxity, a disguised sexual negativism, "the object of which is to compel everybody to quench their thirst with a kind of state-subsidized root beer, guaranteed to contain not more than $2\frac{1}{4}\%$ eroticism." And further: "If we try to reduce the natural sense of sin to the least possible, the result for most people will be less knowledge of both the sweet taste of forbidden love and the healthy and refreshing taste of innocent love."

Obviously, if the church should stop preaching about sin, then a good many things would lose their refreshing taste: not only love in reality, but also love in the novels. Remove man from his state of tension between divine commandment and Satanic temptation, and there is little left to make a fuss about.

One might perhaps have expected that the main result of the Christian doctrine of sin would have been the general all-around improvement of mankind. Well, perhaps it is. But this is not what justifies us in talking about Christian culture, but the plain fact that that is the home of Christian ideas of right and wrong. One thing is certain: Christian influence on culture does not result in the division of mankind into an upper and lower class according to degrees of moral principle. If this division exists (and it is seldom absent), it is neither decisive nor final. The tension between destiny and fall is there in all of us: the commandment is so exalted and the fall so deep that no one can boast of having kept the Law. This is no static principle of division, but a dynamic restlessness that is constantly causing revolution in our laws and customs, simply because we can never consider ourselves finished with it.

But the Law of God is only one side of the central fact of Christian culture: the fact that there is a church there.

The presence of worship and prayer is not in itself a distinguishing feature of Christian culture. Pull down the churches and stop people praying and you will not only have de-Christianized society: you will have done something far worse. Such an attack would be aimed at humanity, as well as at the faith. It is dehumanization. Obviously the church must combat this kind of multilation of human life. But when the church teaches us to pray, and when it builds places of worship, this is much more than merely the creation of a breathing space for a *humanitas*. It is the forgiveness of sins. It goes without saying that this must set its mark on laws and customs in a Christian culture. It was undoubtedly an aspect of the new understanding of justification by faith, when Olaus Petri instructed his judges to acquit rather than condemn.[1] The same thing can be seen in art and literature. We see it in an unusually pure form in the work of the novelist Lars Ahlin, who is very far indeed from wanting to write "Christian novels" (what are Christian chairs, Christian clothes, Christian books?), perhaps because he has penetrated so deeply into Luther's interpretation of grace: "When one encounters one's sin one in fact encounters one's salvation." It cannot be merely a matter of chance that he, and no other, has interpreted the task of the writer, by

[1] Olaus Petri (*ca.* 1493-1552), architect of the Reformation in Sweden, served from 1524 to 1531 as secretary to the city council of Stockholm, and from 1531 to 1533 as chancellor to King Gustav I. His judicial rules (*Domareregler*) mark an epoch in Swedish jurisprudence.

analogy, as that of an intercessor: "To be the one who identifies—that is my great and shameless joy, my passionate desire, bread for my inner hunger." That is the way it is. When an author immerses himself in the situation of mankind, he is entering upon a way that only one man has followed to its end.

This is the great source of inspiration for a Christian culture. In the last resort neither a doctrine nor a principle, but a personality, in whose spirit Bernanos can say "Hell is to be unable to love." Christianity is the novel about the love of God, a novel written into our history with the blood of Christ and the martyrs. It is not a doctrine, but a face that one sees when a voice says, with the miser in Mauriac's *The Snake Pit*, "Perhaps God didn't come into the world for you righteous folks, if he came; perhaps he came for us. . . ." And this way of looking at mankind is one that can be seen in the work of many authors who know nothing of its source.

I have tried in this essay to discern some of the footsteps of Christ. The subject is almost too attractive. We must not forget the final chapter in the Christian view of culture: the eschatological chapter. That is important. If Goethe was Christianity's ally; if Erik Axel Karlfeldt was a Christian poet;[2] if Thomas Mann has sung the praises of the Christian view of life. Yes, it is all most edifying. In front of me I have a copy of the figure of one of the Three Kings, taken from a south German medieval stained glass window. A wise man. The king shines like a jewel, as he stretches out his hands in worship to someone who is not in the picture. I remember the words of the Danish poetess Elle Andersdatter:

> And let all kings bring thee
> their homage.

Sing a *Te Deum* for the kings, by all means. There is still more joy in heaven over one sinner who repents. And if culture should be dechristianized? If the church should lose all its influence? "Where is your God now?"

---

[2] Erik Axel Karlfeldt (1864-1931), Swedish poet, won the Nobel Prize for Literature posthumously in 1931. Associated all his life with the province of Dalarna, his poetry is technically brilliant, and consistently "local" in its coloring, but his ideology is humanistic rather than expressly Christian.

That is precisely where Christianity begins. All the rest is no more than footsteps and reflections. What gives us confidence in our struggle for Christian culture is the strange absent-mindedness that results from the fact that the church faces east, towards eternity. The pilgrim draws a few letters in the sand, and moves on. Call it culture if you like. But why should we be so nervous? What is Christian culture? Teasing the devil in the waiting room.

15.

THE PROBLEM OF CHRISTIAN SERVICE

The Swedish word *samhällsdiakoni* is not easily translatable into some languages. In English, for example, it would be a tautology, the word which might be used to translate *samhälls-* ("social") having already been pressed into service to describe the church's work of individual benevolence. This is significant. There has long been a liturgical diaconate, active in prayer and preaching, and alongside it various kinds of care of the poor, more or less private. The category of divine service and the category of individual service have been separate. Social service seems to have been considered by many far too worldly to deserve the name of diaconate.

Although I cannot share this view, I do not want to give the impression that I think individual service to be dispensable. This, too, is a social service, in that it does not take place merely for the sake of the individual, but ensures that the machinery of society be kept moving, a lubricant to prevent the whole thing from seizing up. If imprisonment is changed to supervision outside the walls, it means that this kind of social care can only, as things stand, function in the context of personal relationships. Another example would be the attempt to remove maladjusted young people from institutions and place them in foster families. A necessary aspect of the diaconate will always be to complement and widen this "general" care by means of personal work, and thus to humanize it. Without a degree of personal involvement, not even a machinery as impersonal as that of society can be kept going in the long run.

However, we must beware of treating personal work in such a way as to evaluate the voluntary benevolence of the rich towards the less well situated as more Christian and more humanitarian than the social help that these people (and as others) pay for with their taxes. To suppose that the poor need, or even want, some kind of personal relationship with the rich is a middle-class myth. Sometimes the best method of individual and personal care demands that people be left in peace, to create individual and personal relationships in their own individual and personal way. I am reminded of Lars Ahlin's interpretation of the Parable of the Good Samaritan —that the money left by the Samaritan in the inn served as his representative. I think, too, that money and medical care did more to unite the Jew and the Samaritan than any personal conversation at table could have done, particularly since Jews and Samaritans were not in the habit of eating together. In the same way, modern social assistance, which makes friends by means of the riches of impersonal Mammon, may often be a better instrument of a personal diaconate than was the old-fashioned workhouse.

In all genuinely Christian service it is the person in need of help who occupies the central position. The personal element in this work consists in understanding his personal distress and his personal needs. Most important is not the personality of the helper, but the personality of the one helped.

The personality of a Jew was not merely an abstraction, derived from the fact of his belonging to the Jewish nation. Nineteenth-century Christian service tended sometimes to treat the individual as though he could be picked up with a pair of tweezers and removed from his social context; if he were to be helped, it would have to be outside the framework of this economic and cultural reality. One might just as well try to help a baby bird—purely individually—by taking it out of the nest. This is the most cogent of the complaints made by the modern working-class movement against the church, that in a period of great social distress she attempted to love and help the individual on the basis of the assumptions of an individualist bourgeoisie and an individualist form of piety, instead of encountering the needy in the midst of their real need.

If it is true that today, in the light of modern developments in the social sciences, we have reached an understanding of the dependence of the individual on his social situation, it follows that this insight cannot be restricted to his finances, his health, his education, and so on. It is a matter of the whole man, and that includes his religion. All service, and not only what we normally call "social service," must involve society as a whole. When someone becomes a convinced Christian, the repercussions reach not only to his soul, but also to his trade union and his political party; and any form of pastoral care that has an eye to nothing beyond the individual's soul is inadequate. It must involve the whole man, judge the whole man and reconcile the whole man. And it must be helped by a society-oriented Christian service.

I can imagine three paths that Christian service of this type might follow.

First, the path of research. For example: A woman is about to have her seventh child. The doctor says, "She just isn't strong enough; her life is in danger." The social worker knows that her life would not be in danger if she were not carrying a double load of work as housewife and seamstress. The psychiatrist knows that if she has an abortion, the weight of sorrow over the lost child will certainly outweigh the double burden of work and pregnancy. But these three do in fact compare notes and share experiences: in Sweden, teamwork of this nature has been inaugurated by Christian representatives of these professions. This is the Christian diaconate in society. But suppose that the woman asks her minister what she ought to do, what is he to answer? Is his answer merely a reflection of his theological specialty, or does it involve insight into her medical, financial, and psychological situation? If she comes to him *after* the abortion, because her conscience tells her that she has killed her child, what does he say then? If he gives the same answer as her conscience, why has he not conducted the child's funeral? He may answer that the doctor threw the baby away, because it was only a few inches long. Next question: *Has the minister discussed the matter seriously with the doctor?*

But if the woman who has consulted the authorities lives in India, where it is said that there are too many children, or in France, where there are too few, then a whole people joins the woman in asking, "What am I to do?" The question goes to the historian, then to the economist, and finally back again to the theologian. If this child or this people is to be saved and allowed to live, what is this precious life for? What is lost if a person or a people is not allowed to live? No doubt the three authorities will provide three entirely different answers, as each does his best to guard and justify his professional reputation, but this does nothing to help the one in trouble, who is placed in an intolerable tension between them.

Sometimes the partitions that divide scientists of one discipline from scientists of another are torn down—as happened some years ago in America, when a few scientists saw, literally in a flash, that what they had produced was not merely a "result," but a concentrate of life and death. "I am afraid"—the expression has passed into history, but not everyone has understood that the real cause of one man's fear was not the possibility of a natural catastrophe, but the fact that a specialist had opened the door of his lecture-room and found that the university had gone. Gone, and the abyss yawned at his feet. This is a dangerous situation.

The diaconate of research can help in the rediscovery of *universitas*. The first thing that has to be done is to provide opportunities of research in a number of boundary disciplines. For example: pedagogics, ethics, and psychology; or industrial economics, group psychology, and the Christian doctrine of work. It is of the utmost importance that theology should be dragged out of the threefold rut of exegesis, church history, and systematic theology. Theologians and philosophers must be made to involve themselves in cooperative ventures with the social sciences. When someone asks what has gone wrong, someone else may look up from his individual "cases," plunge into social diagnosis, and say "Hegel," or "Rousseau." The diagnosis may be correct. It is hardly likely that the patient, visiting the doctor with a heart complaint, will be told to stop reading Sartre. But perhaps that is what he ought to be told. What is certain is that the doctor will examine the poor Sartre addict's heart. And as long as we are talking about *society*, that is exactly what the doctor ought to be doing. The diseases of society ought to be treated psychosomatically, by specialists in the working fellowship of a team.

In fact there already exists a diaconate of the kind I have been talking about, at least at the experimental stage. As an example I might mention the exchange of ideas between German scientists carried out under the auspices of Professor Metzke in Bad Boll. A distinctive aid to anyone wanting to undertake an informed exploration outside the area of his own specialization is provided by the Sigtuna Foundation Archives, which contain almost a million press-cuttings from the Swedish cultural debate. A further example would be the Scandinavian Society for Christianity and Culture, one object of which is the setting up of a Scandinavian university based not on the high school but on the "folk high school"—which would mean a real renewal and extension of the concept of the university.

The second way we might call simply "the conference diaconate." This work, which is now being carried on in all parts of Europe, and which began in Sigtuna in the 1920s, when we assembled workers and students, employers and employees for discussions, seems to be more than ever necessary now that our culture, with its *hybris* and its lack of a common language, has come to resemble more and more the Tower of Babel. The bringing together of representatives from different linguistic levels of society is also a work of Christian service.

The work that we began in Sigtuna in the 1920s is now being carried on by a number of Swedish organizations, not least in the "contact conferences" that are held in the diocesan guest houses. Our task in the Sigtuna Foundation is to bring new groups together and most of all to call conferences of experts in which leading authorities have the opportunity to cross the boundaries of one another's disciplines. Developments elsewhere in Europe are following similar lines.

Of especial importance in the conference diaconate is to avoid the apologetical temptation. The conviction seems to run in the blood of us ministers that when all is said and done, *we* are the ones who are in the know, and we are going to tell the others (perhaps with the help of a kind of play-school for adults) all about it. At a conference for ministers and doctors we are far too prone to treat the doctors as outsiders, now at last brought into contact with the church, as though ministers —*most of all ministers*—did not need to be dragged out of their specializations and saved into the world, and as though laymen were unable to serve the church as laymen without adopting the ministerial air. When a bridge is built between two social groups, it is a work of Christian service, even when none of the highways across it has a church at the end.

But suppose that a conference should end in mistaken views and an un-Christian consensus? Well, even then it is better that these things should be said in the shadow of the church than from a place where the delegates cannot see the cross on the church spire. In some countries, honest opinions can be expressed nowhere but in the church—and that, too, is Christian witness.

The third way in which Christians may serve society is through the arts. I ought to mention, however, that the three ways I am discussing have a great deal in common. There are conferences for research, and research into conferences. As far as research into art is concerned, it is absolutely necessary that this be carried out from the theological point of view, an aspect that all too often has been disregarded. Only in recent years has the Evangelical church been carrying on a genuine debate on the subject of the relationship between art and faith. Many a conference institute has come to recognize how important conferences can be to the diaconate of art, and a great deal has taken place in this area during the last few years that would have been altogether unthinkable not long ago.

But there is good reason to deal with art separately. In the first place, art opens the way to a total view and to perspectives that must always remain closed to research and to conferences. Art is the writing of letters from outposts of humanity, where the situation is open and unprotected by social and personal barriers. Here the specialist is out of his depth: the equation is polished, and man is left in the presence of God and his neighbor.

Second, art is much more than a function of society and a witness to the social situation; it provides a refuge from the totalitarian claims of modern society. Here the individual comes to experience his insufficiency, a forbidden fruit in these days of intensive demands that man be more and more efficient and productive. When art is what it ought to be—the penetrating gaze of one's fellow man—the individual knows that he has been recognized. Someone has seen him; society is not totally blind. This is catharsis; this is Christian service. Third, I speak of the diaconate of art because art is a method for some to escape the totalitarian claims of the church, and because the church is unwilling to concede that the means of escape are necessary.

When we confuse the conventions of certain groups in society with the work of the Holy Spirit, or, to put it another way, when we confuse the total claim of Jesus Christ with the totalitarian claim of the church, we are doing a great deal to impede every form of Christian service in society. For by this deception we place the peculiarities of a social group between Christians and the world, as though these peculiarities were sacred. Those who are parties to the deception are apt to suspect art; and they are right to do so, for art has no respect for convention. At times art is so unconventional as to be reminiscent of the gospel.

It is not uncommon to find free art persecuted by the empirical church, just as it has been by totalitarian regimes. (Although the church sometimes understands distress of body, she seems to have little enough understanding of the distress of soul brought about by the demands of society: a strange materialism.) What we need is a form of Christian service that recognizes the life of art as a creation of God, and, when necessary, rescues it from the church.

The diaconate of art must mediate between the artist and his public, and that is supremely a work of information. But what is so seldom understood is the need to guard the sources of art; for instance, by providing the artist with a place where he can work undisturbed and by making the local congregation aware that the artist as a human type has a place in its midst. This is not an easy task, since there are so many who believe that before the Fall Adam was a respectable middle-class citizen. But the task itself is a noble one. Another task is to work to provide the artist with a decent living wage in society, and in the church—something that is long overdue.

But why do I call all this Christian service? Why not simply call it "work" and "service"? These things do not become any the holier for taking place, for example, in a Christian conference center. The service of one's neighbor is in itself an act of Christian worship and the service of God.

The same applies to the act of service that went astray, the task we failed to understand on account of our shortsightedness; it applies, too, to the service that is offered in the midst of the conflict of duties, where there is no possible way out without sinning against someone. One of the tasks facing what I have called the social diaconate is to try to find a way for collective man to obey his own individual conscience. But if he obeys and yet makes a wrong decision because he is convinced that the other decisions he might have made would have been still more disastrous, he must be enabled to do even this as a Christian. God sometimes calls us to recognize what is his will, and in obedience either go under or keep our life and property —but sometimes he calls us *not* to recognize that will clearly. It is an act of Christian love to be able to explain to one another the situation in which our work takes place, but we can never reveal all the forces involved. Nor can artists and poets —though they are sometimes, unfortunately, called the prophets of our day and age. Remember that prophecy, too, will disappear. Our service is often carried out blindfolded. It is certain that we have often, all unknowing, helped people to gain new strength and discover new possibilities, with which they have gone on to serve the devil. But the service is stronger than the devilish context in which it is carried out. For the Law of God is there, one of the secret signs of the coming of Christ.

One thing is certain, however: the service of our neighbor includes our open criticism of his views and his work; that service has been laid upon us by the Law of God. To serve and to love is not the same thing as to flatter and to keep silent; it is, as far as our resources permit, to help with bread and truth.

Once more the question: why am I speaking about Christian service? Because service is the impatience of the church. All the tasks I have mentioned are the responsibility of society, but when what must be does not happen, then the Word says to the nearest bystander—even if it does not happen to concern his profession or his specialty: "*You* do it!" And it becomes Christian service.

And so, when the diaconate opens a path from the altar out into the world, at the same time it opens a path from everyday life in towards the altar. What I mean is that the distinction we are so apt to draw between the social and the sacramental is wrong. Wrong because it denies the incarnation. In the early church the deacons, at the moment of the offertory, collected bread and wine from the members of the congregation and took it up to the altar; in the same way work is intercession, and intercession carries the reality of our social and cultural life to the altar. We place before God industry and painting, love and politics, liturgy and entertainment. The world must be told, not merely that all things must be changed and brought to God, but that they are there already, under his judgment and his blessing. God has summed up all things in Christ. Christian service, it has been said, is "to spread the canopy of the church over everything." For we do not belong to God only with a special religious segment of our lives. Just as the sermon proclaims the gospel to the whole of human life, so our action must affirm that the whole of human life is God's, and that its goal is to be found only in him.

This is a matter for all of us, but because most people still think that God and society have nothing in common—many because they are so secularized, others because they are so religious (in this context two sides of one and the same phenomenon)—someone must be the first to open the way between work and the altar and, as it were, carry our daily bread from the baker to the minister, and back again to the baker; that is the worship of men's hands, that is Christian service. I sometimes wish that the bread we use in the Eucharist were not so smooth and white. I wish that it were coarse and black. Then people might see that it is indeed "our daily bread," that it had been grown in the soil, harvested in sweat and toil, ground between the millstones of our industry, baked in the ovens of working men, and distributed along roads and highways that are used by taxicabs and buses, bicycles and boots.

16.

LITURGY AND THE THEATER

Overspiritual worship and the secular theater have one thing in common: they are both dull. I am not here thinking primarily of lack of liturgical unity or loose dramatic composition (not necessarily their worst faults). Worship is dull when it comes before God bringing only a fraction of our human reality —a "religious" fraction—leaving out all the rest on the grounds that it has nothing to do with God, and that God could not possibly be interested in it. And the theater is dull (in the opinion of a minister who sometimes goes there) when it presents us with human reality in the style of a post mortem, for the information of an audience (especially the drama critics) and no more than that. Actors and audience between them represent the world. God has nothing to do with the theater and the theater has nothing to do with God.

To be quite honest, I believe that the theater is very seldom completely secularized. It assumes, as a rule, that life is remarkable enough to concern someone more than the person actually living it. Or it ought to. When we have finally come to terms with this attitude, there will be much less drama in the world. What is the point of Oedipus tearing out his own eyes? Why should we take any notice of "The Condemned Man" when he says "there is something the matter with this room"? Of course, we do not have to discern the presence of the Christian God behind the scenes—he might equally well be Zeus or Vishnu or Humanity (a modern form of ancestor- or progeny-worship). But there is still an altar there.

And wherever there is an altar, there are the beginnings of liturgy. I wonder sometimes whether all those desperate efforts to move the stage down among the people are not symptoms of our quest for a lost liturgy. The same might apply to the "realist" and "symbolist" attempts to inject reality into the theater, or, in other words, to overcome dullness.

As long as a drama only offers an imitation of reality—for who knows whether there is an audience on the other side of the last curtain?—the tension scarcely penetrates beneath the surface: such tension as there is, is on the level of the family album. Drama borrows its drama from "real" life; nothing actually *happens* at the theater. What the audience sees is an imitation of something that has happened, or something that might happen. It may be a passable likeness, like Aunt Helga's picture on the wall. Or it may draw its characters from "real" life, sheep and foxes and all, but build up an artificial tension only in the interests of ultimate relaxation.

Of course, this game of "let's pretend" may capture some part of our interest by virtue of the "truth" of its "lies"; but that is another matter altogether.

In the liturgy, the chancel of the church represents heaven; that is where we find the pictures of saints and apostles. But faith claims that when the Eucharist is celebrated, heaven is actually there. It is not enough merely to remember "the night in which the Lord was betrayed"; the night is there, and covers the whole of our earthly reality. Reconciliation, too, is there. God is there. This is the point upon which the whole of the liturgy converges. And it is therefore of only secondary importance (though not unimportant) whether the liturgy is carried out skillfully or not. Perhaps there were critics present, of some kind or another. But the important thing is that God was there; that explains the striking sense of reality that is found in worship. It does not represent or imitate; it is. At the end of it all, what we have seen is not a performance, but reality unmasked. Something has happened, something in comparison with which all else is of comparative insignificance.

The "footlights" across which this drama is played are at the altar; on the other side there is the great darkness, out of which gaze eyes that no one on this side has ever seen. The whole of the art of worship is turned in this direction (that it faces east is a further confirmatory act of symbolism). Great sections of the liturgy, such as the lessons and the sermon, are of course directed toward the congregation, but the point of this is to involve the congregation in what is taking place. Choirs, hymns, psalms, and prayers then join to hurl the action across to the other side. There is no audience, no dualism between actors on the one side and observers on the other; there is a congregation, consisting of ministers, choir, and people. And even if the people sit dumb and motionless, they are still not an audience; for they are being overheard. What is happening is not a performance for their entertainment; it does not perform: it presents. That is why the members of the congregation ought to sense their affinity with what takes place: *tua res agitur:* "it is your case that is being heard." Paul is particularly concerned to have it stated clearly: "how can anyone . . . say the 'Amen' . . ." (1 Cor. 14:16)? "Amen!"—this is not applause; it is involvement. But consider how much less apparatus is necessary to convince a congregation of its involvement than to persuade an audience that it is bound up in a performance.

When liturgy degenerates into theater the footlights and curtains go across the end of the chancel, and however wide may be the gulf which in some churches separates ministers from laymen, it is never deeper or wider than when the church is divided into a stage and an auditorium, and the people separated into actors and audience. Although there have been innumerable experiments having to do with the placing of the proscenium, the dualism is unavoidable; for there is no altar, no focus of everyone's attention, no day of judgment beyond the temporal sequence, in which all things are summed up. The theater has gone the whole way and made the audience into its god; its last judgment is pronounced by the critics. It seems that this god is omnipotent in the control he exercises over the drama. Instead of the veil of the temple he has a mirror. The audience is on both sides of the curtain; the audience wants to see itself referred to and, above all, dramatized; the audience wants to appear to be interesting—though in all likelihood gripped by the nagging doubt that it is not. And the little symbolical gesture is often lost in the welter of "theatrical" posturings; after the liturgical dress, unchanged for centuries, come (after various intermediate forms) the costumes, changed as and when required. The theater becomes a fashion show. The work is completed as the scenery goes up. But let the theater posture all it likes before its new god, he remains on the outside. The audience is a deposed congregation.

This is of course a very rough description; the historical development has been far more complex. Some of the phenomena I have mentioned can also be explained on other grounds than the loss of the cult. So, for example, the secular theater need not necessarily be realistic. But I am convinced that these phenomena would be inconceivable in any form of drama with liturgy at its core. This means, among other things, that the illusion of realism is difficult to maintain satisfactorily, even when the theater is influenced by the cult. One effect of liturgical influence—and here I am speaking only of the influence of Christian liturgy—is to render unnecessary the attempt to imitate; particularly since imitation, compared to the brief, allusive symbol at the altar, appears little short of barbaric. There is no need to drag pieces of scenery around when a gesture will suffice.

It is a fairly certain fact of history that drama begins in worship. In the beginning was the liturgy, but it is there no longer—or it is rare. And I think that it is worth considering what might perhaps have been different if drama had not lost, or almost lost, its orientation towards the altar. It may still not be too late to recapture some lost values.

I repeat: this does not mean that the theater should become a church, or even a pulpit. We do not put crosses on our factories; nor should we put an altar in our theaters. But the actual connection between church and theater—as well as that between church and factory—should be recognized and made manifest. They do not exclude one another. Church services need the direct language and the knowledge of life outside the church walls that are found in the theater. The theater needs a new insight into the category of intercession, since all genuine drama is intercession (though often to an unknown god).

The missing link between them is liturgical drama, in which liturgy and drama are united without either becoming insipid. There is no lack of notable experiments in this direction, the best being perhaps *Murder in the Cathedral*, but many un-Christian church walls and theater proscenia will have to be pulled down before St. Genesius can reoccupy his rightful place in the chancel and on the stage.[1]

---

[1] St. Genesius was a Roman actor (*mimus*) in the time of Diocletian (284-305), who was called upon to parody Christian rites on the stage. However, he was converted by the divine power of the rites; he confessed his faith from the stage and was martyred.

17.

THE DILEMMA OF CHURCH DRAMA

The subject of church drama is being widely discussed these days, both in international circles, where a remarkable cooperation is developing across national and confessional frontiers, and in Sweden, where it appears to be in process of becoming an important form of church activity. But each new phase in the development of church drama reflects a theological and a literary debate. At the moment one can discern, with respect to production on the one hand and theory on the other, the emergence of two apparently incompatible tendencies.

One of them may be traced back to the purely illustrative aspect of medieval church art, which was originally intended as a *Biblia pauperum*, giving the illiterate faithful some measure of easily understandable Bible teaching. But why go back to medieval patterns? Living pictures can be found much nearer home. Simplest of all would be to move the theater into the church, turn the chancel into a stage, the altar into a decoration, and the congregation into an audience. Theatrical properties make themselves cautiously at home in church: a throne (T. S. Eliot, *Murder in the Cathedral*), a cedar bed (Walter Gutkelch, *Der grosse Mut des Hiskia*), or whatever the imagination may require to help it escape from the church. Additional help is readily forthcoming from costumes and masks.

Now I am not criticizing these things in themselves, provided that the plays in which they appear proclaim the gospel and show some respect for the architecture of the church building; this means, among other things, that at least the altar ought not to be hidden. It is just that there is no real reason for calling these plays "church" drama, since they could equally well be performed in a theater or in the street (incidentally, one of the aspects of the modern church drama movement is the revival of the religious street-play). The fact that a play is performed in a church and that the chancel offers a suitable setting is in itself no real reason for labeling it as church drama. The fact that it may perhaps have been written in the Middle Ages does not help, either; the problem is how the modern church drama movement is to avoid sharing the fate of the medieval mystery play, and losing its altar.

This brings into the picture the second tendency: the liturgical tendency. It would seem that this element has been largely forgotten in our discussion of medieval developments; we talk endlessly about the church's preaching, but seldom about her prayer. As a matter of fact, the liturgy contains enough dramatic material to explain the origin of religious drama: when the tropes in a tenth-century Easter service of mattins are reshaped into a dramatic dialogue, or when St. Francis prays before the crib on Christmas Day 1223, it is not merely a matter of winning the attention of the masses; it is adoration in dramatic function.

It is not a question of finding some means of making prayer and preaching more "interesting," an advertisement aimed at making public worship more popular and attractive—although this is the fundamental aim of drama. If the Word is, as it were, given its head, it will never rest content with abstract monologues. If it can be spared the burden of "methods" and pedantry, then the tongues of fire will settle on more than one head, as they did at Pentecost or in the medieval passion plays. Then, too, the dramatic action will burst forth from the spoken word; metaphors will become visible and powerful signs, as they were with the prophets (1 Kings 11:29ff.) and as they still are in the African churches. The same applies to the liturgy: in his *Weltgeschichte des Theaters* Gregor has stressed, rightly, that the liturgical response is in itself dramatic. Liturgical drama is no mere appendix to the liturgy; like Bach's cantatas, it is a branch from its trunk.

That is why the biblical texts and the church's liturgical tradition provide church drama with its content. Church drama is like "the Nordic Orpheus," the fiddler who for seven centuries has been crouching high above the altar in Trondheim Cathedral, his bow laid to the strings, listening to the worship far below him.

In the matter of form, too, church drama is determined by the liturgy. At this point it diverges sharply from the theater.

There is nothing to stop the theater from borrowing material from the church, but church drama has to be subject to the same laws that apply to church music and church art—and that is something that does not concern the theater.

The most important of these is its orientation towards the altar. This characteristic is one which may be traced as far back as to the twelfth century, but as church drama became more and more of a wild public entertainment, it must have declined in importance. Not until this orientation has been restored can we speak without more ado about a "renascence" of church drama. A few years ago I saw at Oxford a production of Eliot's *Murder in the Cathedral*, at which the congregation behaved like an audience, and the atmosphere in the cathedral was that of the theater. But the view of the altar was shut off, and when the actors prayed they turned to face the audience.

Originally, too, illusion was in no way indispensable; illusion always faces the audience, for when it turns to face the altar it becomes merely ridiculous. In the twelfth-century French drama of the Good Samaritan, two platforms were sufficient to represent Jerusalem and Jericho. At a later date, it was demanded that there should be much more of a "resemblance"— as many a medieval altar-piece witnesses. It is particularly interesting in this context to take note of the costumes. A thirteenth-century Swedish manuscript, closely related to a tenth-century dramatization of the meeting of the three women with the angels at Jesus' tomb, stipulates that those taking part should be dressed *in cappis* and *dalmaticis*—liturgical dress, despite the fact that the Swedish historian Schück translates these words by "shawls" and "long dresses." But it is certain that copes and dalmatics were unacceptable in the Valenciennes productions of the sixteenth century. And it would be impossible to count the skin-clad shepherds, the crowned wise men, the cloth-armored soldiers and the toga-bearing Pilates that stalk nowadays through the churches of Europe! I may perhaps be allowed to mention in this connection that the Swedish Fellowship of Liturgy and Drama is trying to find another way out—the first step being the seamen's tunics in *Prophet and Carpenter*, where an anchor is considered enough to show what they are supposed to represent.

Otherwise, this approach has had a marked effect on the movements used by the participants in church drama: instead of the febrile trotting back and forth we are so accustomed to, more use is being made of statuesque scenes, in which slight gestures and movements symbolize, rather than illustrate, what is taking place. And as far as entries and exits are concerned, we have learned to ask why the participants should pretend to have no further part to play in the service when they are not actually speaking their lines in the chancel. Do they disturb the action if they sit at the front, visible to everybody, as they used to in the medieval liturgical dramas? Well, they may disturb the illusion, but they certainly do not disturb either the proclamation of the Word or the prayers.

A further consequence of the renewed link between church drama and the liturgy will be a new understanding of the role of the chorus in the drama. The chorus is closely connected with the worshiping congregation, and was there from the very first in medieval liturgical drama, as it once was in the drama of classical antiquity. In the liturgical tradition it represents the congregation, and voices its intercession. On an occasion it may take its place among the cosmic powers, as in the Greek Orthodox mass, where it represents the angels. When the congregation is demoted into an audience, and when the cosmic perspective of the drama is lost, the chorus is put out of work. But when God's people are once more assembled in a common act of worship and adoration, facing in the same direction as the action of the drama—eastward, toward the altar, Paradise, heaven—there will be no need to try to find work for the chorus to do; it will reoccupy its own proper place.

This has happened, but it has happened far too seldom. Church drama is still afraid to turn its back on the people. Far too often the faces of the actors are turned towards the critics, "to be seen of them" (as the Scripture says of the Pharisees); far too often there is an invisible proscenium in the church, with the result that we have once more the theater's dualism of actors and audience.

The dilemma of church drama is not that it is an ancient form trying to make a comeback. As we have seen, it is not enough merely to try to forge links with the Middle Ages. We must penetrate behind the medieval drama, back to its living source. And that source is neither the *Quem queritis* dialogue of St. Gall nor some *Biblia pauperum;* it is much nearer at hand, in the liturgical life of our own church. If church drama is prepared to submit unconditionally to the liturgy, the dilemma is solved, and at the same time transformed into a task—a task of importance for both the liturgy and drama.

18.

DRAMA AND TRUTH

The formation in 1958 of a church drama society in Oslo led to a violent debate in the Norwegian press. A similar debate had taken place a few years earlier in Finland, in connection with a performance of *Prophet and Carpenter* in Helsinki; articles and letters were written on the same subject, with the same degree of involvement. One accusation commonly heard in situations like these is that church drama is deficient in truth; the accusation appears in a variety of guises, either as a theologically motivated reaction against the claim of church drama to function as worship, and to be a medium of sacramental reality, or as naive indignation against the "lies" of drama. As a Norwegian versifier expressed it:

> A play is a mixture;
> Another man plays it,
> The writer disowns it,
> Its phrases are empty.

Those who are actively involved in the work of church drama may be tempted to ignore their critics, particularly since these appear in many cases never to have seen a church drama. Anyone who has experienced the sheer realism of liturgical drama may well consider without more ado that he knows what it is all about, and that further explanations are unnecessary. But without some attempt to express the theoretical basis of this realism, and the conditions under which it is to be found, there is a very real risk that the realism itself will be lost, and that it will become progressively more difficult to communicate it to others.

In these pages I shall attempt a preliminary analysis of the problem of drama and truth, as it is experienced within the liturgically oriented church drama movement. It will be necessary in this connection to touch upon a number of related questions in the area of Evangelical faith and theology.

In the Beginning Was the Drama

Human speech itself is basically at one with what we call "drama." Words are signs and symbols of reality, but they are not identical with reality. Sometimes they may attempt to provide an illusion of reality, as for example in Tennyson's poem "Ring out, wild bells, to the wild sky." The words imitate the sound of bells when they are read aloud, but does that necessarily mean that they are a lie? Perhaps they might be if someone were to declaim them and at the same time assert that he was a bell—but apart from this unlikely eventuality, the imitation has a closer relation to reality than we would find in words having no such dimension of illusion.

Pictures, too, provide a link with reality. Suppose that I have a photograph of my father, and want to tell a stranger what it is I have in my hand. I may perhaps say, "This is my father"—obviously a lie, if taken literally; and yet the portrait helps me to recall my father, providing it is a good portrait.

In many alphabets the signs representing letters, syllables or words began as pictograms—images of objects. These bear the same relation to reality as does drama: they are not themselves reality, but they are reminiscent of reality and they refer to reality.

At this point the Reformed Churches call a halt. They say that images in church tempt the worshiper to lie, in that he may come to worship an image of God instead of God himself. It is easier to introduce church drama into these churches than it is to introduce a crucifix.

But the boundary between image and action is as fluid as the boundary between word and image. The action is there, in the image, and in point of fact the imitative action is probably more original than the imitative drawing or painting or sculpture. The child who has just seen a horse will after a little while remind himself of the pleasant experience by stamping, tossing his head, and neighing like a horse. It is certain that drama of this order existed before the first word for "horse" and before the first pictogram representing "horse." In the beginning was the drama.

200

Symbol and Truth

The problem of the "truth" of any symbol has to do with its relationship to two realities: on the one hand the subjective, that is, the person using the symbol; and on the other the objective, the reality to which the symbol refers.

As far as the subjective aspect is concerned, none but God can in any real sense be regarded as identical with his word: "The Word was God . . . ." In the world of men it is of course unreasonable to speak of any identity between the speaker and what is spoken; this is not the fault of original sin, but belongs rather to the conditions of our existence in space and time. It is rather different when we come to consider our own personal lack of objectivity, which evidently has to do with a trace of devilry in our own inner life. This inability to be entirely truthful in our self-expression is all the greater since it would seem that we are unable even to know ourselves in any comprehensive way. There is no lack of evidence to suggest that total self-knowledge would lead to total insanity. This inner untruthfulness is not, of course, limited to those occasions on which we are literally talking about ourselves, since our egocentricity leaves traces on all our interests. It would seem that even scientific work is not altogether immune from egocentric motivation on the part of the one who is carrying it out. Our egocentricity is constantly presenting us with spectral ideal images of what we are, with the result that we confront the world with what we imagine ourselves to be, instead of with those fragments of the truth about ourselves that are accessible to all of us.

It is therefore true, generally speaking, to say that we lie more consistently when we play ourselves than when we manage to express other realities, or when we lend our voices and other means of expression to someone else. The Pharisee who stands in the temple and thanks God that he is not like other men lies more thoroughly than the actor who tries to represent the nature of the Pharisee. The soldier who stands at the head of his regiment and says "God save the king and our country" expresses, at that moment, the relationship between the army, king, and country; it is not altogether improbable that he is, at that moment, closer to the truth than when, his voice trembling with emotion, he uses the identical expression at an election meeting. Life is full of such role-playing; the occasions on which we make ourselves the mouthpiece of someone or something else are by no means limited to the theater.

Playing a role becomes an actual sin—a living lie—when we steal a role, like Köpenick, or when we pretend to be something we are not without telling anyone that we are pretending, like Albert Svensson in *Holy Masquerade*. That is why it is so important that we should call drama drama, and theater theater. The great lie in Israel was not that the children on the square played weddings and funerals, but that adults did more or less the same things *and claimed to be serious about it.*[1]

If, on the other hand, by "truth" we mean correspondence between the symbol and the objective reality, it might be as well to consider the role assigned by the Old Testament to human speech in the work of creation. "So out of the ground the Lord God formed every beast of the field and every bird of the air, and brought them to the man to see what he would call them; and whatever the man called every living creature, that was its name" (Gen. 2:19). Creation was not complete until man had seen the creatures and, with the help of language, given them a definite place in his own world. Only in this dimension did they reach completion. Man, therefore, was made God's fellow-creator by virtue of his capacity for shaping symbols; as such he became a sharer of the secret of the divine Word: "all things were made through him, and without him was not anything made that was made" (John 1:3). As God "calls into existence the things that do not exist" (Rom. 4:17), so man creates his own universe in and through the arts.

As Berdyaev has pointed out, this capacity may be a temptation for sinful man to forget his sin and imagine himself divine. If man falls into this temptation, this does not mean that he becomes the god of the symbols, but that the symbols become his gods; we recall Paul's words about those who "exchanged the glory of the immortal God for images resembling mortal man or birds or animals or reptiles," who "exchanged the truth about God for a lie and worshiped and served the creature rather than the Creator . . ." (Rom. 1:13, 25). This untruthful-

[1] Cf. Matt. 11:16-19.

ness, so pronounced in all idolatrous symbolism from Aaron and the golden calf to Valéry and *l'art pour l'art* is, however, not the special province of priests and artists; the tendency is there in us all, built into every nature. Even language is involved in our fall: ". . . no one does good, not even one. Their throat is an open grave, they use their tongues to deceive" (Rom. 3:12f.). This means that we are unable, merely by our words, to fish for secrets across the fence of Paradise and truth. "That which is, is far off, and deep, very deep; who can find it out?" (Eccl. 7:24). We have lost touch with the source of being; therefore "our prophecy is imperfect" (1 Cor. 13:9), and our symbols all contain something of untruth. That is why many mystics and poets, after having attempted in vain to capture the truth in words, have retreated into total silence. This untruth attaches to all human communication, with the result that when we draw back in fear from drama to "plain words," thinking that there we have some guarantee of truth, we deceive ourselves, since words are subject to the same risks as drama.

However, the sins of language that we are constantly committing are not merely a matter of a metaphysical lack of congruence between word and reality. They consist of the following types of misuse: *carelessness*, by which language is made obscure or misleading or meaningless; *cheating*, by which words are made to say that reality is other than it is in fact; and *ostentation*, by which words replace reality and draw attention exclusively to themselves.

It is of the utmost importance that the dividing line should not be drawn between symbolic foundations, for instance, between the account of (that is, a series of symbols for) a historical event and the account of (that is, a series of symbols for) something that has not taken place but which is a symbol of something that has taken place. Nor between different kinds of symbol: figures on a piece of paper are just as much, or just as little, lies *per se* as a play in the theater. The dividing line goes between, on the one hand, a drama (or a figure, or written or spoken words) that points beyond itself to some reality, and, on the other, the same phenomena that point to a nonexistent "reality," or which set themselves up in the place of reality.

This is borne out by the use of symbols in the history of salvation.

The Salvation of Symbols

Despite what we have been saying, God has spoken in human terms, and in so doing has used human language. The absolute has assumed relative form, and expressed itself through our ambiguous words. The people of the Old Covenant exercised the utmost care with respect to the words through which God revealed himself. The tetragrammaton symbolized God, but might not be pronounced, at least in late Judaism. It was forbidden to make any image of God, nor might anyone impersonate God. This is the consequence of the Fall, through which man lost his capacity to represent God, either in word or action.

But throughout history God has used all manner of "drama" to proclaim his will and his purposes: the words of the prophets and the Holy Scriptures, the cherubim on the throne of grace and the processions of the Feast of Tabernacles. At the center of it all there was, in ancient times, a cultic drama that has left many traces in the Old Testament, not least in the ritual fragments that have found their way into the Psalter: a drama that in late Judaism still has its place at the heart of religion in the ritual of the Passover lamb. The meal at which the lamb was eaten is a dramatic representation of the events of the Exodus. The prophets used the same language on important occasions, as for instance in 1 Kings 11:29ff. and Jeremiah 27:1ff. Similar "dramas" are also to be found in the New Testament—Matthew 21:19ff., Revelation 10:8ff.

It is important to note in this context that the Word of God might be transmitted through what we would call fictitious events, and not only through historical events and the narratives about them. Or are we to suppose that the episode of the rich man and the poor man's ewe lamb "really" took place exactly as the prophet Nathan told David? Or are we to accuse Jesus of untruth, if historical research should demonstrate that the unjust steward or the king who gave talents to his servants or the good Samaritan are not historical personalities in the same way as Augustus or Alexander?

In Christ the identity between word and subjective reality returned to our earth. He is the prophetic word that existed before he was born; he is also identical with the gospel that is proclaimed after him. And this identity applies, not only between Christ and the spoken Word or between Christ and the written Word, but also between Christ and the acted Word. He is identical with the image of him that we have in the broken bread and the poured wine. When our other realities gather around the Word and the sacraments, and turn toward the altar, they become participants in the drama in which God reveals himself. This is the forgiveness of sins for the whole of our history, understood as a drama about God. In themselves all our words and actions, understood as expressions of our relationship to God, are mere lies and pretense; through Christ, in the Word and the sacraments, they are lifted into the dimension of saving truth.

Here, too, the symbols receive a new meaning, together with the objective reality to which they point: all things are on the way towards a new heaven and a new earth, where we shall see face to face, and where there will be a new and wonderful relationship between persons and their names, both when the names are pronounced by themselves and when others use them.

"I will give him a white stone, with a new name written on the stone which no one knows except him who receives it" (Rev. 2:17).

Church Drama and Reality

The danger of sinning by word is greatest in the church, since it is there we stand before the Reality of all realities, and if our symbols there are empty or misleading, we risk our souls. There, too, the temptation to set the symbol in God's place is greatest, since the sacred room gives an aura of sanctity to everything that takes place within its walls. Therefore whenever a word is spoken in church, there must be observed the same reverence for reality that the old Israelites showed for the name. Therefore church drama, while it allows itself in humility to be filled with the reality of the Word and intercession, should confess in humility that it *is* a drama—signs and symbols—and turn the attention of all to the real presence—the presence known at the altar in Word and sacrament. For whatever reality church drama possesses is not brought in by the efforts of the participants, but by the reality that is the subject of the drama, from which it radiates and to which it refers. Close attention must be paid to the liturgical dimensions of the drama.

The danger of idolatry is less marked in the theater, which means that the drama can spread itself out more generously, with eloquence and sweeping gestures. Naturally enough, the theater can imitate reality without the danger of anyone falling down and worshiping the drama instead of the Reality of realities. The New Testament does not issue a warning against elaborate cloaks as such, but does stress that there is a danger in wearing especially large tassels as a sign of *piety*.

Elsewhere I have emphasized that there is a cultic tendency in all theater, derived from the liturgical origin of drama. And although the danger is less marked in the theater than in the church, there is a great need of theological criticism—far different from the usual criticism, however—to draw attention to every tendency to manufacture surrogates for reality (and for other, more positive reasons; for the theater embraces a great deal of disguised theology, and theology should be judged in theological terms).

As far as church drama is concerned, it should be pointed out that its risks are shared by all forms of liturgy. The dividing line goes, not between drama on the one hand and the written and spoken word on the other, but between the acted, written and spoken word as a servant of reality and the acted, written and spoken word as a distortion of, or a surrogate for, reality. The sermon that attracts the emotions and reverence of the congregation by its pious prolixity or by the personality of the speaker, the sung liturgy that seems to belong in the opera house, impressing upon the people nothing but the quality of the minister's voice, the "free prayer" that spreads out the piety of the minister for everyone to admire—all these are pure idolatry and untruth, principally because they are trying to imitate reality instead of humbly confessing their symbolic character and standing expectantly before the reality that is Christ and the gospel (Col. 2:17). However, when the preacher or the leader of the prayers considers himself more truthful because he is not an actor, he is guilty of Pharisaism.

"And whenever the living creatures give glory and honor and thanks to him who is seated on the throne, who lives for ever and ever, the twenty-four elders fall down before him who is seated on the throne and worship him who lives for ever and ever; they cast their crowns before the throne . . ." (Rev. 4:9f.). We do not know how close was the connection between this vision and the liturgy of the early church. But if it is true that the rather unassuming men who for the most part constituted the "elders" of the church were in the habit of celebrating mass dressed in the imperial insignia, their contemporaries must have regarded the whole business as blasphemy against the divinity of Caesar. And the Christians knew well enough that they were "a race of kings." But they did not perform for the benefit of the crowd. Their actions were centered on the "throne." The twenty-four emperors fall on their faces before the altar and lay down the whole of their majesty before the royal reality. That is liturgy. That is church drama.

The relationship between church drama and liturgy demands, finally, a couple of applications of what we have been saying about the relation of drama to objective and subjective reality. If church drama is a part of the life of the worshiping congregation, this implies a twofold restriction.

First of all, drama, as a tributary of the liturgy, must not imitate the liturgy, which is its subject, not its object. It is not possible to imitate a celebration of the Eucharist, although it is possible to celebrate the Eucharist in the course of a church drama. If the drama has to do with the wedding at Cana, the minister cannot pretend to join the couple in marriage, since prayer and the Word of God have the same effect in church drama as they have in all forms of worship. There is, on the other hand, nothing to prevent a real wedding from being set in the context of a church drama, for example a drama based on the wedding at Cana. This means that church drama is immune from the criticism that claims that it "plays" prayer and weddings and the Eucharist. In church drama prayer is always prayer, weddings are always weddings, the Eucharist is always the Eucharist.

Church Drama and the Participant

The second restriction has to do with the subjective reality of those who take part in church drama. The actress in *The Fiery Furnace* who prays for Babylon—is she not committing a form of perjury? How are people supposed to believe what the church drama has to proclaim if it is performed by actors who do not mean what they are saying, but only pretend. The question is answered in and through the fact that the drama is subject to the Word. The praying church is its subject. The actors in church drama do not as it were exhibit themselves in a store window in order to tell the congregation who they are and what they feel. The prayer and proclamation in church drama is the prayer and proclamation of the church, and not the private concern of the actor. The problem is therefore identical with that of the prayer and proclamation of the minister or priest. There comes a day when the minister is utterly exhausted, near desperation, and yet he stands before the altar and says, "Praise the Lord, my soul!" His voice is not cold and impersonal: it actually sounds joyful. Does that mean that he is committing religious perjury? Certainly not, because he is lending his voice to his congregation. It is another matter altogether that he ought to allow the praise of the congregation to comfort his own heart; in the same way the participant in church drama ought to allow the prayer and proclamation that belongs in the context of the congregation to penetrate into his or her own heart and transform it. As a matter of fact, this is what is constantly happening in the church drama movement. That is why it is somewhat risky to join; there is a very real risk of being converted.

Church drama, when it is rightly studied and rightly carried out, is in fact an excellent training in biblical realism and liturgical rectitude. It has proved to be the case that in church drama, when the individual is compelled to be not merely a hearer of the Word, but a doer of the Word, the contact with reality that is communicated thereby is almost frightening. He does not act himself away from the sacred realities; he marches straight into them, body and soul.

19.

SYMBOLISM IN CHURCH ART—
INHIBITION OR INSPIRATION?

If we are to try to restore a little order to the frequently confused debate about the importance of symbolism in church art, we must begin by asking *for whom* it serves as an inhibition or an inspiration.

As a rule this question is approached from the angle of the artist; and that is by no means an unimportant angle, particularly since the artist's reactions do not always fit into one particular aesthetic pigeonhole. The artist, in fact, is extremely concerned that there should be some kind of order in other areas of the totality he is trying to serve. Now it is not uncommon to find that by "inhibition" and "inspiration" the artist means hindrances and helps toward the expression of his own personality. He demands an instrument for his religious individuality, a prism for his experience, and an idiom for his ecstasy. This being so, it goes without saying that the symbolism of the church may often present itself to him as a hindrance. What, after all, is an artist supposed to do with all those crosses and triangles?

To which the assembly of the faithful immediately answers that it does not regard its church as a symbol of the soul of the artist. It is not in the least interested in what kind of associations the silversmith finds in the ruby he is mounting on the chalice, or in the experiences that may have inspired the artist to paint his incomprehensible figures on the church wall. The pious mind regards personal symbolism of this kind with the same kind of distaste as it feels when it learns that Leonardo da Vinci is said to have given the Christ of his *Last Supper* his own features. Or when it remembers that seventeenth-century noblemen, restoring their parish churches, placed their own portraits where the images of the saints had once been.

But is the church not the home of the congregation? Ought it not to share something of the character of those who live there, something of their personalities and views?

To be sure, at times the artistic self-consciousness of the faithful has led to noble results. I am reminded of Fra Angelico, of whom Argan has said that his art was "an expression of the apostolate of preaching, turned always in the direction of a living fellowship, an *ecclesia*—whether a small monastic community or the great multitude of the faithful." Those artists, and others, who may not belong to either of these communities of believers, of course find in Fra Angelico a certain beauty, quite apart from his somewhat inaccessible symbolism. But for most people, his imagery remains an aesthetic or historical curiosity, and its *docta pietas* is experienced by secular man much as he would experience a barbed-wire fence.

We ought perhaps to add, with regard to what the faithful generally take to be symbolism, that this symbolism tends to reproduce itself in perpetuity. There is in "religious" circles a conservatism that most artists probably feel to be an insuperable barrier to any kind of art that aims to pass beyond repetition and reproduction. This nostalgic anxiety often gives rise to a degree of banality that is frequently mistaken for homespun sincerity. There is a "Christian" view of art that is not far removed from that which is to be seen in some Communist countries, as illustrated, to take only one example, by the great Meissen mosaic on Leipzigerstrasse in East Berlin.

But there is another voice claiming to be heard. In the course of an art debate in a Swedish journal, Teddy Brunius made reference to the painting of Beuron, which he felt had been overlooked in the discussion. This is what he wrote: "It does not meet the needs of secular man in the cities, but in closed religious circles these works have filled, and continue to fill, a definite function." This is "the world" speaking, in conscious opposition to the group of believers. One might be tempted to think twice about the tone in which the article in question was written, as though Brunius were in some way disturbed that Beuron had been overlooked. It may have been a purely scholarly dissatisfaction over the fact that not all the authorities had been quoted. But it may equally well have been an expression of "secular man's" common concern for the religious conventicle. He treats it with a mixture of irony and respect, but is rather pleased that its boundaries should be so well marked, and that it should take such good care of the niceties of its own tradition. He is decidedly irritated, however, at the thought that the conventicle might be opened, so that some of its religion could leak out. Should the assembly of the faithful suddenly turn and address the world, evidently believing that the world "needs" Christianity in some way—and take pains to make their address intelligible—his irritation develops into a rage.

Sometimes this is quite understandable. I am reminded of an altarpiece somewhere in Sweden where the artist, acting on the instructions of the rector, painted the way of life and the way of death, the broad way and the narrow way. The clouds gather soon enough over the way that leads to destruction, but the path to heaven leads from beauty to beauty—at least once the narrow gateway has been passed. It is very likely that the outsider will experience this patently obvious demonstration that the Christian is always privileged to be happy, as a naive piece of propaganda, expressed in terms of abrupt contrast merely in order to appeal to the simple-minded. Perhaps, too, one has the impression that this propaganda has been careless with its facts, as they are in present-day Christianity and as they are in the Bible.

An interesting attempt to satisfy both the closed group of the faithful and the curious public has been made by Matisse in Vence, where the nuns of the Dominican Order sit by themselves in a little transept on the north side of the church, with St. Dominic facing them on the south wall of the chancel, while the congregation is as it were surrounded by the Virgin Mary on the south wall and the passion on the west. So the nuns are given the symbolism of the convent, and the people the symbolism of the church. But neither the missionary zeal of the Dominicans nor the secular interests of the architect have been able to prevent the church from turning its back—a most forbidding back—on the tourists, while opening its arches on the convent garden, from which the common people are excluded. The point of this symbolism is obvious. The church's symbols of rejection have never been difficult to understand.

Occasionally, "the world" may try to impose its own religious images on a center of worship. The most obvious examples are in crematoria, where specifically Christian symbols have given place to more general concerns. But all these wheatfields and trees of life and suns and hills and lights, however artistically interesting they may be in themselves, are as insipid, from the point of view of religious symbolism, as all attempts to talk religion without the help of the religions. Why should religious art succeed in uprooting itself from the soil of tradition, and live on abstract speculation, as yet devoid of all history save what it has managed to acquire as a substitute for faith?

Should these three—the artist, the community of the faithful, and the outsider—be permitted to continue this particular debate, it is unlikely, whatever else may happen, that it is going to lead to any kind of artistic inspiration. But there is another voice demanding to be heard: the Word of God. The voice is not unknown to the other participants, since the Word has something to say to all of them. But none of them has a monopoly on the Word. The distinction between the faithful and the world disappears in the light of the gospel, since there is no guarantee that it will be better understood by the one group than by the other. One of the signs that the Word has borne fruit is that the same confession of sins is called forth, and the same mercy received, in the one place as in the other. This means that the artist has more important things to express than his own personality; it also means that the social and traditional identity of the congregation is relegated into a secondary concern. The Word stands over all those who have so far spoken in the debate, uniting them in the task of listening and passing on what they have heard.

In this light, we must ask to what extent the symbols used in church art are hindrances, or open channels, for the Word.

First of all, we must note that the Word is itself prolific of symbols. Should it be proclaimed in the open air, the points of the compass become symbolic. The closed room, too, becomes a part of the Word itself. The upper room, in which the Eucharist was instituted while the night pressed, black and threatening, outside, is transformed by what took place to an image of our Father's house, of which Christ spoke.

The room in which the Word is proclaimed and the Eucharist celebrated becomes a frontier, where earth and heaven meet in the means of grace. The place where the forgiveness of sins is pronounced and the kingdom of heaven is at hand divides the whole of existence into "before" and "now," into death and life, into the questions of history and the answers of salvation. It is inevitable that the entire room should be drawn into this symbolism.

We should also remember in this connection that there is a law of symbolism, *pars pro toto*, which means that the part set aside for a certain purpose becomes, by virtue of its separation, an image of the whole. The stage becomes an *imitatio mundi*, representing the world. The fact that Sundays are set aside as holy days does not mean that the other six days of the week are unholy, but that every day is a holy day. In the same way, the setting aside of a room as a center of worship makes the room a summing-up of the whole of existence. It is the task of church art to fulfil this symbolism, created by the Word itself. What is proclaimed there is not the holiness of the church, but the holiness of the entire world.

It follows from this that in some liturgical traditions the chancel becomes an image of heaven and the choir the representatives of the angels, while the rood screen and the triumph crucifix mark the torn veil between heaven and earth.

A further factor is that the word proclaimed in that room is itself rich in imagery. It is scarcely necessary to paint symbols on the church walls; the imaginative listener will see them for himself. A medieval church, full of signs and figures, gives the impression that the proclaimed Word has, as it were, been splashed all over the walls, and stuck there.

Some of these symbols are of figures from the Scriptures, whose sin and pardon presents them to us as types and examples, for our comfort and emulation.

There is a window in the Church of St. Peter in Paris, on which the artist has depicted the footsteps of Peter on the water—the footsteps of the first witnesses, one might say—first on the surface and then disappearing into the depths. The application to the lives of ordinary sinners is clear. The figures of saints on the altarpieces fill the same function; they are not there to be admired, but to remind us that we can follow them despite our shortcomings. It is therefore more important in

Evangelical church art that the repentant thief, Magdalene, and Zacchaeus should have their places in the chancel than that we should have to look at a collection of models of virtue who do nothing but hide the gospel of the love of God from the rest of us.

But there are biblical figures who are symbolic in a different sense. In the New Testament we find a mass of names and events from the Old Testament that serve as "types" of Christ and his reconciliation. The story of the prophet Jonah is thus "typical" of the death and resurrection of Christ; Moses' serpent in the wilderness represents the mystery of salvation through the cross of Christ; and the passage through the Red Sea typifies Christian baptism. The apostles read the Old Testament in this way, though they never forgot the historical drama that led from Genesis to Christ. Anyone who has learned to recognize this symbolism has been given access to a rich and inexhaustible world of images. Some of these "types" have had their content fixed once and for all; others appear in different guises for different ages; others again are still waiting to be discovered.

Using this key, church art has often tried to unlock the secrets of nature and history. The effort has not been altogether unbiblical, since not only the Old Testament, but also the creation and the history of our own times is summed up in Christ, as Paul reminds us. Snowflakes and gearwheels bear his mark; events show signs and signals, from age to age, that he is coming. In our day, too, there is no lack of such symbols for the one who has eyes to see. The pillar of cloud in the desert, spreading into its characteristic mushroom, anticipates the last judgment—a sign that the artist is learning to use.

But if this kaleidoscopic mass of symbols is really to serve the Word, and not hinder it, it must become a part of the liturgy and submit to its laws; that means it must facilitate, emphasize and clarify the proclamation of the Word and the blessing of the sacraments. It must not draw attention to itself, but lead attention to what is happening at the altar and in the pulpit. In the best church art the great liturgical types are there, but often expressed with such reticence as to escape the attention of all but the initiated. The dimensions of Solomon's temple are incorporated into many a Swedish parish church, while the concourse of the blessed, as depicted on the high altar at Ghent, makes us realize how much of heaven there is room for in an ordinary chancel.

The close connection between the church building and the Word is further emphasized by the fact that in some churches the line from the nave to the east chancel wall is not straight —reminding us that at the last, Christ's head fell to one side. When church art refuses to be satisfied with providing a setting for the Word, and is itself drawn into the task of proclamation, it becomes an element in the life of the Christian community, and thus a witness to the mystical unity of Christ and his church. The bent center line is a confession that the congregation is part of the body of Christ, and an aspect of the life of the Savior on earth. It is the mystery of the Eucharist interpreted in stone.

However, this world of symbols contains both tensions and possibilities within the service of the Word.

I have already suggested that the relationship between function and symbol is not always without its special problems. A detail of the liturgy may live on, and serve some sensible end, long after its original function has ceased to be of significance, or even remembered. The candles on the altar were once held by acolytes, while the minister read the Word: to give him light, and perhaps to honor him. Then they were left on the table; and there they have remained. In our church we find them natural, since we put candles on our dining tables, and they have gradually gathered a large number of symbolical meanings. As long as they do not usurp the place of the chalice and the book, they neither hide nor hinder the liturgical function of the altar; they emphasize it, rather. But it is not unknown for a liturgical detail that no longer serves its original function to become a symbol that confuses the liturgical action. For instance, an altar at which no Eucharist is ever celebrated is a liturgical monstrosity. A so-called "baptism altar," like the altars that are found in most Swedish cemetery chapels, serves only to put books on, and, to some extent, to say prayers beside. For both of these functions a prayer desk would be much more useful and practical. Make the altar into a book rest or a prayer place, and you have obscured its function as a communion table. Symbols like these, working against or contradicting a liturgical function, are from the point of view of church art, sheer irrelevances.

It is also necessary in this connection to stress that every detail in church art must take its place as an organic part of the whole. A cautionary example is that of the little church at Assy, to which a number of modern artists have contributed excellent works. But however beautiful the details, they do not work together to provide a beautiful whole, such as we find in the Vence chapel. This is important, not only with an eye to the collision of styles that takes place when a number of artists make unrelated contributions, but also when it is a matter of bringing together various symbols to communicate a tolerably coherent message.

One practical aspect of this subject is that when a new church is being planned, those consulted should include the painter, the sculptor, the silversmith, and the textile artist, and not only the clergy, the church council, and the architect. These should all be involved in planning from the very first, while the craftsmen who are to carry out the work should also be present from an early stage.

The relationship between tradition and creation in art is one that always implicitly involves a considerable degree of tension. Because the symbolism used in church art contains such vast possibilities for creative insight, it tends in time to incorporate into itself many dead symbols. The living tradition speaks with a thousand voices; in ancient churches the centuries can be heard calling to one another; but those symbols that were once particularly up-to-date and "modern" often strike later generations as pointless and incomprehensible. On the north wall of Bromma church just outside of Stockholm, there is a picture, one among many, of a lioness standing over her newborn cubs and roaring. Once this was an excellent symbol of resurrection. In the Middle Ages it was believed that lion cubs were born dead, and were given life through the roaring of their mother. Not that the incomprehensible is unattractive; the observer is often willing to penetrate the mysteries gradually. But one cannot expect everyone to know enough about medieval zoology to be able to make a living symbol out of the lioness. Instruction and study is necessary if the historical heritage is to be incorporated into our living present.

If this does not take place, then the present will be much the poorer. It is in those ages that lack a sense of history that the church artist is tempted to repeat *ad nauseam* the few symbols he considers comprehensible to his contemporaries. And the result is that the crosses, triangles, stars, and lilies become a real inhibition instead of an inspiration.

In our day we are discovering afresh how to use half-forgotten truths and symbols in the life of the church. What we have to do now is to confront these newly discovered truths and symbols with the reality that belongs to our own day and age. Biblical symbolism needs transplanting: when the sower goes out to sow he uses, not a tiny basket, but an enormous machine; when the Bible talks about the potter and his clay, we see the factory that makes cups and plates. If the church artist can draw on industrial life for his symbols, this is to confess the church's doctrine that the heavenly Father is still at work. He seeks to be comprehensible; but this is not a merely intellectual problem: the gospel demands proximity and relevance. The church artist often has to choose between the atmosphere of the storybook and that of revival. Nevertheless he must remember that he is working for coming generations, and not only for his own. The problem of tradition versus creativity is implied in our attitude to the future, and not only in our attitude to the past. It is a matter of "whatever you wish that men would do to you, do so to them," for if we wish that certain past generations had been somewhat less self-centered and more catholic in their interpretation of the gospel, we must recall in our own work that when we build churches, we build for more than one generation. Our situation is no more than a temporary phase of the meeting of God and mankind at the altar; it is as it were a detail in the order of grace, lived out in sacred symbolism. And although the order of grace is an ancient order, it will remain until the last judgment.

This is our great task, to bring the concerns of time face to face with the concerns of eternity. But how are we possibly to do this without the aid of symbols? After all, Christ himself felt it necessary to teach in parables, even though he was eternity in our midst.

20.

CHRISTIAN ASPECTS OF THE NOVEL

In this essay I deliberately avoid talking about "the Christian novel," for two reasons. In the first place, because the expression is ambiguous: a novel may be considered Christian because a Christian has written it or because it has been published by a denominational publishing house or because it defends the Christian faith or because its contents alarm no one and shock no one, dealing only with noble and edifying matters. These various alternatives belong together, and tend to support the view that any writer who wants to be regarded as a Christian ought ideally to write books defending the faith, or at least books dealing with the higher aspect of life; "mere" love, or "mere" social problems, on the other hand, are too petty to concern such a man. But I wish to avoid the term for another reason: because it approaches the problem of how to write novels about Christianity from only one angle, the angle of the Christian believer—as though he had a monopoly of that particular art.

My term, "Christianity novel" (*Kristendomsroman*), formed by analogy with such terms as "social novel," "Western novel," and the like, means a novel that deals with "the religion based on Jesus Christ"—as a Swedish encyclopaedia defines it. If it deals with Christianity as practiced in everyday, profane life, then it is quite clear that it is in fact a matter of practical Christianity. There is no reason whatsoever why this kind of framework should be pro-Christian. Aldous Huxley's *Point Counter Point* is just as much a Christianity novel as is Graham Greene's *The End of the Affair*. It may also happen that a Christianity novel is written, as it were, by mistake; the author himself has no idea what he has done, although a theologian ought to be able to see the point.

The purpose of this essay is to try to describe some of the ways in which novelists, and in particular modern novelists, have approached the subject of Christianity. We might begin by examining the fairly common, albeit rough, distinction between naturalistic and symbolical novels.

I am not in this context using the word naturalism in any pejorative sense; I use it merely to refer to a literary method similar in scope to descriptive science. Just as historical dissertations differ from one another, depending on the frames of reference of the scholars involved (compare, for example, Erik H. Erikson's *Young Man Luther* and Roland H. Bainton's *Here I Stand*), so, too, Christianity novels differ. Some novelists work on a basis of Marxist patterns; others against a Freudian background; while others again derive their knowledge of human nature from Christian devotional classics. But whether this knowledge comes from *Zentralblatt für Psychoanalyse* or from Christian Scriver's *Seelenschatz* (1675), it is reality that is being described, and as such something capable of empirical verification.

The question of the Christian legitimacy of naturalism depends, of course, on the purpose to which it is put. For instance, as a *diagram of society* it can scarcely come into conflict with faith—always provided that it does not claim to say all there is to be said about human existence. From the Christian point of view there is no more reason to be suspicious of extreme realism than there was to be suspicious of certain sciences. Jaspers has recently pointed out that Western man's interest in scientific fact springs from a Christian belief in creation. The same might be said of naturalism: facts can never be a matter of indifference to anyone who believes that God has made them. It is also remarkable how the church has adopted naturalism; a Swedish bishop in his pastoral letter has criticized modern literature for contriving problems and conflicts, and thus giving a distorted picture of reality: "Great areas, the most important areas of life, are either ignored, or else treated with undue brevity in literature. The workaday world; married couples doing their best to stay together, to care for their children, to live decent lives; the joy of work, not least the pure joy of intellectual effort—all these are left out altogether." None would be more surprised than Zola to find himself regarded as being hand in glove with the church!

If we look at the Swedish Christianity novel with this in

mind, we have to admit that the writer of these words was right at least in that there is a great deal which is left out, both of faith and of conduct. And although it would be altogether incorrect to call the various forms of Swedish piety a well-worn subject, nevertheless if we put the various descriptions together, we can get a rough map of Sweden. But the result would be far too much like a tourist guidebook. In order to penetrate beneath the surface we have to ask different questions. Bernanos, in his *Diary of a Country Priest*, has more important things to do than to describe French Catholicism; in the same way Julien Green's book *Moïra* is concerned with more important matters than the functioning of certain types of American Puritanism. There is a type of naturalistic descriptive novel, dealing with Christianity, which we might classify as the *verification novel*. Behind this kind of novel there is a religious experience or a dogmatic conviction; it results from the author's concern to tell the believer (or the unbeliever) exactly what happened, to describe how it works, to compel the reader to adopt a personal attitude to phenomena that confirm that something has, or has not, happened beneath the surface of life. And the author meets the doubter on his own level; he appeals to verifiable facts, and to events that can be re-experienced. With the help of naturalism he sets out to verify—or deny—that which is beyond nature.

To this category belong primarily those novels dealing with religious conversion: an excellent example is Bernanos' *Sous le soleil de Satan*. And just as there are novels that bear witness to Christian conversion, there are those which have to do with the same phenomenon, only vice versa. A good example is James Joyce's *A Portrait of the Artist as a Young Man*. Both types verify a personal decision, and do so using similar means. Similarly, the novel may give an account of experiences having to do with the growth and development of the spiritual life. The supreme example here is Dostoyevsky; I recall how the light from Father Zossima is reflected on to the other characters in *The Brothers Karamazov*. But similar experiences can be effectively illuminated from the opposite direction, as, for instance, in Huxley's *Point Counter Point*.

An interesting and exceptional case is provided by C. S. Lewis' *The Screwtape Letters*, which gives an inverted picture of Christian pastoralia. The book, as is well known, is made up of a correspondence between two devils, one of whom has been given the job of carrying off a human soul to hell. This is to say that the framework is metaphysical; but the psychology is thoroughly empirical. When the apprentice tempter showed signs of losing his prey (the subject having fallen in love with a Christian girl), his immediate chief "inadvertently allowed" himself to assume the form of a large centipede. Throughout the book as a whole, the inner conflict is supported, for the reader's benefit, by the kind of material that corresponds closely to probable experiences of the reader's own. This book is a modern equivalent of Bunyan's *Pilgrim's Progress*—and is worthy of the comparison, perhaps even more so than Lewis' "deliberate" counterpart, *The Pilgrim's Regress*.

However, the process of verification need not refer to an experience attested by an individual or by the church; it may have to do with a doctrine or a dogmatic scheme. Thus Mauriac's novel *Le nœud de vipères* is an interesting witness to the fact that the doctrine of salvation by God's grace alone is not unknown in the Roman Catholic setting. The first time I encountered this work, my immediate reaction was, "This is exactly what an Evangelical novel ought to look like."

It would often seem to be the case that verification is best carried out by means of understatements. *The Power and the Glory*, in which the hero of the faith dies a miserable coward, is more convincing than *The End of the Affair*, despite the fact that in the latter Sarah dies a saint. Mauriac has also pointed out that the reason why *Sous le soleil de Satan* is so convincing to the reader is that "Bernanos, guided by his literary instinct, finally discovered and demonstrated that in this elect soul [l'abbé Donissan] there is nevertheless a weakness, a hidden fault in the vessel." Father Zossima shows no such signs of weakness; if he were to be separated from the vast verification of evil that surrounds his story with an aura of Satanic credibility, he would be much less credible as a character.

But does any author ever succeed in verifying God? Or is Mauriac right when he says that "God escapes every poet's attempt to capture him"? There is a phrase in the book of Exodus which is worth considering in this connection: when

Moses worked his miracles, "the magicians of Egypt did the same by their secret arts" (Ex. 7:22, etc.). Should someone give us a vision of heaven reflected in a saintly soul, there will always be another artist waiting to demonstrate that the re-flected image comes from more earthly—or subterranean—fires. The dream that the poet might be able to "reveal God," as Maritain says, and do it by psychological means, is in point of fact nothing but a kind of literary spiritualism. When God is revealed, our difficulties in verification have to do with prob-lems other than God. But there is another type of verification than that which has to do with matters of proof; in biblical language it is called "testimony"—to "reveal God" is normally left to Christ.

Before we leave the naturalistic verification novel, we must take account of a type of novel that apparently moves farther out than others into fantasy. I refer to what we usually call "science fiction." I say "apparently," because in this type of writing the author is constantly appealing to facts that verify the *possibility* of what he is recounting.

Socialist and Marxist authors have described society as it might be after the victory of socialism (an early example would be William Morris' *News from Nowhere*); similarly, R. H. Benson, in his novel *The Dawn of All* (1911), described the state of the world after the final victory of Catholicism over socialism in, say, 1973. In this utopian vision the author has the opportunity of demonstrating a Roman Catholic cul-tural synthesis in which scientific facts are incorporated into a dogmatic structure, and in which doctors prescribe prayer much as they would prescribe other medicines. The system of dogmatics, science, and politics is so closely integrated that the author is able to note with satisfaction that a pious and peace-ful heretic is condemned to death. To this extent, then, the book is a verification novel. C. S. Lewis' trilogy of space novels, of which the first, *Out of the Silent Planet*, may serve as an example, provides more edifying reading. The central figure of these novels, Ransom, is a philologist (and thus to some extent a reflection of Lewis himself), and finds ample scope for his gifts on Mars, but the outstanding feature of the trilogy as a whole is the alliance between their science fiction frame-work and their author's Anglican theology. A militant materialist, with certain Hitlerian characteristics, Weston, manages to get to Mars and there to do a certain amount of damage, but is finally made fun of by the entire planet, and sent packing by its ruler. Weston and Ransom both return to the earth, "the silent planet," whose ruler is the fallen angel of tradition, and where the creatures are shut off from fellowship with the remainder of God's cosmos. In the second novel of the trilogy, *Perelandra*, which is set on a Venus in a state of primeval innocence, Weston is killed by Ransom in hand-to-hand combat; and in the third, *That Hideous Strength*, the forces of good and evil are pitted against each other on earth. Oddly enough, in these novels Lewis manages to give a more convincing verification of orthodox Christian faith in a new cosmology than many who concern themselves solely with "established" facts.

The naturalistic Christianity novel has, however, another variant, the *identification novel*. This term I have borrowed from a Swedish novelist, Lars Ahlin, who uses it to describe his own work. In point of fact, here the fence around the Christianity novel is torn down; before the author knows what is happening, he is outside the area of the Christianity novel, *for it is not Christianity he is identifying himself with, but with humanity*. Should Christianity enter the writer's field of vision, it is because the men and women he is writing about are either interested in, or come into collision with, Christianity. And yet it may well be that the writer practices his Christianity most intensively from outside its boundaries. Christian authors often regard themselves as being too "spiritual" to develop this craft. But there is no denying that the work of Christ and the Holy Spirit had a great deal to do with perfectly ordinary, profane distress.

The verification novel is often concerned with the defense of Christianity; the identification novel, on the other hand, frequently defends men and women against Christianity, or against its degenerate forms. This may take the form of a direct attack; as when Laxness[1] compares the sufferings of Christ with the sufferings Christ has brought upon mankind. But when Greene in *The Heart of the Matter* asks the church about

---

[1] Halldór Kilian Laxness (b. 1902), Icelandic novelist and winner of the 1955 Nobel Prize for Literature.

the suicide Scobie, or when Dostoyevsky refuses to buy eternal bliss for the price of a child's tears, this is a criticism of Christianity having its roots in the New Testament. There are, however, examples of another type of identification than identification with the defense; there is also identification with the prosecution, and there is a type of novel in which Christianity is made to face its accusers. Alan Paton's novel of South Africa, *Cry, the Beloved Country*, is one such, in which social injustice is so intolerable because of the universal presence of Christianity on the scene. This accusation in this novel is all the more radical for its lack of histrionics: without indignation it follows an African Job to the depths of his tragedy—and allows him to keep his faith.

Identification need not be turned "downward," in condescension, as though the writer felt morally or intellectually superior to the people he is writing about. It will suffice, for the purpose of illustration, to mention Sholem Asch, *The Prophet*, and Gertrud von le Fort, *Die Letzte am Schafott* (dramatized by Bernanos as *Dialogue des Carmélites*).

Finally, an observation concerning the naturalism of authors dealing with Christian themes: it is often surprisingly free in the intimacy of its descriptive writing—especially when it deals with matters from which sugar-candy Christianity recoils. This tendency is particularly noticeable in those writers for whom Christianity has been a discovery, and not an inheritance. We do not, for instance, find it in Mauriac, but we do find it in Greene. Occasionally one has the impression in Protestantism that a writer will do almost anything to avoid being classified as a puritan. There is evidence that this is not merely a matter of sensitivity to the reactions of the secularized public; for many an author it seems to be more of the nature of a literary conscience: the mere fact that some people think that some things ought not be said is enough to ensure their being said—a phenomenon that, let it be said, looks suspiciously like inverted puritanism!

One might suppose the *symbolical novel* to be easier to handle, from the Christian point of view, than the naturalistic novel. But a symbol—any symbol—is apt to have a life of its own, and does not always conform to the wishes of the author.

In Paul Gallico's *The Foolish Immortals*, a substance with remarkable qualities (it confers immortality on the one who eats
it) becomes a symbol of selfishness and materialism. In the
end, Gallico has to try to dispose of the symbol by revealing
it to be mere superstition. But in vain—the biblical myth of the
tree of life breaks through and retains its hold upon the reader,
with an entirely different group of associations from those the
writer intended. Charles Williams is more successful in giving
his symbols of power—the Holy Grail in *War in Heaven*, the
"living stone" in *Many Dimensions*—intrinsic qualities corresponding to his intentions. He succeeds, on the one hand, because his use of these symbols is motivated by a profound
respect for their theological and mythological roots, and on the
other, because the best figures in each book lose their lives in
the affirmation of the meaning of the symbols. This is to say
that Williams approaches his task along a way diametrically
opposed to that followed by Gallico.

Here we approach a characteristic that can be noticed in
most symbolical Christianity novels—the tendency either to
imitate biblical figures or to create an outline corresponding to
their history; by this means the symbol is given a focus that
is not easily lost sight of. In other words, the symbolical Christianity novel often becomes a *typological novel.*

This term calls for closer definition. Its background is provided by two peculiarities of the biblical narrative. One of
them has been observed, for example, by Thomas Mann in his
Joseph novels. When Joseph is thrown into the well and then
rescued, there is more to it than meets the eye; there is a
pattern of fate, and this pattern is represented in the oriental
cult. Mann has not written this without association to the death
and resurrection of Christ. In fact he draws parallels not only
with Near Eastern religions in general, but also with the Old
Testament, in the same way as the New Testament writers
were constantly doing. Jonah, despite his disobedience, is a
type of Christ, who was also swallowed up by death and
arose on the third day; the children of Israel wandered for
forty years in the desert, and Christ's forty days in the wilderness thus recapitulated the history of his people, which was
fulfilled in him. Theologians call these *types*, or *prototypes.*
This way of looking at the Old Testament has often been used

in ecclesiastical art—think only of the Gothic church paintings, in which episodes from the life of Christ on the north side of the church are often accompanied by their Old Testament prototypes on the south side.

Exegetes have also pointed to another biblical use of typology: Paul, for example, tells his readers that "I received mercy for this reason, that in me, as the foremost, Jesus Christ might display his perfect patience for an example to those who were to believe in him for eternal life" (1 Tim. 1:16).

His personal history, like that of Peter, has become an object-lesson to all Christians, because it contains such typical characteristics: sin, conversion, and service have been outlined in such a way that even the most insignificant of Christians can recognize themselves in the narrative. The typological narrative continues in the legends of the saints, though in these cases the emphasis is placed on the ideal and the example: the saint's sins are as a rule passed over in silence.

It may be that a number of harmless naturalistic Christianity novels are in fact continuing the tradition of saints' legends, though neither their authors nor their readers are aware of it. They have neither the bright colors of naturalism nor the other dimension of symbolism; accepted patterns of ideas have prevented their authors from studying reality, while what they imagine to be a desire for realism has prevented them from learning anything from the symbolical side of church art.

According to this latter line of development, the narrative of some "example," the typological novel is a modern costume in which to parade events from sacred history, or else an archaic mantle in which to dress modern Christian problems.

Among the variety of books that try to answer the question of "what if it were to happen now," we may mention Charles Sheldon's *In His Steps*, a novel without literary significance, but which was very popular in the 1890s. In this book the imitation of Christ is depicted in puritan terms. For instance, if Jesus were a newspaper editor he would do everything in his power to fight the saloon, and he would resolutely refuse to issue a Sunday edition. But in social questions, this puritanism is so radical that it is worth noting purely on that account—this kind of radicalism is by no means as common, even in typological novels, as one might think. " 'My plan,' replied Dr.

Bruce slowly, 'is in brief the putting of myself into the centre of the greatest human need I can find in this city and living there.'" *The End of the Affair*, Graham Greene's attempt to write a modern saint's legend, is, of course, on quite a different literary level. But is his intention fully worked out? The reader may imagine that he is reading a perfectly ordinary naturalistic love story, but a story with a number of disturbing peculiarities: for instance, there is the matter of Sarah's baptism, which she knew nothing about, but which had such far-reaching consequences; and then there are the miracles, which appear to be stuck on as an unnecessary afterthought. There would appear to be a certain degree of competition between the naturalistic love story and the medieval saint's legend; the two do not quite mix.

Many novels retell the story of the past in the imperfect tense, but in such a way as to allow modern problems to shine through—despite the fact that the purpose was accurate historical depiction. The situation is quite different in the case of Merezhkovsky's book about Julian the Apostate, *The Death of the Gods* (1895, Eng. trans. 1901), in which the naturalistic framework is nothing but an elaborate barge into which are loaded the author's philosophy of history and his belief in a coming cultural synthesis between Christian and anti-Christian. Pär Lagerkvist, with less elaborate means and much greater effect, has made the figure of Barabbas represent both alienation from Christ and affinity with him—a combination which has little enough to do with conditions in Barabbas' own day, but a great deal to do with conditions in the author's time.

Conscious anachronisms of this kind are well known in preaching, and it would be well worth investigating to what extent these apparently common methods can be put down to transference from the pulpit to the novel, or vice versa.

Modern saints' legends often involve examples having the character of prototype—though it would probably be better to use the term *antitype* (cf. the Greek *antitupon* in Heb. 9:24), since it is not a question of an example, but of a copy. For instance, Morris West's novel *The Devil's Advocate* tells of a British deserter in World War II who comes to an obscure village in south Italy, where he comes to be regarded as a saint.

Finally he is martyred, shot by the Communists. The olive tree to which he was tied for execution resembles the cross, and the deserter himself becomes an antitype of Christ.

A better integration into an overall picture is the antitypical passage in the novel *A Man and his Conscience* (*En man och hans samvete*), by the Finnish writer Jarl Hemmer. The minister, Bro, is certainly no Christ-figure: he suffers moral shipwreck in an attempt to save a girl from the street; he is put in prison; but a friend comforts him by saying that "God doesn't lift up many clean souls to heaven; most of them he fishes up out of the filth." Later, working as a chaplain in a Finnish concentration camp for Bolsheviks, he runs away because he cannot tolerate the victors' way of treating their enemies. But he runs *into* the camp, not out of it; he disguises himself, and becomes a prisoner among prisoners. Finally he goes to the wall, and is shot instead of one of the prisoners. In the camp they had called him "Little Jesus."

In this case the antitype is almost as clear as the prototype in Isaiah 53: "upon him was the chastisement . . . ." If Hemmer's story reminds us of vicarious suffering, the nineteenth-century Swiss novelist Jeremias Gotthelf has drawn an antitype to the so-called classical doctrine of the atonement, Christ as the conqueror of the devil. In his novel *The Black Spider*, Gotthelf tells of the young peasant Christen, who tries to save a newborn child from the power of the spider by taking it for baptism to the priest. On the way he meets the poisonous creature, sends the child on its way in a boy's care, and enters into combat. He takes hold of the spider, and carries it to the hole in the cottage wall where it had previously been shut in. "The fire in his hand was terrible; the spider's poison penetrated to every part of his body. His blood turned to fire. His strength ebbed, his breath became labored, but he prayed and prayed and kept God constantly before his eyes. He held out in the very fires of hell." When Christen had completed his task, the priest came to take up "the same battle in which his predecessor, in once winning the victory, had laid down his life. But God did not demand that he make such a sacrifice; another had already won through."

And what of Melville's *Billy Budd?* In the decisive meeting with Captain Vere and the Satanic Claggart, Billy is unable to utter a sound in his own defense; even Captain Vere's fatherly effort to reassure him only worsens his vocal paralysis, ". . . bringing to his face an expression which was as a crucifixion to behold." Then with a single blow, in full view of the Captain, he kills Claggart, causing Vere to exclaim, "Struck dead by an angel of God! Yet the angel must hang!" Melville's account of the execution leaves the reader in no doubt that he is describing an antitype of Christ. As the last signal was given, ". . . it chanced that the vapory fleece hanging low in the East was shot through with a soft glory as of the fleece of the Lamb of God seen in mystical vision, and simultaneously therewith, watched by the wedged mass of upturned faces, Billy ascended; and, ascending, took the full rose of the dawn."

The author's intention is not always as clear as in this instance. But an antitype is a literary, not a psychological phenomenon, and it is of little account whether or not the author intended it. In Ingmar Bergman's film *Winter Light* (*Nattvardsgästerna*), the manuscript of which was published more or less in the form of a novel, Märta receives *stigmata* from her eczema in accordance with the marks of the wounds of Christ —without Bergman ever thinking of, much less intending, such an allusion. If the intentions of the author were to be decisive for the prototypes in the Old Testament, there would be hardly any at all; what did the prophets know about Christ?

Now should anyone imagine that this is merely a way of fathering Christian offspring on to agnostic writers, it would be as well to recall that there are such things as negative antitypes, and that the most Christian of authors runs the risk of producing them—as when R. H. Benson makes the church into the executor of his hatred of heretics. The vital test is whether or not the biblical motif shines through the narrative. The causes of the phenomenon—unconscious theological impressions on the author's part or the unavoidable cultural infection of Christianity or Jung's archetypes or what you will—can be discussed later. The same applies to un-Christian phenomena in the world of Christian writers; we recall that Gide has assured us that there are demons everywhere.

Female antitypes in literature are a separate chapter. Of course, they refer more often to Mary than to Christ; for instance, Aurelia in Gerard de Nerval, and perhaps also Temple

in Faulkner's novel *Sanctuary*, though in this case the antitype
is negative. But just as Roman Catholic popular piety tends
more and more to incorporate Mary into the godhead, so one
encounters at times in Protestantism a tendency to weave
Christ imaginatively into a female figure. Is this a secret affinity
with the cult of Mary? Or is it perhaps simply a case of "any
port in a storm" for needs that have not been able to find their
way into any church (bearing in mind that these authors as a
rule have little or no connection with the church)?

I ought perhaps to point out that the antitype of Christ does
not have to be the most important thing in a Christianity novel.
Adrian Leverkühn says, meeting his friends for the last time,
"*Wachet mit mir.*" And when paralysis pushes him over the
brink of mental breakdown, he falls over his instrument with
his arms stretched out—an evident symbol of the cross, as a
Swedish scholar has pointed out. But these allusions to Christ
are merely a counterpoint to the main theme of Thomas Mann's
Doktor Faustus, which is an antichrist theme.

Just as the naturalistic Christianity novel may on an occasion
be set in the universe as a whole, so the typological novel may
occasionally attempt to incorporate Everything That Is into its
scheme of things. But it is by no means as practical, in this
context, to undertake a voyage into space as to try to sum up
Everything in a tiny focus.

When a literary cosmos is constructed around an antitype it
is assisted by two literary phenomena. First, the fact that the
biblical narrative itself often sums up the whole world in one
item: "The kingdom of heaven is like . . . ." The passion narrative is the consummation of all things, a consummation which
is constantly being repeated in the Eucharist. And secondly,
the drama is a source of inspiration. The Swedish literary historian Staffan Björck has pointed out the way in which the
modern novel has made use of the means of expression of the
stage, and has also suggested some of the causes of this development. It is relevant to ask, however, whether the quest for a
cosmos, the All, the consummation, may not be of importance
in this connection. It is a well-known fact that in the Middle
Ages the stage was a microcosm of the universe, with heaven
in the East and hell in the regions of the setting sun. And the
most important thing that was represented on this stage was

the death and resurrection of Christ. Now, as the Christianity novel builds its literary cosmos, it would seem only natural that it should be influenced by the powerful constellation of Golgotha, Eucharist, and stage. Let me give two Swedish examples.

Gunnar Edman's novel *Now at the Sixth Hour* (*Men vid sjätte timmen*) begins at the Eucharist, with the message that God is dead. He follows the news as it spreads, and notes the various comments that are made—a precise naturalistic description against an irrational background. But then the theme returns in a different form. A marriage becomes the field in which the death of God is to emerge victorious: constantly returning in the Eucharist or in parable; constantly waiting to take form in human love. But the death of God also follows another path. The contradiction that permeates the whole of our history strikes a member of the family, Conrad; his mind gives way; and the couple's mental wrestling with their problems is never far removed from the fate of the wife's brother. Not until Conrad dies is there liberation for them. The man is an antitype of Christ. Thus the novel has a number of "strata": a naturalistic verification (the comments on the death of God, the love story); a mass of theological arguments, interwoven with these events and the narrator's emotions arising out of them; a couple of antitypes (the Eucharistic parables, Conrad); and finally, what is told of the Eucharist itself. The antitypes are the pins that hold together what is happening now with what happened two thousand years ago and in eternity. This last is the most important, for what Edman is retelling has no boundaries.

Walter Ljungquist's symbolical novel *Azalea* is also a literary cosmos—a typical characteristic is that the island on which the main figures land is egg-shaped. John Karlzén has pointed out that the most important female character in the novel is what I have called an antitype of Christ. Over against Azalea stands Dr. Gempel, though after her death he becomes much more human than Satan can ever be—an example of the point that the antitypes do not have to be carried through to the bitter end; they can be described in terms of a role, which someone assumed in a particular situation and then abandons. After Gempel has said "forgive us our trespasses" by Azalea's coffin, someone remarks that "he looks like an actor who has lost his makeup." This approach makes it easier for us to accept the consequences of the fact that in this novel the author himself is identified with the Creator. The other six characters do not have to be made up for their roles: they are humanity yesterday, today, and always. It is precisely this unity of time, place, and action—this limitation—that makes it possible in this novel to sum up world history, and to identify it with the history of the sufferings of Christ. Edman has written, as it were, a prelude and fugue for organ; the Eucharist is the *cantus firmus*, while the other parts are on the one hand the antitypical line, and on the other the naturalistic line. Ljungquist has taken his inspiration from the drama, and placed the history of the world on a little stage in the middle of the ocean: three acts between two bursts of bird song, with the mist, the wind, and the thundercloud as the chorus, observing and commenting.

The whole idea is reminiscent of Chesterton's *The Man Who Was Thursday*, in which an anarchist society of detectives in disguise (none of whom is known to any of the others) hunt a mysterious chief, Sunday, who finally proves to be none other than God, the hidden and suffering Creator. As a Swedish literary historian has said, "The riddle of Sunday is the riddle of this world."

The types of novel which I have tried to describe in this essay have, of course, many hybrid forms. There are antitypes in naturalistic novels, and the details of typological novels often demonstrate that care which is so typical of naturalism. In other words, the various approaches to the subject of Christianity which are to be observed in the modern novel are by no means exclusive; any or all of them may be found in one and the same novel.

NOTE: This essay is an abridgment by the author of a much longer essay, in which most of the illustrative material was drawn from modern Swedish literature.

THE CHRISTIAN FAITH

AN INTERPRETATION OF
THE APOSTLES' CREED

I believe in God the Father Almighty, maker of heaven
   and earth.

What does this mean?

I believe in a love which works the miracle
of existence
light glistening on the water
the spark which existed before there was light and distance
galaxies beyond the reach of light
the stones below my window.
And everything that has breath has been created by it
the deer grazing in the glade
the ants scurrying to save their eggs
as I lift the turf
the teeming sea and the gulls crying over the herring shoal
and in the clear drop on my windowsill
a wilderness I cannot see but full of life.
And all this exists today,
world, things, I myself
who am able to see it, hear it, feel it, taste and smell it,
it exists at this moment
because at this moment someone is saying:
"exist, exist, exist!"
—a love

I believe in a love at work
in the world of men
in peoples and cultures.
Even when evil begets evil and men
stand helpless
that love is at work
unseen but near
those who are of a contrite heart.

I believe in a love—it is turned to me
with the eyes that look upon a child
and all I do and all I say
is a response to a love
my joy a game before Someone
my distress a lament before Someone
and I call his Name who is God
his Name who is Father.

✿   ✿   ✿   ✿   ✿

And in Jesus Christ his only Son our Lord,
Who was conceived by the Holy Ghost,
Born of the Virgin Mary,
Suffered under Pontius Pilate, was crucified, dead and
    buried:
He descended into hell;
The third day he rose again from the dead;
He ascended into heaven,
And sitteth on the right hand of God the Father Almighty;
From thence he shall come to judge the quick and the
    dead.

What does this mean?

I believe in a love that was betrayed
by me and all men—
leaving me alone
separated from God and my brother
from life and blessedness;
an enemy had done this.

But love became my brother
Jesus,
God of God, Son of Mary.
Through him the world had come into being
the myriad creatures—
now he himself became one of them
flesh of our flesh, blood of our blood
a fetus in a womb
a child under the stars
left at the mercy of laws and powers.
So he bore a human destiny
from the womb to the grave.
He went about helping the helpless
he bore our sorrows—and our guilt.
At the last he entered the ultimate horror
the ultimate agony the ultimate separation.
So he took upon himself all execration all condemnation.

But that night in which he was betrayed by me and all men
was too small to measure the love.
Death itself was filled by it. By life.
And to the end of time must call his name—
Jesus.

For death burst on the third day
and henceforth neither time nor space can
imprison him
or exclude him.
So he destroyed enmity
and for those who love him
there shall be no more separation.

                          *   *   *   *   *

I believe in the Holy Ghost;
The Holy Catholic Church; the Communion of Saints;
The forgiveness of sins;
The resurrection of the body,
And the life everlasting.

What does this mean?

I believe in a love
at work in me and through me.
Not as though I had accomplished it
or won through to it
love has won through to me
in the Gospel
has taken me in its arms and carried me into the Church
where Christ lives
forgives sins
heals the wounded
loves the world
the same today.
Although I still live in a divided reality
and am a sinner
the Gospel makes me one with Christ
and in him with apostles and prophets
and a company no man can number
out of all peoples and tribes and nations and tongues.
I am a fiber in a great tree
a voice in a chorus of praise like the sound of mighty waters
that carries my prayer, my home, my work
toward a far coast
whither all things are moving redeemed from loneliness
to the home of all. To God.

There is an ache in all things
the stones, the clouds, the roots of the grass.
Homesickness
All things die. We with them. One day the elements shall burst.
But the bursting of the earth shall be not as a bomb, but as a seed.
There is a resurrection
in which the humanity of God
with its roots in earth, twined in companies,
praying, working, longing,
shall be transplanted into a new reality
which no eye has seen and no ear heard.
One thing I know about God's new world.
I shall always be with the Lord.
I shall see God.
Eternal life.